Other books by
Margery Reynolds

One Summer at Ril Lake
One Winter at Ril Lake
One Autumn at Ril Lake

Also

The Reynolds Collection of Journals

And by
D. M. Rutherford

Reflections From Doteaga
(A compilation of poetry and recipes)

Published by

The Golden Pencil ✎
Copyright 2024 Dale Margery Rutherford

(aka Margery Reynolds)

All rights reserved.

Library of Canada Archives and Publication
ISBN: 978-1-0691820-0-5 (paperback)
ISBN: 978-1-0691820-1-2 (e-book)

by
Margery Reynolds
www.margeryreynolds.ca

Cover designed with Canva,
by D. M. Rutherford and Jennifer Merivale

One Autumn at Ril Lake

A Muskoka Cottage Novel

By
Margery Reynolds

For

Lynn & Evie

Sisters of the heart

Canasta Forever!

One Autumn at Ril Lake

Chapter 1

If there was one thing Julie Wight didn't want, it was complications. It had taken her two years to achieve a sense of calm, since the last big disaster in her life, and that's how she wanted it to stay. Her quiet life and her home on Ril Lake offered her exactly that: peace, tranquility, and solace. To some it was serene, to others it was paradise, but to Julie Wight it was pure magic. She'd even crafted an enticing new description for Cottager's Magazine, hoping to attract like-minded people next cottage season.

Picture yourself, at Julie's Haven, in a wooden deck chair, at the end of a dock overlooking a crystal-clear lake, a beverage of your choosing in your hand. Whispering pines surround you. Chipmunks scurry at your feet. The tree-lined horizon displays a glorious array of colour and as you tip your head to watch the birds soaring through the sky, all you hear is the coo of a dove, the trill of a sparrow, and the gentle swoosh of the water lapping against the shore.

Julie's Haven was a two-acre parcel of land at the end of Ril Cove Road, where a point jutted sharply into Ril Lake. To the east, the rocky outcrop led to the larger, open side of the lake where the wind could turn your kayak around a hundred and eighty degrees if you didn't have your wits about you. To the west lay a sheltered cove with sparkling calm waters and a half a mile of white sandy beach; the perfect place to swim or sunbathe on a hot summer day. Julie's home was in the middle of the property at the top of a circular drive, with two all-season rental cottages nestled into the woods on either side.

Labour Day weekend marked the end of the cottage season for renters and now that most of them had gone home, the entire area was blissfully quiet, and Julie was enjoying a peaceful existence once again.

Yet something about Felicity Pierce's vehicle pulling into her driveway that Friday morning, late in August, told Julie that things were about to change. That Felicity wasn't alone made it seem doubly so.

Even though she and Felicity had been neighbours and friends for years, Julie wished she'd had a little warning that her friend was dropping by with guests. She would have changed out of her dust-covered yoga pants and the faded Blue Jays baseball shirt she was wearing to refinish the kitchen chairs. And she most certainly would have done something with her hair other than shove it into a messy bun. But with no warning, Felicity and her friends would have to take her as they found her. When Felicity pulled into the circle and parked, Julie dropped her sandpaper, dusted her hands on her thighs and left her project behind.

The afternoon sun sifting through the leaves sent flickering shadows across the gravel and there was something in the air that said autumn was in the offing, even though this Labour Day weekend had been one of the nicest all summer.

"Felicity!" Julie called out, as her friend climbed out of her vehicle and met her halfway up the drive.

"I'm sorry I didn't call earlier, but I brought some people to meet you. Julie, this is Michael Adams, and his three daughters. Joy, Faith and Hope."

"The new village doctor," Julie said.

"Apparently so," Michael said rather sheepishly as he stepped forward, hand outstretched to shake Julie's.

A handsome face was pleasant enough, but the traces of his British accent made him even more appealing. The single women in Baysville were going to be lining up to make appointments at the clinic, she thought.

"It's nice to meet you and your daughters." Julie returned his smile and his handshake. "I teach grade two at the school in the village and there's a Hope Adams on my class list this year."

The girls hovered in the background for a moment until the youngest stepped forward.

"I'm Hope," she said, displaying confidence her sisters didn't seem to share. A spray of freckles danced across Hope's sun-kissed nose. Her hair, a mass of bouncing brown curls poked out haphazardly from beneath a pink Barbie baseball cap and when she smiled up at Julie her dazzling blue eyes sparkled with flecks of gold. Julie felt a twinge in her heart recalling the children she'd imagined she might have one day. They would have looked just like Hope.

The little girl clutched a stuffed bear who was missing both eyes, had one arm precariously close to falling off and sported drastically matted fur, as if he'd been tossed in the washing machine a few too many times.

"This is Blind Bruce," Hope said, holding up her bear. "He used to be just Bruce until he lost both his eyes."

"He looks like he needs to see a doctor," Julie said, flashing a grin at Hope's father.

"It's beyond this GP's skills, I'm afraid." He seemed a little embarrassed at his lack of sewing skills.

Faith, who appeared to be about eleven or twelve with bright blue eyes like Hope's and long braids hanging over her shoulders, was holding tight to a copy of The Hunger Games. Julie pictured herself at the same age, riding in the back seat of the car, missing all the scenery because her nose was stuck in a book, much to her mother's chagrin.

"Who's your favourite character?" Julie asked as Faith's arm timidly looped through the crook of her father's.

"Katniss is very brave, but I'm more like Primrose," she said timidly, her gaze immediately directed toward her feet.

"I like Rue, but I'm not very fond of President Snow," Julie said.

"No one likes him," Faith said, nudging a stone with the toe of her shoe. "We're not supposed to because he's the villain."

"Very true." Julie wondered if she would have figured that out when she was Faith's age.

The eldest Adams daughter was about fourteen or fifteen, with darker hair than either of her sisters, a paler complexion and her father's hazel eyes. She kept her distance from the others, arms crossed over her chest as she surveyed the surroundings, lifted her nose in the air and sniffed.

"Is that poo I smell?" Joy asked, lifting her feet to check the soles of her shoes.

"Felicity and Ben's dog sometimes wanders over here, so it's possible," Julie said, sending Felicity a knowing smile.

"Eeww!" All three girls said at once, though Joy's voice was the loudest.

"You're being overdramatic, Joy," Michael said, after her shoes revealed nothing. Felicity checked Faith's shoes, just to be sure, while Hope turned her runners up for Julie's inspection.

"No mishaps," Julie said, satisfied her guests wouldn't be taking any dog business home with them.

Felicity had been on the selection committee who'd hired Dr. Adams, along with Julie's colleague Rebecca Vickers, so Julie knew something of the process they'd been through to find Dr. Adams. Once the decision had been made everyone in the village had expected the new doctor's arrival but no one, least of all Julie, anticipated personal visits. She couldn't help wondering why Felicity had brought him here.

"I'm happy to meet all of you," Julie said. "I hope you'll enjoy living in Baysville."

"You see, that's just it," Felicity said. "Ideally, Dr. Adams would like to live in the village, close to the clinic, but there's nothing available right now, so we've been up this way, hoping to find a suitable all-season cottage for them." She inclined her head toward Julie's recently renovated rental cottage.

"You mean my place?" Julie asked. She hadn't been expecting to rent it out again until next summer, so while it was empty, Julie had hired Joe Hewitt to do some renovations inside.

"It's available, isn't it?" Felicity asked.

"I haven't finished cleaning since Joe's crew was here." Julie turned to the doctor. "It's only three bedrooms. I'm not sure it will be what you're looking for."

"Nothing else is suitable." Felicity's head inclined in Joy's direction, which to Julie was a sign Joy was being fussy. Not surprising, given the 'poo' incident just now. "Couldn't they just have a look around?" Felicity asked, a desperate *you-are-my-last-resort* look on her face.

"I suppose, but you'll have to pardon the mess," Julie said. "I haven't vacuumed or dusted anything yet."

As she led them up the front step and in through the door, Dr. Adams said, "I'm sure we can look past a little dust, can't we, Joy?"

In the kitchen, Felicity pointed out the ample cupboard space gushing over the new countertops, and the easy to maintain flooring. Julie pointed out the appliances weren't exactly the latest models.

"But they're all in good working order," Felicity said quickly.

Julie thought Felicity had missed her calling and should have been a real estate agent.

"It's great," the doctor said with a satisfied nod. "Roomy and bright, especially with that large window overlooking the driveway. The girls and I enjoy sitting down to supper together as a family, so an eat-in kitchen is nice."

"But there are only three bedrooms," Julie cautioned.

"If the girls don't mind sharing, we could make this work. Right, girls?" Dr. Adams said. "Shall we look at the rest of the rooms?"

When he followed his daughters to the living room, Felicity held Julie back. "What's the matter with you?" she whispered.

"What do you mean?" Julie frowned and squinted just a little.

"It's almost as if you don't want to rent this place."

"Well, I don't. After a long summer of renters, I was looking forward to a little privacy for a change."

"Privacy? You rent the other place to Sirona. How is that giving you privacy?"

"Sirona is different, Felicity. She's an angel, and except for playing cards on Saturdays, I hardly even see her."

"It's only for a year. Just until something in town becomes available. Not only would you have help toward your mortgage, but you'd also have something you've always wanted. A ready-made family, living right next door."

"Don't start. You know I'm not in the market. Not after Eddy."

"Why not? Dr. Adams is a widower. He's your age and you can't deny he's drop dead gorgeous."

"He's your age, too, my friend."

"But I have Ben," Felicity reminded her.

Julie shook her head. "Men only complicate life, and I'm all for a quiet life these days."

"Suit yourself, but I know Rebecca Vickers was keen during the hiring process. She couldn't say enough about him."

"She's vicious with men. Recently divorced and rebounding all over the place. I can't imagine a man with three daughters would be interested in someone like that."

"You're probably right. Besides, there's gossip in town that she's seeing someone." Felicity nudged Julie's elbow. "So that means Dr. Adams is all yours."

"Let it go, Felicity."

"Fine, but don't say I didn't try." Felicity ran a finger through the builder's dust on the counter. "I'll think I'll go see how they're getting along."

Alone in the kitchen, Julie got out the spray cleaner and some rags and cleaned up the worst of the mess. She was just wiping the kitchen table when Dr. Adams came back from the living room. Felicity trailed along after him, having left the girls to check out the bedrooms.

"I noticed that the road goes all the way around the lake," he said. "How far is it? I'm hoping it will make for a good run in the mornings."

"It's nine kilometres. Julie runs it every morning."

"Do you?" Dr. Adams looked at Julie with sudden admiration.

"It's hilly though," she warned. "So not for the faint of heart."

"Sounds perfect," he said.

There was something about the tidiness of Dr. Adams, the neatly trimmed dark hair, the clean-shaven face, the well-fitted slacks and casual button-down shirt, which left Julie with a good feeling about this man. He seemed genuinely interested in the place and looked like the kind of person who would take care of it. She also could not deny the rent money would help, especially since there would be a huge bill from Joe coming in thirty days. Maybe there were viable reasons to rent the place out, and if she was going to do that, the doctor and his girls seemed like decent folks.

The girls were flitting between the smaller bedrooms of the three, giggling and speculating on which would be whose. The doctor plied Julie with questions about all the pertinent things, like heat, water supply, the hot water tank, air conditioning, a generator if the power goes out and Wi-Fi.

"We're so far from civilization," he said. "Joy called this the land that time forgot."

"We are a little remote," Julie agreed.

"Twelve kilometres from town isn't bad at all. But she couldn't get any cellphone reception most of the way up here from town, so she's a little worried."

"We have Wi-Fi out here," Felicity said, "It can be a little slow, and it's not always reliable. But we manage. I'll leave you two to discuss the details while I go see how the girls are getting on."

When the doctor leaned against the doorframe and ran a hand over the back of his neck, Julie smiled sympathetically. "Not a lot of places to choose from, I suppose," she said.

"I guess it's obvious Joy is the cynical one in our family. It's been a struggle to get her to agree to anything."

Julie smiled. "She's probably worried about missing her friends."

"She is, but when I was offered this position, we all agreed this would be a fresh start for us, but now that we're here, she's a little reluctant."

"The secondary school in Bracebridge is excellent. I'm sure she'll do well there."

He nodded. "Joy would do well anywhere. She's clever, and she takes school seriously. But she can be a bit stubborn. She plays the eldest child role to perfection. She's protective of her sisters and of me." He grinned sheepishly. "She'll push away friendships if they are going to interfere with family."

"And the other two?"

"Faith, my bookworm, is shy and sometimes that's mistaken for rudeness, so she doesn't always make friends easily."

"I was a lot like her when I was young."

"Really? That's surprising, for a schoolteacher. You don't seem shy now."

Julie laughed. "Oh, I can be sometimes, especially in crowds. What grade is Faith in?"

"Starting sixth," he said.

"Ah. There are two young ladies in her class who share her enthusiasm for reading, so I'm guessing she'll be just fine. She'll have lots of books to choose from, between our school library and the public one just down the street. She'll have an endless supply of books at her disposal."

"That's good news. Of course, there's always Amazon, but at the rate she reads, I'd be penniless in a month."

Julie smiled at the thought.

"What about Hope?" she asked. "Does she have any concerns about moving away from home, or what Baysville will be like?"

He shook his head. "Oh, no. Hope is happy wherever she is. She's bold, maybe a little too sassy for her own good, but she has a commonsense approach to everything." His eyes drifted to the window and beyond. "This really is a lovely cottage. The nicest we've seen by far."

"You won't find it cramped? There's no basement, and just the three bedrooms."

"Not at all. We were living in a tiny townhouse in Niagara Falls. The girls had their own rooms there, but the rest of the living space wasn't as big as this. We didn't have a dining room. Our kitchen was the size of a matchbox, and you've got that sunroom on the back. I believe Felicity called it a Muskoka room."

"My father added that room years ago. Most of the cottages up here have one. You can't beat the sunsets, and you have a spectacular view of the lake."

"That sounds wonderful. After the rat-race of the city, I'm all for a quiet life." He leaned against the counter and crossed his arms over his chest, a contented smile on his face. "I guess all we need now is the girls' verdict."

As if they'd heard him, the girls came from the hallway and Hope bounded across the kitchen and stopped at her father's side.

"Can we live here, Daddy? This place is the best! There's a hammock outside, and a firepit and the lake is right there! Right outside the door."

"Not quite," Joy corrected. "It's down the steps and across the yard. But it's closer than the other places we looked at." She looked at Julie to ask, "Does the lake freeze in the winter?"

"It does," Julie answered.

Felicity was close behind the girls. "But you must be careful. Sometimes the ice is thin, so stay close to the shore and never go without an adult close by." She looked at the doctor. "Well," she asked. "What do you think?"

He asked the girls for their opinions, cautiously. "Faith, you and Hope will have to share a room, you know."

"That's okay," Faith said. "As long as I can have the bed by the door."

Hope nodded. "Works for me."

"What do you think, Joy?" Felicity asked.

"I suppose," Joy said, skimming her fingertips across the countertop Julie had just cleaned. "If we have to live way up here, at least this one has potential."

Dr. Adams' wary glance at Julie confirmed what he'd said earlier. Joy was hard to please. He clapped his hands together enthusiastically.

"Alright then. Where do I sign?"

"We haven't even discussed the rent," Julie said. "Are you sure?"

"Whatever the cost, I'm happy to pay," Michael said. "We just need a place for a year and then we can look at something more permanent. If it all works out here, that is."

"Okay then. I have lease agreements at my place," Julie said, waving toward the front door.

Faith pulled on her father's arm. "Can we go to the lake while you sign the papers?"

He glanced at Julie in hesitation, then said, "I don't think that's a good idea. When we leave here, we'll go get something to eat. I don't want you to be full of sand, or worse yet, be soaking wet."

Moans of disappointment from the girls had him shoot Julie a look of desperation, as if he was asking for her help, yet, how could she, the single, childless woman in her mid-forties, understand the nagging, pleading, and agonizing looks of his daughters.

"We're only going to put our feet in, Dad," Hope pleaded.

"I'm a qualified lifeguard now," Joy reminded him.

"And you can see us from Julie's window," Faith added, pointing to the bank of north-facing windows across the back of Julie's place.

Faith was right. Julie had panoramic views from the windows in her kitchen, the Muskoka room, and her bedroom, which ran the length of her place. They could watch the girls from there.

The doctor caved when Felicity said she would stay with the girls. "I'll stick my feet in too," she said. "I'm not going to a fancy restaurant for supper."

"Don't go in above your knees," he called out when the girls took off for the beach.

His smile was such a dad kind of smile, Julie couldn't help grinning. "They'll be fine," she said.

"I'm sure they will, but I guess there's no point in hoping they'll stay dry."

They followed a path through a narrow stretch of woods and came out onto Julie's driveway.

"This grove of trees goes almost to the shoreline," Julie explained. "It gives a little privacy between the two places, but it's not so big you could get lost in it. Just a few rows of trees that have grown tall over the years."

"Have you lived here long?" he asked, as they climbed her front steps and went inside.

"Every summer for as long as I can remember, but it's been my permanent home for the past fourteen years. I love it here. It's the closest thing to heaven I can imagine."

As Julie led him to the kitchen, they heard the squeals of delight coming from the beach. They both laughed, and he shook his head as he looked out the window.

"Something tells me even Joy might grow to like it here," he said, smiling fondly as his girls chased each other in and out of the water.

Turning to business, Julie waved him to a chair. "I'll just get the papers, but I was thinking about the furniture. Do you want me to put all my stuff in storage? I'm sure you'd prefer to use your own things, wouldn't you? It will take some time, but I can arrange it."

"No need," he said. "I'll find a storage unit in Bracebridge, but we will want some things from the moving van. When would I be able to arrange that?"

"If you give me the rest of the day to clean, you can have the place tomorrow. Then you can take the rest of Labour Day weekend to move in." Julie thought about that for a moment. "Oh, but those chairs. I'm refinishing them. That's what I was doing when you all arrived."

"My kitchen set was the last thing on the truck, as it happens. We'll use our chairs. That way, you can take your time with those. Or, if you like, I could finish them for you. I don't mind. I'm handy with things like that."

"I couldn't ask you to do that," Julie said. But maybe she would because no matter how hard she tried, when she put a coat of varnish on anything, she invariably got dust stuck in it. At any rate, she could stack the chairs in the garage for a year, and who would care?

"You didn't ask. I offered."

His smile seemed genuine, so Julie nodded.

"Okay then. But first we should make this official," she said. "I'll just get the papers."

Julie kept a small writing desk near the window in her dining room and in the top drawer, she had a file folder of blank forms for renters who didn't book online. She went to get one and was just opening the drawer when she heard his voice behind her.

"Your home is lovely," he said.

"Goodness!" she gasped. "You shouldn't sneak up on me like that."

"Sorry. I thought the creaking floorboard gave me away."

"Guess I'm just used to it. I didn't notice."

He wandered the length of the room, commenting on the subtle shade of grey on the walls, the landscapes her grandmother had painted in her *artsy days*, as she had called them, and finally he commented on the furniture, old but beautifully finished, with room for eight to sit comfortably. The windows were open, and a gentle autumn breeze fluttered the curtains.

"I'll bet this room has some memories," he said, eyes floating up to the chandelier overhead.

"It certainly has."

"Bedrooms upstairs?" He didn't wait for her to answer. "That's why you have so much space down here."

"Yes, three bedrooms upstairs and a full basement below. It was my grandparents' forever home. They bought the property in the 60s, when my mother was a little girl. When she and Dad got married, they built the cottage you just saw. That's where I spent all my summers."

"And the little cottage where the beach curves around the point?"

"A rental place my grandfather built to help pay his mortgage. Sirona lives there now. You and she have something in common. She's a naturopath."

"Is she? Interesting." Although his tone suggested it wasn't interesting at all. "Not quite the same though, is it?" His head cocked to one side questioningly, as if wanting her to explain.

"Well, you're both in the business of healing." She hadn't taken him for a snob, but perhaps when it came to his profession, he was.

She turned back to the desk drawer and retrieved the folder she'd wanted. "Here's what I'm looking for."

Back in the kitchen, sitting down at her table, Michael twisted the lease agreement toward himself and jotted a figure down on the amount to be paid line.

"That's too much," Julie insisted.

"It isn't. I checked. It's the going rate out here. And I'm thrilled to have a good neighbour living next door. Your place is exactly what we need." He signed and dated the agreement, then turned it back to her. "Is an e-transfer, okay?"

"It's very okay," she said.

"Done," he said.

Julie heard a ping on her phone and confirmed she'd received his payment. "Welcome to Julie's Haven, Dr. Adams."

"Please call me Michael, or Doc, if that seems too informal, but I don't answer to Mike or Mick. Sorry, it's a pet peeve of mine."

"Okay. And I'm Miss Wight at school and Julie here. But never Jewls. A little pet peeve of my own."

"I'll remember." A contented sigh escaped his lips as a gentle breeze wafted through the open window. "Is it always this quiet up here?" he asked.

She nodded. "Most of the time. It's my little piece of heaven because up here, the most complicated my life gets is choosing what kind of wine to drink while I watch the sun go down."

Chapter 2

The following morning Julie was still in her pjs, filling the coffeepot with water, when she heard the rumblings of a truck making its way up Ril Cove Road. The grinding gears, the tires crunching over the gravel and the whine of the engine echoed off the lake. It could only mean one thing. The doctor's moving van had arrived and that meant it had to get into their circle. Her neighbours would know it too, because apart from the odd buzzing of a saw, wood chopping or occasional repairs, it really was quiet this time of year. She wondered, for the briefest of moments, if there would be room to turn the truck around in her circle and hurried to dress in case they needed someone to direct them.

Julie pulled on a pair of jeans and a yellow hoodie, then stuffed her hair into a messy bun. But she needn't have worried, because when she got to the front door, the truck was already in the driveway and Michael was speaking to the man inside. A moment later, the driver shut off the engine and two men jumped down from either side of the truck.

Michael turned back and saw Julie standing on her porch. "Sorry, I hope we didn't wake you," he said, coming her way.

Her hand went unbidden to her hair, tucking an errant strand back in place. "Oh no," she said. "I've been up for ages. I was… reading." That sounded plausible, didn't it?

The rear doors of the truck swung wide and the younger of the two men hoisted himself into the back—a monumental feat, given the distance from the ground and the tiny space for him to stand.

"Kitchen chairs?" he called down.

"Yes, please, and those boxes we discussed," Michael answered.

"Coffee?" Julie called out, and the three men all nodded at once.

"Love some," Michael said. "But only if it's not putting you out."

In her kitchen, Julie brewed a full pot of coffee instead of her usual two cups, then went to tidy herself up. When she looked in the mirror, she was horrified at the sight of the woman staring back at her. No wonder Michael had asked if he'd woken her. She brushed her hair and put it in a single braid down her back, then washed her face and applied a thin layer of eyeliner. As an afterthought, she added two splotches of blush on her pale cheeks and blended them in. She didn't want it to be obvious she'd put on makeup.

The ding on the coffee pot beckoned her back to the kitchen, where she organized a tray of cream, sugar, spoons, and four mugs of coffee. By the time she was back outside, the men were finished unloading the things Michael wanted.

"That's everything?" she asked him, when the young fellow jumped down and closed the doors.

"We needed very little off the truck. Personal things mostly, and those chairs."

"They're almost exactly like mine," she said, a hand running over one of the bow-backed chairs. "Except yours look much nicer."

Michael grinned, taking a cup of coffee off her tray and adding cream. "I got them at a secondhand shop, like everything else in our townhouse," he explained.

"You stripped these and redid them?"

He lifted a shoulder. "Piece of cake. I'll do yours too. If you still want me to, that is. Wouldn't want to push in."

"Well, maybe once you're settled in and have some time." Julie set the tray of coffee on the top box in a stack, clearly labelled FAITH'S BOOKS, and called out to the delivery men. "Coffee's ready."

Michael drained his coffee and set his cup on the tray. Then, with a small smile to her, he picked up two of the chairs and headed to his cottage.

Julie saw little of Michael or his daughters the rest of Saturday, though she heard all of them coming and going down the drive, their voices calling to one another, car doors closing with an echoing thunk. Most noticeable of all was the screen door slapping the frame every time it closed. She should fix it, soften the sound so it stopped reverberating clear across the lake. In the summer, it was a rather satisfying sound, but just now, she found it annoying. Maybe Michael would get annoyed with it, too, and fix it so she wouldn't have to. If he could refinish the kitchen chairs, maybe he could take care of a few other things, too. Another plus for renting to someone who would stay longer than a week or two.

She turned back to the lesson plans she'd been working on all afternoon and the sounds from next door muffled into the background. Eventually, when she retrieved a novel she wanted to finish, the sounds disappeared altogether, and she was transported to another place and time.

It was dark when she closed her book with a satisfied smile, set it on the coffee table and went to the kitchen to make something for her supper. It was quiet across the lake, the sky a beautiful shade of purple except for the tiny hook of the slivered moon, peeking out from behind a cloud. Nothing disturbed the water below, not even a ripple. It reflected the sky above, like a mirror, giving the impression you could step onto it and walk all the way across the cove to the other side. This was what Julie lived for: peace, quiet, serenity and no complications.

She was in the middle of making a tuna sandwich when she heard footsteps on the deck and the soft rap of someone knocking at the back door.

"Yoo Hoo. Okay, to come in?" Sirona called out.

"Goodness!" Julie said, clutching her throat. "I'd forgotten it was Saturday." She hurried to answer the door. "You've brought carrot cake!"

"Of course." Sirona handed over a round plastic container. "I made two. I took the other one next door. Lovely fellow, that new doctor, don't you think?" Sirona glued her matchmaker look to her face and smiled at Julie. Ever since Julie and Eddy had split, Sirona had been hinting it was time Julie got back on that horse. But she wasn't interested.

"I'm sure he is," Julie said. She'd agreed when Felicity had commented on the new doctor's good looks, and she wouldn't argue with Sirona's comment either, but as far as she was concerned, both her friends could just stop meddling in her life.

"And those girls! They're just precious. Bright as pennies and so polite." Sirona settled herself down at Julie's kitchen table and pulled a black silk bag out of her pocket. She slid her Tarot cards out of the silk bag and shuffled, waiting for Julie to brew their tea.

"We're not doing those tonight, are we?" Julie said, filling the kettle. "I thought we were going to play Canasta."

"Don't we always? But what can it hurt to see what the cards have to say? Now come and shuffle, while the kettle boils."

Julie did as she was instructed. Refusing Sirona was never an option, so she might as well just let her do this reading and then they could get on with playing cards, and tea and a little gossip from town, not that Julie cared either way. She wasn't one to talk about others, but Sirona had this unspoken need to impart her knowledge, though it was always with the concern for the greater good. Or so she said.

"Look here," Sirona said with a gasp as she laid out the cards on the table. "The Ace of Cups. You know what that means."

"No, can't say as I do." Julie put a cup of tea at Sirona's elbow and settled into her chair opposite. "What's the Ace of Cups?"

"A new romance." Sirona's eyes flitted toward the other cottage. "I told you."

"Oh, for goodness' sake, Sirona! Give it a rest. What do the rest of these mean? Here this one." Julie tapped the ten of swords. "That guy looks like he's about to keel over with all those sticks in his arms."

"Well, yes, you could say that. But it's in the past, you see, which means the bulk of the heavy lifting is over for you, and isn't it just? You've got that place sorted out and you have a good tenant now, so you can rest easy and enjoy…" She tapped the Ace of Cups.

Julie smirked. "Sometimes, Sirona, I'm convinced you just make this stuff up."

Sirona gathered the cards and indignantly stuffed them back in their silk pouch. "I never make this stuff up," she hissed. "If you don't want to believe the message, that's up to you, but I never, ever, make it up."

Chapter 3

On Tuesday morning, Julie woke, as she always did the opening day of a new school year, refreshed after a good night's sleep and eager to meet all her new students. Most of them, she knew because they'd been in Rebecca's grade one class last year, but there were two unfamiliar names on her class list. Hope Adams was one, although she wasn't unfamiliar now. The other was Piper George. She and her brother had been homeschooled until now, but when their parents had split and Piper's mother had returned to work, she'd registered the children at Baysville Elementary. Piper was in Julie's class, her brother would be in grade four.

Julie recalled seeing the George family at hockey games when she and Eddy were still together. Ian, Piper's father, and Eddy had played on the same team in the men's league in Huntsville. Occasionally she and Piper's mother had watched the games together, but Vivian George hadn't gone to the pub for drinks after the games, because she had two children to take care of. Ian hadn't missed his chance for a beer, and Eddy and Julie had always taken him home afterwards. She wondered who was driving Ian home from the pub now that Eddy had moved away.

There was something about a new school year that Julie loved, probably as much as her students did. Maybe it was the return to a routine, after a long structureless summer. Or the promise of autumn, her favourite season. Or maybe it was the excitement of an eager group of students, just waiting to have their heads filled with endless knowledge. That morning, Julie was up before dawn, eager to get her run in and then get to school, a little early if she could. She dressed in her running gear, did her stretches in the living room, then slipped out her front door.

As she came to the end of the trees separating her driveway from the one next door, Julie ran headlong into Michael, colliding with such force it nearly knocked them both off their feet and onto their backsides.

"Sorry," he said, reaching out to save her from falling. "I should have… God. I'm so sorry."

"It's fine. Doc. No harm done." She tugged at her ponytail and jogged on the spot. "You want to join me?"

"Sure. Yeah. I'd like that."

When she'd regained her rhythm and headed for the road, he moved in beside her, keeping pace as they made their way out of the circle and onto Ril Cove Road.

"Getting settled?" she asked when they came to South Ril Lake Road and turned left.

"Surprisingly, Joy has been a big help."

"So, she's adjusting to life here in the *land time forgot*." Julie made air quotes around the words and grinned.

He laughed. "Yeah. Something like that."

They came to the first of many hills and by the time they reached the top of it, Julie could see he wasn't used to them. "Doing okay there, Doc?" she asked, a grin spreading across her face.

"Of course," he said, sounding a little winded. "I'll manage. Are all the hills this big?"

Julie picked up the pace across a flat stretch. "What's the matter? Afraid you can't handle it?"

"Something like that," he half mumbled under his breath. "I'm more of a sprinter than a long-distance runner. You know, built for speed, not endurance."

"Ah. Well, you can turn back any time if you like."

"Ha! Not going to happen."

After a bend in the road, Julie picked up a little more speed. Michael sprinted to keep up with her. "Jesus, you can't keep that pace for the whole nine K, can you?"

"I'm used to it."

"I'm okay with the distance, but I usually go to the Y and run the track."

"No indoor tracks around here. I just don't have that luxury."

A hundred yards later, Julie pointed up toward Lookout Point. "There's a staircase to the top and a bench when you get there. Best place around to watch the sunset."

"Good to know," he said, glancing toward the embankment that led up to the Point. "Looks steep."

"Hence the steps."

They continued in silence after that because there was little else to note. Their surroundings were more of the same: trees, cottages, little laneways that trickled off the main road, and the occasional view out over the lake. Usually, Julie ran solo and with no one to talk to, so that all she ever heard was the slap of her feet on the road, the distant call of a bird and the occasional whine of a boat motor somewhere out on the lake. It was a pleasant change to have someone else huffing up the hills alongside her that morning, although by the last leg of their trek, Julie was a little concerned her new running mate was struggling. She opted to take the shortcut through Annie and Joe Hewitt's place, which brought them out to the beach, where they splashed along the shore the rest of the way back.

"I'll get us some water," she said, when Michael collapsed in a deck chair by his fire pit. A moment later, she returned with two bottles of ice-cold water and handed him one.

"Thanks," he said, unscrewing the lid. "Can we do this again tomorrow? I really need someone to challenge me."

"Sure." Julie took a long drink, letting the cool water rush down her parched throat, then set the cold bottle to her neck. "You said you're a sprinter, so I assumed you keep up a good pace." She was still panting a little, catching her breath. "But that run was a little fast for me."

"Thank god. I thought I was just getting old."

"We're all getting old, Doc, but we can take it a little slower tomorrow."

"Yeah, like that'll help with those hills." He tugged his shirt over his head and wiped the sweat from his body.

Julie wanted to avert her eyes, but she couldn't help following his movements, over the muscles of his arms and then to his chest, bare, except for the tidy little cropping of curls across his pecs. She felt a flush of heat rising in her cheeks and tried to turn away. Too late. He'd noticed her blush but had the good manners not to say anything. Instead, he gulped back the last of his water, recapped the bottle and handed it to her.

"Thanks again," he said, still huffing a bit. "Have a great first day back."

"You too," she said, then went home to get ready.

It was just before eight in the morning when Julie opened the door to her classroom and slid the windows open to let in the September breeze. She placed the infamous treasure box where she kept small rewards for her students on her desk. It was a curiosity piece made of intricately carved wood, with a jewel studded domed lid that looked like it was something out of a Harry Potter movie. When she'd seen it at an auction house several years ago, Julie knew exactly what she wanted to use it for.

On the first day of school, each of her students could choose an item from the box. She had a friend in Huntsville who made zipper charms, which Julie bought and put in the box just for the first day. Julie's friend crafted some each year with her students in mind and this year there were gold stars and bright red hearts, miniature hockey sticks and even some baseballs with fake autographs on them, anything that seven-year-olds might like. Throughout the year, Julie would refill it with other things, fancy pencils or fun things she found at the dollar store, but on this first day, the selection was a little more special.

Her desk was organized. The classroom was tidy and waiting. A glance at the clock told her she had fifteen minutes until the bell went. Across the hall, Rebecca seemed to scramble to get the Grade One room ready. She could offer to help, but Becs preferred to do things her own way, so Julie picked up the giant number 2 sign she would hold to let her students know where to line up and headed outside.

Baysville Elementary had a student population of just over a hundred, ranging from Kindergarten to Grade Six. Most of the students rode buses to get to school, but those that walked were already filling the playground and the soccer field beyond when Julie went outside. A huddle of sixth-grade girls, obviously eyeing the sixth-grade boys who were playing basketball on the tarmac, lingered at the edge of the playground. Other groups of girls huddled near the older student's entrance, while the younger children occupied the playground equipment near the Junior entrance.

It surprised Julie to see the Adams' car pull into the school driveway rather than the one across the street at the new clinic where Michael should be going. He got out of the car, a suit and tie replacing his running attire from earlier. As he approached the playground gate, he squinted into the morning sun and gave her a little wave.

"Are you sure the girls are alright on the bus?" he asked, when she went to talk to him.

"Helicopter parenting, are we?" Julie teased.

He frowned. "No, I wouldn't call it that. I just worry."

"Try not to. They're on Turtle Ted's bus. He's the best, and they will be fine."

Across the street, Gwen Sheridan pulled into the clinic parking lot. The unmistakable blue bungalow had once belonged to Wally and Doris, who owned the local mechanic's garage but was now converted to the new clinic.

"Do you have patients this morning?" Julie asked.

Michael glanced over his shoulder where Gwen was unlocking the door and going inside, then shook his head. "Nothing on my schedule until eleven. Mrs. Sheridan said she would catch me up with how things work."

"Well, they don't work. At least not yet. I'm sure they told you that you're the first doctor in the village, so I expect you'll call the shots." He grinned, and Julie winced, realizing the unintentional pun. "Oh, that was bad, wasn't it?"

The corner of his mouth twitched up in a smile. "I rather think she will be the one calling the shots," he said.

"Touché!"

"Sometimes I'm on point."

"Okay. Enough. Stop it!" she insisted. "Remind me never to hit you with a pun again."

He laughed and cast one last look over the playground. "Well, I should be on my way. I don't want to be late. I have a feeling I'll be in for it if I am."

"Don't let this get out," Julie said. "But Gwen is really a sweetheart."

"Head nurse in a hospital ER for over thirty years? I seriously doubt that."

He pushed off the fence he'd been leaning against and headed back toward his car with a little *see-ya-later* salute from behind.

If Michael only knew how right he was about Gwen Sheridan, Julie thought. She'd come out of retirement to run the new clinic, at the request of the village board. Everyone knew she would run a tight ship and heaven help the patient or the doctor who got in her way.

At ten to nine, the last of the four buses that serviced the catchment area for Baysville Elementary rolled into the parking lot. Ted Sheridan, Gwen's husband, who all the students called Turtle Ted because he collected toy turtles of every shape, size and colour, swung the door open wide.

The first two passengers to disembark were Ali Hewitt and Hope Adams, who descended the steps, sporting their new backpacks. Hope had a shiny pink *Barbie* one, and Ali's was lilac with multi-coloured rainbows, pink hearts, and sparkling white unicorns. Ali's favourite bear, Fred, peeked out of the back of hers, while Blind Bruce, who wasn't blind anymore, stuck out of Hope's.

He fixed Blind Bruce! Julie thought, and a smidgeon of pride for the doctor made her smile. That he'd accomplished this task on his own, despite his comment that it was more than he could manage, spoke volumes about the father he was to his daughters.

Julie had been sure that Ali and Hope would be best friends the minute they met each other, given their natures. She could picture Ali eagerly watching Hope get on the bus and the first thing she would have said is, *'sit with me.'* That's all it would have taken for them to be on their way to a wonderful friendship.

"Good morning girls," Julie said, holding the sign with her name and the number 2 a little higher so all the children in the schoolyard could see it.

"Morning Miss Wight," Hope said, with a proud grin, because she'd remembered that at school she must call Julie by her proper name.

"How was the bus ride?" Julie asked.

"Great! I sat with my new friend, Ali Hewitt. She lives near us." Hope nudged Ali's shoulder.

"Hi Miss Wight," said Ali with a grin. "Noah says hi too, but he's ignoring me, because he thinks he's too cool to talk to second graders now that he's in grade three."

Noah Hewitt and his cousin Ryder sped past to line up in front of the grade three teacher, Sarah Gillespie, who stood a few feet away holding up her own sign. Both boys had been in Julie's class last year, though Ryder hadn't enrolled until just after Christmas. He'd been a little shy at first, but soon gained a foothold with the other boys, when he proved himself to be an outstanding hockey player. Ryder had suffered a tragic loss when his mother had died of cancer just over a year before. Now he lived with his Uncle Joe and Aunt Annie Hewitt, and they all seemed to get along well.

Noah was anything but shy and loved to tell jokes. He was already planning a career in standup comedy and loved to corner people and tell them his jokes. No matter how corny they were, everyone laughed.

"Have you got a joke for us today?" Julie asked Noah as he hurried to get in line.

"Here's one just for you, Miss Wight. What time would it be if Godzilla came to school?"

"Hmm." Julie thought for a moment. "I give up. What time would it be?"

"Time to run!" Noah said proudly, then burst into a fit of giggles.

By now there was a growing din of children's screams of pleasure as they met up with friends they hadn't seen since June. When the five-minute warning bell broke through their laughter, they all scrambled to find their place in their respective line.

"Line up over here, grade twos!" Julie called out, holding her sign high in the air.

Rebecca Vickers was beside her, doing the same for her grade ones with Sarah Gillespie on the other side of Julie, watching for her threes and fours.

A parent might have thought it utter chaos, but amid the laughter and excited cheers, Julie organized her class and led them inside, down the hall past the office and the Kindergarten room, until they arrived at hers. Inside, Julie stood next to her desk while her students scrambled to identify their hooks, which Julie had labelled with their names, and find a desk of their choosing. She would reorganize their seats if the chatter got out of hand, but for now, she wanted them to settle in comfortably. After opening exercises, and a get acquainted time, they got started with their first lesson of the day.

Julie had yard duty at morning recess and when she went outside and walked around the playground area, Faith waved and ran up to see her. Trailing, though not far behind, were two other girls Julie recognized. Joanna Morgan and Shelby Mason had both been helpers in Julie's classroom.

"Hello girls," Julie said.

"Hi Miss Wight," they chimed in unison.

"I see you've made some friends, Faith," Julie said.

"I have. They're readers like me." Faith was almost bubbling over with enthusiasm. "Joanna is already on the third book of The Hunger Games series. She's going to lend me Catching Fire when I finish the first one."

Joanna was eager to share some news they'd been discussing. "We three are going to write a play as part of our English project," she said. "We were thinking of a Thanksgiving theme, a modern day take on the pioneer's story."

"That's a great idea," Julie agreed. "Maybe you'd let the grade twos act it out for you."

"Could they?" Shelby asked. "That would be so much fun."

"I'm sure we can arrange it. Let me know when you have a rough draft ready and we can talk about it some more," Julie suggested.

"Cool. But we're going to skip now. I've got a new rope, and Faith says she can do over two hundred in Double Dutch." Shelby held up a neon green skipping rope in the air and a crowd of girls called them over to an empty spot on the tarmac.

As they went, Julie felt as if things were falling into place nicely for at least two of the Adams children. Hope had befriended Ali and now Faith seemed to have found her niche, too. With any luck, Joy was having an equally good day at Bracebridge and Muskoka Lakes Secondary and they would all be happy their father had moved them all the way from Niagara Falls.

When a shadow fell across the tarmac a few feet away, Julie turned to see Rebecca Vickers heading her way.

"Everything okay?" Julie asked, seeing the worried look on Rebecca's face.

"Fine. Fine. I just… never mind. Was that Faith Adams you were just talking to?"

"And Joanna Morgan and Shelby Mason."

"Yes, well, I know those two, obviously." She crossed her arms over her chest as her eyes drifted over the field. "Where's the other one?"

"Other one?"

"The other Adams girl. She's younger. In your class, I believe."

Julie shaded her eyes from the sun and searched the playground until she found Ali and Hope standing next to one of the soccer posts.

"There," she said, pointing in their direction. "That's Hope, with Ali Hewitt. Instant best friends."

"Hmm. I see."

"You see what, exactly?" Julie asked, wondering why Rebecca was so interested in the new girls. Piper George and her brother were new students too, but she hadn't asked about them.

"It's nothing. I was just curious."

Then Julie figured it out. "You were on the selection committee. You knew about Dr. Adams and his three daughters."

"I was just curious. You know, bachelor, mid-forties."

"A widower, actually, and I wouldn't go there if I were you. You have a love 'em and leave 'em kind of attitude with men. Even you've admitted that."

Rebecca held up her hand. "I am aware, thank you very much. But if I don't keep my options open, I might miss Mr. Right. So, unless *you're* interested in him, Julie, maybe you'll get the scoop for me."

"The scoop?" Julie stifled an outright laugh.

"You know what I mean. What kind of wine does he drink? What does he do for fun? You know. Find out what makes the guy tick."

"I will not do that. That's not who I am."

"Well then. I might just have to break an arm or get the flu or something, so I can visit the new clinic." Rebecca rubbed her stomach and scrunched her face into a grimace. "In fact, I feel queasy right now. I think I'm coming down with something."

"That was sudden." Julie almost laughed at Rebecca's performance.

But Rebecca wasn't listening. She was heading toward the gate. "If I'm late getting back, tell Vince. Maybe he can send one of his students to supervise my class for a few minutes."

"Wait! You can't…"

But Julie's words fell on deaf ears as Rebecca headed down the driveway, across University Street, and up the steps of the new medical clinic.

Chapter 4

During the rest of the first week of school, the usual things took place to prepare the staff and students in the event of emergencies. They had a fire drill on Wednesday, followed by a visit from two volunteers who came across the road from the fire station. The lockdown drill was on Thursday, which seemed redundant to Julie, because she found it impossible to imagine an event like that could ever happen in a tiny village so far from anywhere that mattered.

It was required by the board, so Officer Darren Meyers of the Bracebridge Police Department, who was a recent graduate of the police college, was the policeman who visited that day. Darren's grandfather was Slim Meyers, who lived on the other side of Ril Lake. Julie's family and the Meyers had known each other for years, and no one was prouder of Darren's accomplishments than Slim.

"Remember," Darren said when he was getting ready to leave Julie's classroom. "Three sharp rings of the bell mean you must go to the safe place inside this classroom. So, tell me again, what should you do if you hear it?"

"Go to our classroom. Gather in a safe place away from the windows," all the children chimed in unison.

"Good, and Miss Wight knows what to do next, so watch and listen to her for further instructions. Now, I think that about covers it so, I'll say goodbye, children."

"Goodbye, Officer Meyers," they all had shouted as Darren closed the door behind him.

On Friday afternoon, just before dismissal time, Julie settled her class down to write stories about their summer holidays. It was a great way to gain insight into her students' interests, and to give an indication of their spelling and grammar abilities, which would help her prepare lesson plans going forward. When the bell rang to end the school day, she collected their stories and tucked them into her satchel. She couldn't wait to read them over the weekend.

Rebecca cornered her on her way to her car. "Find out anything I should know?" she asked Julie.

"You're the one who went over there the other day."

They both looked toward the building across the street. "He wasn't taking patients on Tuesday, so I made an appointment for next week."

"I hope your queasy stomach doesn't get worse." Julie tossed her satchel onto the passenger seat of her car, a small grin curling her lip. She knew exactly what Rebecca was up to and it had nothing to do with being sick.

"Got any plans this weekend? Why don't you invite me up for a drink? We could sit on the deck. I'll bring a pizza or something, or…" She batted her eyelashes. "Are you keeping him all to yourself?"

"Sheesh, Becs. They're tenants. That's it. I hardly see them at all." Except that wasn't quite true because every morning, for the past four days, she and the new doc had been running the Ring Road and once or twice they'd sat on her deck or his, sipping wine and chatting until the sun went down. It was their plan for this evening too, to talk about their work week, after the girls settled to watch a movie. But first he was taking them out for dinner—a celebration, he'd said, of their first week in their new digs.

Rebecca wasn't giving up. "Just renting. Sure. I seriously doubt that. But if you're so sure there's nothing going on, then how about I come by on Saturday? In the afternoon and…"

"I'll be reading papers all weekend. Don't you have lessons to plan or marking to do?"

Rebecca nodded. "I can work around that. What time should I be there?"

Julie got into her car, shaking her head. It really was ridiculous the way Becs was carrying on, and she hadn't the slightest idea what more she could do to dissuade her. As she started the engine, Rebecca knocked on the passenger side window.

"I'll see you tomorrow, around two."

"Fine." Julie waved her away from the car and pulled out of the parking lot and down the long drive out of the school grounds.

All the way home, she turned over the conversation with Rebecca in her mind, getting more annoyed by the minute. What was her deal? Did she really have to push so hard? It would never work between her and Michael, anyway. He'd already told Julie a couple of evenings ago that he wasn't interested in a relationship. The girls were his priority and had been for the past seven years since he was playing a dual parent role.

Julie pulled into her driveway moments before Turtle Ted stopped the bus and opened the door to let the Adams girls out. They waved to her as they crossed the circle, then disappeared behind the trees that separated the two properties. Joy had a determined look on her face and was hurrying her sisters along. She stopped when Hope dropped Bruce, then nudged her down the drive. Julie retrieved her satchel from the car, pushed the lock button on her fob, and went inside. She couldn't help thinking the doc had been right. Joy really was taking charge.

A change of clothes and a cup of tea later, she was sitting on the back deck, reviewing the first week of school in her mind, when she heard a knock on the wooden railing below.

"Permission to come up?" She smiled, recognizing the voice of her new neighbour.

"Of course, Doc," she called out. "Want a cup of tea? I've just brewed a pot."

"Tempting as that sounds," he said when he'd reached the top step. "The girls thought it would be nice if you joined us for dinner, and I do, too."

"That's kind of you. I... Um..." Julie was feeling relaxed in her casual *hanging around the house clothes*, and wondered what excuse she could give him. But she had nothing pressing to do, so why not?

"Sure," she said finally. "I'll need to change, though. Can't go to town in sweats. Where are you going, by the way?"

"Gwen suggested a place in Huntsville. *That Little Place By the Lights*. The girls all love Italian food, so it sounded like a good bet."

"Great choice! Okay. I'll meet you in the driveway in... is ten minutes, okay?"

"Perfect. See you in ten."

When Julie stepped out her front door, expecting to take her usual path through the trees to the cottage, she found Michael's car in her driveway. He held open the passenger door for her, then closed it when she was inside. The girls, lined up across the back seat, were grinning like a row of proverbial Cheshire Cats.

"Hello girls," Julie said, wondering what the joke was all about, and if she was the brunt of it. "Is my skirt riding up or is my bra strap showing?" She knew neither were true, but she waited for an answer, anyway.

"You look nice, Miss Wight," Hope said, then giggled behind her hand. "I mean Julie. We're not in school now."

"Thank you, Hope. You all look nice, too."

Michael got in behind the wheel, with a quick glance in his mirror at his three grinning daughters.

"What's gotten into the three of you?" he asked.

"Nothing," they said in unison.

He shot Julie a questioning glance. "Did I miss something?"

"If you did, I missed it too."

"Okay then. That Little Place By the Lights, it is."

The drive to Huntsville was anything but the quiet ride Julie had expected after the girls' silence. They were bubbling over with news about school, new friends, and their teachers. After a while, when Joy could get reception on her phone, she looked up the restaurant's menus so she and her sisters could decide what they were going to order.

Their preoccupation with food left Julie silently watching the scenery until they pulled into the parking lot behind the restaurant. When they got out of the car and walked up King Street, Joy and Faith hurried along ahead. Hope had to run to catch up, but she did, eventually, leaving Michael and Julie trailing behind.

"I'm sorry," he whispered.

"For what?" she asked in surprise.

"My daughters," he nodded toward the girls. "You didn't notice their not-so-subtle attempts at matchmaking?"

She grinned. "Oh, I noticed. But you can tell them they'll have to get in line."

"Oh?"

"Felicity has already been singing your praises and I believe you've met Sirona, the carrot cake lady, who lives in my other cottage?"

She found it endearing when he blushed and grinned sheepishly at her. "I'm not sure why everyone thinks single people have to find partners."

"Me either. It's been two years since Eddy and I split up. I've been happy on my own. I don't need a man to make me feel complete."

"Is Eddy your husband?" Michael asked.

"We weren't married, but we were together for a long time. He's been gone for just over two years now and I honestly like being on my own."

"Right. I completely understand," he said as they turned the corner onto Main Street. "I'm far too busy raising my girls to even think about a relationship."

Julie wondered if she should warn him about Rebecca Vickers and let him know that someone was hot on his trail. Becs wouldn't be the only one. Any single woman, and some married ones too, would fill his office with unsubstantiated ailments just to get a glimpse of, and maybe a date with, the newest available man in town. But Michael looked as if he could take care of himself in that department, so she said nothing.

In the restaurant, Julie let the girls choose their seats at the table first but wasn't surprised to find the only seat left was the one right next to Michael, with Faith and Hope across from them, and Joy sitting at the end.

"What are you having, Faith?" Julie asked, once they were all settled.

"I'm not sure yet. But I really like your dress." Faith glanced toward her father. "Doesn't Julie look pretty tonight, Dad?"

"She certainly does," he agreed, leaning over to tuck a stray lock of Julie's hair back in place with a conspiratorial kind of smile.

The girls couldn't have been more obvious if they'd come right out and said they wanted them to be a couple.

"Why thank you, Dr. Adams," Julie said, enjoying the game, just a little.

He turned back to the table. "We should try this style with your hair sometime, Faith. Maybe Julie would teach me how to do it."

"Will you, Julie?" Faith asked.

"Of course," Julie said with a smile in Faith's direction. "It's easy. You could do it yourself."

A few minutes later, the girls all got up to use the Ladies' room and when they were gone, Julie lifted her purse from the back of her chair.

"Do you mind if I sit across from you?" she asked. "It feels awkward to talk to you sitting here."

When she had changed chairs, the waiter arrived with the wine and poured some into Michael's glass. He sampled it, swirled it a little, and nodded his approval.

"You can leave the bottle," he said to the man.

"You're driving," Julie reminded.

"You're not, so drink up." He filled her glass and poured a little in Joy's. "Sometimes, I let her have a sip or two. She doesn't really like the taste, but it makes her feel grown up."

"She's lovely, you know. All your girls are. Don't make a big deal about this matchmaking business. I'm sure they just want a maternal figure in their life."

"They do, actually. Joy does her best to mother her sisters, but she's a little bossy something and that doesn't go over well."

His eyes followed Julie's hand as she tried the wine. "That's nice," she said. "I love wines from the Niagara area. You must have been spoiled for choice living there."

He nodded. "Not that I had a lot of time to visit all those wineries." He swirled his glass again, then changed the subject, again.

"Hope told me you'll be discussing family this month at school."

"We will. You've met Felicity Pierce. She's a genealogist and she'll be in our class a few times. We'll talk about our families, and the kids will make an ancestral tree."

There was something about his expression that made Julie want to drop this topic. Having lost his wife, it must be difficult for him to speak about family and those connections.

"How was your first week at the clinic?" she asked, changing the subject. "Did you get Gwen all sorted out?"

"Ha! The other way around you mean. I don't know what I'd do without her. She's organized, she knows the billing, and she's much more than a nurse."

Julie plucked a bun out of the breadbasket, cut it in half and buttered it, wondering what was taking the girls so long.

"Do you think I should check on the girls?" she asked when she'd eaten half the bun, and they still weren't back.

"I'm sure it's fine. You saw Joy grab her cellphone on the way by, didn't you?"

"No. I didn't catch that. You have parental vision, I guess."

He laughed and buttered a bun for himself. "They'll be talking to their grandmother. They usually do on Friday nights."

"Is that your mother or their other grandmother? Or is that being too personal?"

"It's my mother. Grace's parents are both gone. In fact, when I met her, she was alone in the world. I think it's what attracted me to her, that lonely, lost little girl aura she had. I thought I could help, you know... It's the way I am, I guess. Always have to fix everything." He paused as the girls crossed the dining room and returned to the table.

"Here they are," he said.

Joy slipped her phone back into her purse. "Sorry Dad, but you know how precise Grandma is with our calls."

"I knew what you were up to. How's she doing?" He asked.

"She's fine and Granddad says hello too. They'll call you sometime over the weekend."

The waiter returned to take their orders. When he was gone again, Hope told Julie some news. "We're having a sleepover tomorrow."

"That's exciting. Who's coming?" Julie asked.

"Naturally, I invited Ali,"

Hope had been using the word *naturally* a lot in school all week, so hearing it again made Julie smile. Out of the corner of her eye, she saw Michael grinning too. Obviously, it had become part of her vocabulary at home, too. Hope prattled on about the party.

"Joy's new friend Rachel is coming, and Faith invited Joanna. Naturally, we're going to have homemade pizza for supper and pancakes in the morning."

"Naturally," Julie said. "You're welcome to use my canoes if you like. There are enough lifejackets for everyone in my garage." She glanced at Michael. "Sorry, I should have talked to you about it first.

"No, it's a great idea." He nodded his approval. "I might go too," he said. "You could come too, Julie. The girls can take the canoes, and you and I can paddle the kayaks. Keep an eye on them." He flashed Julie a *wait-for-it* wink.

"No way!" Joy cried. "Adult supervision from the dock only, please."

"As long as you keep the canoes close to shore," Michael agreed.

Later, when they arrived at home, Michael pulled into Julie's driveway first, to drop her off. The girls got out of the car and hurried across to their place, leaving the two of them alone.

He grinned. "Sorry, but it seems my little matchmakers are at it again." He got out and opened her door for her. "I didn't mean for this to be a date or anything like that."

"It's fine, and like I said before, it's understandable. They just want you to be happy. You can't blame them for that. Besides, I had a nice time."

"I did too. Are we running in the morning, or do you need a day off?"

"Wouldn't miss it, but since it's Saturday, can we sleep in?"

Julie smiled. "I suppose so. See you at six-thirty instead of six, then."

"That's sleeping in?" he asked.

"Okay, how about seven?" she relented.

"If that's the best I can hope for…"

Chapter 5

On Saturday afternoon after her usual household tasks, Julie sat in the Muskoka Room, tea in hand, reading over her students' summer stories. She had been so engrossed she'd completely forgotten Rebecca had invited herself over (or maybe she'd forgotten on purpose, hoping Becs wouldn't show up) until the knocking on her front door, brought Julie back to yesterday, the school parking lot and Rebecca's self-serving invitation.

She had only three more stories to read, after which she'd planned to visit Felicity for tea. She couldn't help wishing she'd been a little more insistent yesterday with Rebecca, not that it would have done any good. Still, she knew her only motive for coming was to flirt with Michael. Maybe since he was busy with the sleepover, they might not even see him at all.

The girls were on the lake in Julie's canoes. She'd been watching them off and on for the past hour, in between stories. Joy had taken the lead, expertly maneuvering her canoe. Julie wondered if she'd taken lessons. Her strokes were even and sure, and not once did she flip her paddle from side to side, like a beginner would. Faith and Joanna were in the bows while Ali and Hope, much to their loud disappointment, had been relegated to the mid-ship seats without paddles. Their job, as per Joy's instructions, was to watch for rocks, which, given the proximity to the shore, was an important task, indeed.

When Michael had seen both canoes safely off from Julie's dock, he'd looked her way and acknowledged his thanks for letting the girls use the boats.

"You're a brave man, Doc," she had called back. "Six girls at once. I don't envy you."

He had laughed and told her they were having pizza after their paddle.

"Why don't you join us? Joe's here and he's promised to help. Apparently, he fancies himself a bit of a chef."

"He's a great cook. They have neighbourhood dinners at the lodge all the time. You'll be invited now that you are part of the Ril Lake family."

"Join us then," he'd said.

"Thanks, but I've got marking to do and I wouldn't want to spoil any male bonding time you two have planned."

He'd grinned at that. "Suit yourself. You don't know what you're missing."

And then he had gone back to his side of the woods, where Joe was just coming out to the deck, a glass in each hand. It would be nice, Julie thought, for Michael to make some friends here, and Joe Hewitt was just the man for that.

She, on the other hand didn't need friends, especially the fair-weather kind like Rebecca Vickers, who was standing on her porch at that moment, with a bottle of wine in one hand and a me-dium-sized pepperoni pizza in the other. She didn't really want her here, but Julie would not be rude, even if she thought Rebecca was, so she pushed open the door and waved her inside.

"You found the place, I see," Julie said, leading the way to the kitchen.

"We were all here in June for your end-of-year barbeque, so it's not like I didn't know where I was going."

"I forgot about that." Or she'd tried to.

Rebecca had pushed her into hosting the party when no one could decide what to do to wrap up the school year. Rebecca had come up with the idea and wouldn't let it go until Julie finally agreed. She wasn't one for a lot of company, preferring her privacy and couldn't help thinking once others got a taste of her tranquil sur-roundings, they might want to be there all the time. They hadn't, which Julie found curious, but at the same time, she was grateful. Until now.

Rebecca gave a little shudder as she took in their surround-ings. "You really are out in the sticks, though, you know."

"I am. And that's just how I like it. Have a seat. I'll get some plates and napkins."

"Why don't we eat outside on your deck?" Rebecca suggested.

"It's a bit cool, and the sun will set before long."

"You've got shawls, don't you? Isn't that what's hanging there, by the door?"

"I do, but…" Julie glanced out her kitchen window where the girls were now paddling toward shore. Michael and Joe were sitting in deck chairs, ready to help them dock.

Rebecca followed her gaze, and Julie knew it landed on Michael when she said, "Magnificent views from here."

"Since you're not looking at the lake or the tree line, I'll have to assume you mean the guys on the dock next door. The girls are having a slumber party," Julie told her.

"Well then. The more the merrier, I say." Rebecca gathered the pizza, the plates and the napkins. "Bring the wine, will you, Julie?" she called out over her shoulder as she headed for the back door.

Reluctantly, Julie followed Rebecca out to the deck and set the wine on the patio table. But Rebecca had the gas-lit firepit in mind and put the pizza there, mentioning the nicer view from that side of the deck.

"Dr. Adams has a friend. Is that Joe Hewitt?" she said, hovering closer to the railing.

"We are not joining them," Julie insisted. "It's a private party."

Reluctantly, Rebeccas settled into a chair and ate two slices of pizza and guzzled a full glass of wine. While she was refilling her glass, Michael came across to help the girls drag the canoes onto the beach. While they were hanging up their lifejackets, he looked in Julie's direction, waved and repeated his earlier invitation. Before Rebecca could say anything, Julie shook her head and called out her thanks.

"You should have accepted," Rebecca said, with a little pout.

"It would spoil their fun."

"Their fun! What about ours?"

"Let it go," Julie warned, taking a healthy sip of her wine. "Honestly, Becs you'd think you were desperate."

"Maybe I am?" Rebecca's eyes met Julie's. Her frown deepened. "If I was desperate? Would you help me then?"

"Becs come on. You don't mean that."

In some ways, Julie felt sorry for Rebecca. If she wasn't so pushy, maybe she'd find someone nice, instead of all the one-night stands she seemed to have lately. Julie reached out her hand to rest it on Rebecca's arm, but the gesture seemed to unsettle her.

"No." Rebecca said, shaking her head and pulling her arm away. "I'm not desperate in that way. Not what you're thinking."

"I wasn't thinking anything at all," Julie said, helping herself to a slice of pizza. "I don't think you're desperate, but I happen to know Michael isn't looking for a relationship right now."

"Michael, eh? Not Dr. Adams?"

"We're neighbours. What do you expect me to call him?"

Rebecca shrugged. "Are you sure you're not just keeping him all to yourself?"

"Nothing like that. Just friends."

"If you say so." Rebecca placed a half-eaten slice of pizza onto her napkin and dusted the flour from her fingers. "Hey, how far is it across the lake?"

"I don't know the exact distance. Why? Are you thinking of swimming it? The water is a little chilly."

"Hell no. I was just curious. Looks like there are a lot of cottages up here. I guess they're mostly vacant this time of year?"

"I suppose. I don't keep tabs on everyone's places. It's enough to manage my own."

"Yeah. I get it. Well…" She pushed to the edge of her chair, eyes flitting toward Michael's dock, then back again. "I should go. You're busy and I've got stuff to do."

Julie wasn't about to encourage her to stay longer. Rebecca would, Julie knew, eventually hit on Michael, and that left her wondering, for the second time, if she should warn him. Or should she mind her own business and let them work it out?

As she watched Rebecca turn her car around the circle and head out the drive, Julie decided to let it go. Michael was a grown man and he could make up his own mind about Rebecca and anyone else who came along and showed an interest, and no doubt there would be others. And as he'd told her last night, he could handle himself in that department. She certainly hoped that was true.

Chapter 6

There are screams, and then there are screams. The one that came from the cottage next door just after nine that Saturday night was the shrill, ear-piercing kind you'd hear from someone who was frightened beyond belief. It was so shrill that Sirona and Julie, who'd been playing Canasta, shot out of their chairs and raced to the door.

"That came from next door." Sirona's eyes widened as Julie reached for the baseball bat she kept by the back door and headed outside.

While they'd been playing cards, a fog had settled, leaving the night air thick with moisture and the boards of Julie's deck a little slippery.

"Stay behind me," she said, edging her way past Sirona, who had adopted a comical kung-fu kind of pose, hands in the air, ready to do battle with an intruder. If the situation hadn't seemed so grave, Julie might have burst out laughing and teased her just a little. Instead, she grabbed the railing and, with Sirona breathing down her neck, crept down the back steps and into the foggy, black night.

With only a hazy porch light from Michael's deck guiding them, they made their way through the underbrush of the patch of wood between the properties and came out onto the dewy grass on the other side. The night sky was black as pitch, not even a sliver of moonlight shining through the fog. Twice, Sirona reached out for support from Julie.

"You should have waited at my place," Julie whispered.

"Not a chance." Sirona might be in her mid-sixties, have arthritic hips and knees, but if something was going on, she wanted to know about it firsthand. So, on they went.

A few feet further along, as they were passing Michael's firepit, a shadowy figure loomed just up ahead. Julie readied her bat. She'd aim for the knees and take the intruder down in one fell swoop. But as she raised her arms, the figure turned and a beam of light blinded her momentarily. It was Michael, one hand brandishing a poker from the fireplace high in the air, the other holding up his phone, flashlight glaring in their eyes.

"Oh, it's you," he said, lowering the weapon and the light. "Sorry. I thought you were an intruder."

"What's happened?" Julie asked.

"The girls saw someone at our window." He threw the flashlight's beam across the line of trees behind them.

"Poor things. They must be scared to death," Sirona chirped. "Is it alright if I go inside with them?"

"Good idea," he said. "They're pretty hysterical."

While Sirona made her way up the steps to Michael's deck, a rustling sound near Julie's dock sent her and Michael in that direction. Julie's baseball bat was at the ready while Michael, armed with his poker, swept the beam of light from side to side across their path. They held their breath, took one silent step at a time, until a rabbit bounded out of the underbrush and scurried up the hill toward the driveways.

Julie stifled a nervous laugh. "Goodness, he scared me half to death. Maybe we should just call the police."

"I already did," he confessed. "But I figured they'd take forever to get here, so I thought I'd have a look around myself."

"Are you sure it was a person the girls saw and not an owl settling on the deck rail or something?"

"Faith said she saw a woman looking in the living room window. My porch light wasn't on then, and in this fog it's hard to know for sure what she saw."

"So, maybe it was an animal or a bird."

"The thing is, I was just about to tell the girls a ghost story, and Faith has a pretty active imagination, so maybe she didn't actually see someone. Then again, maybe she did."

"It might be someone who's lost or even injured. Her screams probably scared them off, but I still think we should check it out, in case someone needs our help. Tell you what. I'll go toward Felicity and Ben's place, and you can head toward Sirona's. The only way past her cottage would be to go up to the road, so you won't have far to look."

"Why don't you go inside too? I can do this," he said.

"I know the area and what to look for." She handed him the baseball bat. "This will be better than the poker."

He shook his head. "What are you going to do if you run up against someone?"

"I'm good, honestly."

"No, I insist." He tried to return the bat to her.

"You don't know this about me, Doc, but I have a brown belt in karate and three years of kickboxing. I'll be okay." Julie didn't tell him she hadn't used either of these skills in a real-life situation before. Everything she'd learned had been in class, under a controlled setting. "Honestly," she said again, as a sudden rush of adrenaline pumped through her veins.

A half smile curled Michael's lip. "You'll have to tell me more about that sometime."

"Sure, but not when we're chasing trespassers."

Six cottages lay between Julie's place and Felicity and Ben's. They were all dark, vacant, she guessed, since most of the owners had gone home on Labour Day weekend. Still, she ran up the steps of each, shone the light from her phone around their decks, and up and down the paths on each side that led to their driveways. Nothing. She got all the way to the Pierce cottage without so much as a rustle in the trees until she heard Felicity's back door creak open.

"Julie?" Felicity called out, stepping through the fog. "Is that you?"

"Yes, it's me. You haven't seen or heard anyone lurking around, have you?"

Felicity's porch light flicked on, and Ben came out to stand next to his wife. "Julie? Everything okay?"

"She asked if we'd seen anyone around." Felicity told him.

"Duke was barking at something a while ago." Ben draped a protective arm around Felicity's shoulders. "He hasn't come back yet, but you know what he's like. He's always wandering around, poking into everything. Sorry if he bothered you all the way over there."

"He didn't. But one of the Adams girls thought she saw someone looking in their window." Julie shrugged. "They're having a sleepover. Six girls. Maybe they got a little carried away."

"Well, Duke will bark at his own shadow so you can't trust him. I'll help you look around, if you like."

Ben was about to come down the steps, but Julie declined his offer. "No. But thanks. I'm sure it was just a renter who got lost looking for home, if it was anyone at all."

"Probably," Felicity said. "Getting damp at night, isn't it?"

"It certainly is," Julie agreed. "If it's okay with you, I'll head up your path and go back along the road."

"Of course. Let us know if you need anything. See you next week for our family history talk."

"We're looking forward to it. Night Felicity."

Julie made her way past Felicity's cottage, up the hill and down their long drive, until she came to the road. It was dead quiet, as if the fog had muffled all the sounds the way it had blurred the light. Just as she reached the top of her circle, she heard a car inching its way along behind her. As she whirled around, she stared into a pair of high beams that switched to low as she raised her hand to block out the light.

Officer Darren Meyers brought his cruiser to a halt, swung the door open wide and stepped out.

"Hi Julie. I was visiting my granddad when I got the call. Did you see anybody?"

"No one," she told him.

Michael appeared in the cruiser's headlights then.

"Hi Doc. Any luck?" Darren asked.

"No, but one of Julie's canoes is missing. The one with the Canadian flags painted on it."

"Are you sure?" Julie asked. "It might have just drifted."

Darren agreed. "Sometimes we get boats all the way over to my grandfather's place."

"I don't think so. I made sure the girls put them well away from the water," Michael said.

"If it's alright, I'll just pull into your circle," Darren said. "I'd like to have a look around for myself. You should both go inside. I'll let you know what I find."

On the way back to his cottage, Michael handed Julie's bat to her. "I thought I'd brought my girls to a safe, quiet place where nothing dangerous ever happens beyond a pinecone falling on the hood of your car."

Julie grinned. "It is safe, Michael. Honestly. Sometimes people drink too much, and they wander. It was probably someone from Annie's or one of the other cottages who realized they'd gone too far and borrowed my canoe to cut across the lake. We'll probably find it tomorrow on the other side."

Inside, Sirona was on the couch with Ali on one side of her and Hope on the other. Faith and Joanna were curled up on the floor at her feet while Joy was pacing the room, scrolling the local 411 Facebook group, hoping for information. Her friend, Rachel, seemed to be the only one with a clear head as she set a tray down on the coffee table and handed out cups of steaming hot chocolate and tea to everyone.

"It's all her fault," Joy said, poking an angry finger at Ali.

"I'm sorry!" Ali whimpered. "I'm really sorry."

"How could this be Ali's fault?" Julie asked, sitting down beside her.

"She told us about the girl who drowned and how she haunts this lake now."

"Did you mean Abby?" Julie asked.

Ali nodded solemnly. "I told them how she fell through the ice."

"Ali's right. Sixteen years ago, Felicity's daughter drowned in the lake. It was winter, and she went through the ice, which is why we always warn everyone about being careful in the wintertime."

"And now her ghost wanders the cove," Ali said. "That's what Noah told me. That might be who you saw at the window."

Julie put a reassuring hand on Ali's arm. "Your brother was probably trying to scare you, sweetheart. I imagine that when Abby died, she became an angel, not a scary ghost who wanders the lake."

Julie caught Sirona's approving smile before she went on. "Faith, you said you saw a woman, didn't you? So, it couldn't have been Abby. She was only twelve when she died."

"Maybe I didn't really see anything," Faith said. "Maybe I just imagined it because Dad was going to tell us a ghost story."

Michael agreed. "And you were playing with the Ouija board before that, remember? I think you just got overexcited."

"Hello?" The voice calling out and footsteps coming through the kitchen made them all a little jumpy until Darren stood in the doorway.

"Sorry. It's just me."

"Anything?" Michael asked.

"Not a soul to be seen, unless you count Ben's dog wandering around. He was all the way over to your place, Sirona." Darren shifted his feet and took out a notebook and pen. "If it's alright, I'll take down a description. Which one of you saw the woman in the window?"

Faith raised a timid hand in the air while Darren perched on the arm of the sofa. Her details were sketchy and seemed to describe her little sister more than anything. Joy called her out on it.

"Well, she looked like Hope a bit," Faith insisted. "Only older, like Dad. Long hair, and she had a baseball cap on." Faith looked up at Darren. "Is that okay?"

"You did great." Darren pocketed his notepad. "My guess is that someone got lost, saw the light from your window and thought they'd ask for directions. They probably got scared off when the screaming started. I'm sure whoever it was, they're long gone, but just in case they come back, I'll stick close by the rest of the night."

Darren handed Michael a business card and started for the door. Julie followed them to out onto the porch. "I don't suppose you saw my canoe while you were out there?" she asked.

Darren shook his head. "I didn't, but let's keep that to ourselves for now. Those girls are already spooked enough."

As Darren drove down the driveway, Michael glanced at Julie. "Do you really have a brown belt in karate?"

Julie raised both hands in the air, assuming the pose. "Category two, lethal weapons," she said with a laugh.

Michael shook his head and laughed. "I'll consider myself warned."

Chapter 7

"Hello!" Michael stood at Julie's back door, in a pair of navy blue SAXX swimming trunks and an orange Lululemon T-shirt and a wide smile.

"The party's over and my three are knackered," he said. "I don't think they slept at all last night and I know I didn't."

"Welcome to slumber parties, Dad," Julie teased. "I put my parents through a few of those when I was their age."

"I might limit it to one friend at a time in the future and definitely no Ouija Board." He jerked a thumb over his shoulder toward the lake. "I thought if you're not busy, we'd go look for your canoe."

Is that what you're dressed for, she thought? She could have told him his choice of a designer outfit to go canoe hunting was a little comical until she realized she was wearing a Dolce and Cabana top herself. Although she'd gotten it cheap at a secondhand shop.

"Not a good time?" he asked, and she realized she'd been staring at him, mouth open, without saying a word.

His sunglasses were perched on the top of his head, and yesterday's five o'clock shadow was now threatening to become a full-blown beard, but he still looked great. Steady on, she told herself. You don't want to go there, remember?

"I'm not doing anything I can't set aside," she said. "We could ask Sirona to keep an ear out in case your girls need anything. When I saw her last, she was picking blackberries. Let me just grab a hoodie."

Sirona was happy to do a little beach combing between their places, which would keep her close by in case the girls needed something, so Michael put a canoe in the water and they pushed off Julie's dock, her in the bow, Michael taking the stern.

When they rounded Abby's rock and he steered deftly toward the open water, she called out over her shoulder to him. "You've paddled before."

"Once or twice," he said. "University days. Feels like a long time ago, though. I guess you've had lots of practice living up here."

"Paddled my first kayak and canoe in these waters. I learned to swim here, did my first dive off a platform that used to sit just off the end of your dock. My first belly flop too," she laughed. "A lot of firsts up here."

"Sounds intriguing. Tell me more." His tone was teasing.

Julie grinned and pointed to a low boathouse over a dock on the distant shore.

"I smoked my first cigarette in Wilson's boathouse over there. Come to think of it, I tried vodka for the first time there too. A bunch of kids from Buffalo stayed next door to the Wilsons. They had some pot too, which I tried for the first and last time. And…" Julie flushed. "See that dock over there?" She inclined her head to her right.

Michael shaded his eyes and looked toward the shore. "The one with the red chairs at the end of it?"

"That used to be Aaron Bixby's place. I had a serious crush on his son Jordan and apparently it was reciprocated, because he kissed me, right under that maple tree."

"Oh, and how was that?" he teased, spraying a little water off the end of his paddle at her.

She laughed and sprayed him back. "It was terrible. He stuck his tongue in my mouth and I was so naïve, I had no idea what he was doing. I slapped his face and took off as fast as I could."

Michael laughed. "You didn't?"

"I did." Julie slapped her paddle on the water, sending a spray backward, which got him well and truly wet.

"Hey!" he cried. "That's cold!"

"Truce?" she suggested when he grabbed the gunwales and started swaying the boat as if he might tip them both over.

"I think we better or we'll both be soaked." Michael stopped to wipe his face on his sleeve.

"Well?" she said, dipping her paddle in to carry on.

"Well, what?" He caught her rhythm, and they fell into an even stroke.

"Aren't you going to tell me about your first kiss, Doc?"

"Nope."

"That's not fair." She cast him a disappointed look over her shoulder.

"Whoever said life was fair? Besides, I'm much more interested in hearing your adventures."

Julie motioned she was zipping up her lip. "Not until you're willing to share, too."

"I don't kiss and tell," he said with a playful smirk.

She pretended to be indignant then, as they paddled along in silence, taking in the colours of the season around them. The leaves were just beginning to turn, displaying vibrant sprays of golds and orange with the brilliant reds of Japanese Maples mingled among them.

When they had only one inlet left to explore before returning to their little cove, Michael stopped paddling to survey the horizon.

"Maybe they went off into one of the other lakes," he suggested.

"It's possible, but we should leave the smaller ones to Darren. He can access them from the roads. I'm sure he's right. It will it'll turn up, eventually."

Entering the last inlet, Julie pointed to the first dock jutting into the water with a Canadian Flag flying high on the top of a pole. Slim Meyers, Darren's grandfather, stood next to the flagpole, waving to them as if he'd been watching them for a while. Slim's cottage, like most others around the lake, sat high on the slope, a good distance from the shoreline, and Slim spent most of his day perched on his deck, like an eagle in a tall tree, keeping watch over the lake.

"Darren told me you're missing a canoe," Slim called out as they approached. "Can't miss that one with the Canadian flags on it. Haven't seen it, but I'll keep an eye out."

"Thanks," Julie said. "I'd appreciate that. How are you keeping, Slim?"

Slim was at least eighty, though no one would have believed it. He had his wits about him and if his body was failing him, he never complained. He was a bit of a loaner and kept himself to himself, unless he was down at Wally's garage playing checkers or someone dropped by to be sure he was still ticking over.

"Just fine. Just fine. Thanks for asking, Julie. Did you see that grandson of mine graduated from Police training? Makes a man proud, so it does."

"You have a right to be, Slim, and so does his dad. How is Cam? Still teaching at Lakehead?"

"That's right. At the Barrie campus, so he's not far away now. You know, the whole time he was married, I only saw him at Christmas and Father's Day. Now he spends his summers up here and drives me to drink." Slim grinned and let his gaze wander over the lake. "Or maybe it's t' other way 'round." A burst of laughter at his own comment sent Slim into a coughing fit and a lot of thumping on his chest.

"Sounds like you need to make a doctor's appointment," Julie suggested. "This is Michael Adams, our new village doctor."

"The new doc, eh?" Slim bent closer to shake Michael's hand. "I've heard about you."

"All good things I hope," Michael said.

"Well now. The truth is, I haven't heard a thing. Just that we were getting one. I'll come down to see ya on one condition."

"What's that?" Michael asked.

"Come around sometime for a game of checkers and a little snort of the good stuff." Slim winked behind his hand, as if he were hiding a secret from Julie.

"You forget, Slim," Julie teased. "I know where you keep the good stuff."

"Ha! So you do. So you do. Well, gotta go, but I'll let you know if I see that canoe, Julie. Still got your number stuck to the fridge."

"And you'll book an appointment at the clinic," Michael reminded.

"Right you are, Doc."

Slim headed back toward the shore and his cottage atop the hill. Julie pushed off the dock and they headed for home. After following the shoreline for a while, Abby's rock loomed in the distance.

"Did they ever find the little girl's body?" Michael asked.

"They did. On the other side of the lake. It was heartbreaking. Still brings tears to my eyes." It occurred to her then that he had lost someone too, and probably much more recently than Abby's passing.

"I'm sorry," she said. "I'd almost forgotten that you've lost someone too."

"It's fine. Losing a child is a horrible thing."

"So is losing a spouse."

He nodded, but kept his eyes fixed on the horizon.

"It must have been difficult."

He was quiet as they paddled the rest of the way to shore, drained the canoe and hung their life jackets over Julie's deck rail. She wondered if Michael had been thinking about his own loss. Outwardly, he seemed to have adjusted, but Julie knew how overwhelming it could be when someone you loved was gone. She'd felt that gaping hole in her life a lot lately, especially given that in seven years she'd be fifty-two, the same age her mother was, when she died.

"Sorry," she said. "It's none of my business."

"Losing Grace, you mean?" His gaze remained focused on the distant trees.

"You don't have to say anything."

He tilted his head to one side, just a little. "I think I do. Or at least I'd like to. You've been kind to us, Julie, and you're Hope's teacher. It might help her if you know about our past. What would you say to a glass of wine on the dock, after supper, once the girls settle for the night?"

"I'd say, do you want me to bring red or white?"

"Just bring yourself."

Chapter 8

Streaks of purple, lavender and apricot trailed across the horizon when Julie and Michael settled in Muskoka chairs on his dock. He had brought a box with a cushion from the living room, for them to use as a footstool, blankets to throw over them to ward off the damp night air, and a bottle of chilled Pinot Grigio which sat on a small table between them.

"Are we drinking straight from the bottle?" Julie asked, settling into her chair.

"You can if you like." But then he produced a glass from each pocket of his hoodie, set them on the arm of his chair and poured. With their faces tipped to the horizon, they sipped and marvelled at the ever-changing skyline. This is what Julie lived for. The quiet. The peace that could gentle the soul after any kind of day.

"I just can't get over how quiet it is up here," he said. "I've spent time in the Rockies, which are incredible in their own way, but this is quite unique. I'm ashamed to say we've been living only three hours away and I've never made it north of Toronto."

"Don't tell too many people, or everyone will want to come here," Julie said.

Night unfolded around them as the sun disappeared behind the tree line, and a clear night beckoned the twinkling stars. Overhead pinpricks of light twinkled against a curtain of black, and Julie heaved a contented sigh and settled deeper into her chair.

After hastily gulping half his wine, Michael finally broached the subject he'd said they would talk about. "You asked about Grace," he said.

Julie felt a pang of angst poke at her insides. Once someone told you something, especially difficult things, and you knew their secrets and innermost thoughts, there was no going back. Michael was her tenant, a neighbour, and she was Hope's teacher. Would listening to him talk about the death of his wife mean a change in the casual nature of their relationship? Maybe she didn't really want to know about his past.

"Michael, you don't have to tell me anything you know. It's really none of my business."

"Like I said before, I'd really like you to know, some things at least."

"Okay, but…

"Julie. Grace isn't dead," he blurted out. "She's in prison."

"What?" Julie straightened in her chair and looked at him. "You're not a widower? I don't understand. Why would you lie about a thing like that?" Her hand flew up. "No, don't tell me that. It's really none of my business. I wish I hadn't asked."

His eyes told her everything she didn't want to know. Dr. Michael Adams had secrets, ones she had no wish to know.

"Do the girls know this?" she asked.

He shook his head, but did not look away from her. "They believe she died seven years ago, in a car accident. Julie, I…"

She held up her hand again. "I hope you know what you're doing where your girls are concerned."

"Please let me explain."

"You don't owe me any explanations, Michael. This is none of my business. I'm just a… I'm just your landlady, a neighbour, Hope's teacher."

"And a friend, I hope." His eyes searched hers and when she turned away, he said, "I'm sorry. Let's not talk about me or my past or any of it. Tell me about your students, or why you became a teacher, or anything else."

She hesitated for a long moment, unsure if she should call it a night or stay. "There is something I wanted to talk to you about, but it isn't me or my students. I think I should warn you about something."

"Okay, sounds a little ominous."

"You have a patient coming to see you next week who I'm pretty sure is going to hit on you."

"Oh! I see. Is it the woman who visited you yesterday?"

"How did you know?"

"Joe got the impression there was some ulterior motive for her visit. He said she isn't the kind of friend you normally invite for pizza on your deck."

"Joe is right. In case you haven't figured me out yet, I like my privacy and I don't share my deck with just anyone."

He tilted his head to one side as if gathering information from her unspoken words. "If you're warning me about her, there must be a reason, so you may as well tell me everything."

Julie took a deep breath. "I'm not one to gossip, but in this case, I feel you should know she has a history with men. She told us all she's recently divorced, yet she brags about her conquests in the staff room. It's like she eats men for lunch, spits them out and moves on to another one in time for supper. She's trouble, Michael, honestly."

"I'll consider myself warned," he said. "But in that department, I think I can take care of myself."

"So you've said. I hope so, Doc, because she might be the first, but she won't be the last to come calling. As far as everyone is concerned, you are Baysville's only eligible bachelor, except for Darren Meyers. Maybe if they knew the truth, people like Rebecca wouldn't be so eager to hit on you."

"Because having an ex-wife implies that I'm a lousy catch?"

There was a hint of a grin at one corner of his mouth, and Julie regretted what she'd implied. "I didn't mean it that way. I just meant…"

He nodded and rested a hand on hers. "I know what you meant." His hand lingered longer than it should have and Julie felt the urge to pull it away, but he seemed to need her reassurance.

After a moment, he said, "Julie, Grace's prison record isn't common knowledge for a lot of reasons. I'd tell you more, but you were pretty insistent you didn't want to hear it. If you change your mind, just ask. I meant what I said earlier. I feel as if I want to tell you about this, but I'm not going to force you to listen."

Then he lifted the wine bottle to fill her glass, then filled his own again too.

"As long as we're sharing secrets," she said. "I'll tell you why I prefer my solitude, if you want to hear it."

"I'm guessing this has something to do with the man you mentioned the other night."

"It does. His name is Edward Vail. We met at university. I was hopelessly in love. He was the captain of the hockey team, and I was his adoring admirer. He'd score a goal, then skate by and blow me a kiss. *That was for you*, he'd say. It was magical as first true loves usually are and, silly me, I thought it would last forever."

Michael nodded, and Julie wondered if he realized his thumb was aimlessly caressing the back of her hand. She didn't move or stop him. It seemed harmless enough and honestly, just then, she liked the warmth of his touch.

"After university?" he probed.

"I went to Teacher's College. The NHL rejected Eddy and said he needed to do something else for a while, so he went to South Africa to do some volunteer work, digging wells or building hospitals or something. When he was leaving, he said I should date other men. He didn't call it breaking up, but we weren't really together either. He wrote a few letters. We texted now and again, but... Long distance romances are hard to keep going."

"Did you date other men?"

"No one seriously. Eddy was the only man I wanted. I was teaching in Bracebridge when he came home and we fell into the habit of being together again. A few months later, my mum got sick and between taking care of her and working, my father didn't want the hassle of managing these properties too, so I moved out here. It made sense for me to take care of the cottages, since I had always loved it out here."

"And Eddy came too?"

"He did. It seemed like the next logical step in our relationship." Julie heaved a deep sigh. She'd shared as much as she was going to with Michael. Like his secrets, there were some things she didn't want to talk about either.

"But he's not here now, so something happened," Michael said. "Or is that too personal?"

"We realized we saw things differently."

"What things?"

Julie brushed at a tear that welled and spilled down her cheek. "Kids, Michael. Eddy didn't want kids."

"I'm sorry. I shouldn't have pried."

No, you shouldn't have, she thought, then again, she could have kept quiet about all of this.

"I should go. It's late." Julie pushed out of her chair and set her empty wineglass on the arm of it. "There's something you should know about me, Michael. I'm not a gossip and while I don't understand it, I'll keep your secret about Grace. But secrets have a way of coming out when we least want them too and the people we love usually are the ones who get hurt. So, like I said before, I hope you know what you're doing, keeping it from your daughters."

Chapter 9

It was a relief to Julie when her canoe turned up undamaged, on the other side of the lake at a vacant rental property, even if it was two weeks after it went missing. Darren had found it cleverly hidden among some trees, out of sight of both the road and the lake.

"Squatters were living in the cottage there," Darren said, while his father backed his Jeep into Julie's driveway. "Three of them, maybe more."

Cam got out and together he and Darren lifted the canoe off the top of his Jeep and set it at the edge of the Julie's front porch.

"How are you, Julie?" Cam asked, dusting his hands on his jeans. "Haven't seen you for a while." He flashed her an admiring smile.

"Good, thanks. Would you guys like a cold drink? Wine? Beer? Water? It's the least I can do for returning my canoe."

"Water for me, unless you got a Coke," Darren said.

"I wouldn't say no to a brewski," Cam said.

Inside, Julie led them into the kitchen and waved them into a couple of chairs while she got a beer for Cam, a Coke for Darren, and a bottle of water for herself.

"Hey, you've redecorated," Cam said, scanning the room. "The colour's great."

Darren's eyebrows shot to his forehead, but he waited for his father to elaborate. He didn't. It was Julie who confessed all. She grinned at Darren and rested an affectionate hand on Cam's arm.

"You never told him?" Julie asked Cam.

He shook his head. "Ancient history," he said with a sheepish grin.

Julie looked at Darren. "I had a mad crush on your dad when we were kids," she said, glancing at Cam, his cheeks tinged red. "He rescued me when my canoe tipped over, and then towed me to shore."

"Oh, yeah?" Darren nudged his dad's elbow. "Good one Dad."

Cam brushed it off. "Anyone would have done the same. I was just passing by."

"You weren't," Julie said, cracking open her bottle of water. "You were on your dock with your nose in a book. Your dad had that little motorboat, remember? You jumped in it and came out to save me."

"Way to go Dad," Darren cheered.

"I didn't save your life, Julie. I'm no hero." Cam took a swig of his beer and looked away.

"You were a hero to me." Turning to Darren, she said, "I was fourteen years old and my crush lasted the rest of the summer."

Cam's face turned the colour of beets, and Julie grinned and squeezed his arm.

"So, what happened?" Darren asked.

"Nothing," Julie said. "Because your dad was *way* older than me." She laced it on thick to tease Cam. "He was at university already, so you know… *way* older. But I gave up pining for him just before Labour Day weekend when a family rented Shaw's place for the last week of the summer. They had a boy closer to my age, who was an absolute dream." Julie's eye roll sent Darren and Cam into fits of laughter. "We climbed onto the roof of the boathouse and he kissed me. It wasn't my first kiss, but I was so scared I didn't know what to do so, I jumped off the roof and swam home."

"I should have rescued you then," Cam said.

"I don't think you were even here," Julie told him. To Darren she said, "Then your Dad got married, and eventually I met Eddy."

"Good old Eddy," Cam said with a sigh.

Darren nudged his father's elbow. "But you're both single now."

"We are, but I think we're happier that way, right Cam? Older and wiser."

Julie wasn't about to tell Darren that she and Cam had revisited that infatuation just a couple of years ago, when Cam split up with his wife and Eddy walked out of her door. Then, they were both feeling rejected and alone, and the notion that dating each other might work seemed a good one. It wasn't, and they quickly discovered they were just too different. But they'd been friends ever since.

"I know you probably don't understand this, Darren," Cam said. "But I'd rather have a good friend than a bad partner, any day."

Julie agreed. "Relationships can be complicated." And Julie didn't want complicated anymore.

Cam and Julie shared a look of understanding while Darren drank half his pop in one go. "Who knew you were so smart about stuff like that, Dad? I mean, I know you are book smart, but this... well, this is a whole new you."

"What do you know of the person who *borrowed* my canoe," Julie asked, changing the subject when it looked like Cam had had enough of relationship talk.

"Not much. Some squatters have been living in there," Darren said, picking at the tab on his pop can until it broke off. "Judging by the takeout containers, they've been there a couple of weeks. I'll stake it out tonight, but my gut tells me they've moved on."

"If not, they'll get a surprise," Cam said. "I'm going to hang out with him." He reached over and gave Darren a paternal shoulder squeeze. "We make a good team, don't we, Dare?"

Darren just grinned. "I guess. But you're not supposed to tell anyone you're on a stakeout with me, Dad."

"Oh right. So, Julie...you're renting to the new doc," Cam said. "Dad says he seems like a good guy."

"Slim hardly said two words to Doc the other day," Julie said.

"Well, he's a good judge of character, I think." Cam nudged her elbow. "He's always liked you, you know."

Julie flushed at the compliment. "I like your dad too. I used to love it when he and Grandpa played checkers. They always let me set up the board for them and sometimes they'd let me play the winner."

"Yup, now he's just got Wally when he gets up the gumption to go into town." Cam gulped down the last of his beer and fished his keys out of his pocket. He passed them to Darren. "I must be getting old. One beer and my head's spinning. Ready to go?"

Darren stood up and headed for the door and to start the Jeep. On the front porch, Cam pulled Julie aside.

"Might not have just been the beer making my head woozy. You're looking great, Julie." His hand grazed her arm as he looked at her, his dark violet eyes curious and questioning. "You wouldn't want to…"

"I'm flattered, Cam, but we don't want to do that again, do we? Didn't you mean what you said earlier? Friends? Remember?"

He nodded and let his gaze drop to the ground as Michael came down his driveway and waved to them.

"You got your canoe back," he called out.

Julie waved and nodded.

"Is he?" Cam nodded toward Michael. "Are you and the doc…?"

Julie smiled. "Not what you're thinking, Cam." Not that it was any of Cam's business, even if there had been anything going on between them.

Cam pulled her to him and gave her a hug. "You're right," he said. "Friendships are more important."

Chapter 10

The annual *Meet The Teachers* event at Baysville Elementary School had been the topic of conversation in the staff room nearly every lunch hour for the last couple of weeks. The PTA had offered to sponsor a barbeque, Sarah Gillespie organized the school choir to perform at the opening ceremonies and there was talk of a *parents versus teachers* baseball game if the weather cooperated.

It was, fortunately, a perfect fall day, the ball diamond had been prepared for the baseball game, leaving the scent of freshly cut grass mingling with hotdogs and sausages cooking on barbeques by the gymnasium doors.

After the choir sang *Oh Canada*, Vince gave a welcome speech, introduced the teachers and support staff and provided details about visiting classrooms. Sophie Wilcox, president of the PTA, announced that food and beverages were being served outside and Rebecca Vickers told everyone about the Scholastic Book sale taking place in the library. Just before the gymnasium cleared out, Julie slipped down the hall to her classroom to get ready for her students' parents.

The walls of her room were filled with her students' writing and artwork, and their notebooks were set out on the desks, ready for their parents' inspection.

Julie had barely stepped inside when Piper George's mother cornered her to talk about her recent separation from her husband. She'd wanted to know if Piper seemed affected by it.

"She's thriving in the classroom environment, if that's what you're asking, Lexi."

"I'm glad. I miss homeschooling them." Lexi George's eyes drifted to the autumn decorations around the classroom and when they came back to meet Julie's, there were tears in them. "He's not making this easy," she said, eventually. "He was…"

Her pause was filled with the sounds of laughter coming down the hall, and Julie recognized Ali Hewitt's giggles.

She reached out to brush Lexi's arm. "Why don't we have coffee sometime and talk?"

"I'd like that, Julie. Thanks. I don't mean to bring my troubles to school."

"That's why a coffee shop, somewhere else, makes sense." Julie nodded reassuringly. "Why don't you read Piper's story about her summer holidays? It might put your mind at ease."

"You think so? Okay." Lexi took a single step away, then turned back. "Are you and Eddy getting back together?"

Julie frowned. "Gosh no. Why would you ask?"

Lexi shrugged and flipped her hair over her shoulder. "I saw him in Huntsville the other day. He mentioned you, so I thought maybe…"

Julie shook her head. "No. His sister lives in Huntsville. He was probably just visiting her."

"I'm sure you're right. Well, I don't want to monopolize all your time. Let's get that coffee sometime soon."

"Miss Wight!" Ali was waving in Julie's direction, her other hand clinging to Hope's. Behind them, Annie and Joe Hewitt stood in the doorway.

"Give me a call when you have some free time," Julie suggested to Lexi, who nodded and went to read Piper's story.

Julie had talked with all of her students' parents except for one, Michael, when he came through the door, huffing as if he'd run all the way down the hall from the front entrance.

"Daddy!" Hope cried, racing to him. "Come and see my painting. It's our new house and the lake and I even made Sirona's cottage and Julie's place, too." Hope's face grew beet red. "I mean, Miss Wight's."

Julie sent her a reassuring smile. She knew it was hard for students who saw their teachers outside of school to keep things straight, especially at Hope's age. Ali sometimes forgot too.

"Sorry I'm late," Michael said after touring the classroom with Hope. "Thanks for bringing the girls with you. Did it go well?"

"It did. Have you been to Faith's classroom yet?"

"I went past there already, but I didn't see her," he said. "I don't suppose you know where she is?"

"My guess would be the library. That's where the book sale is."

He grinned. "Spending her allowance money, no doubt."

"If you hurry, you can still join the parent's baseball team. They'll be starting the game in about twenty minutes."

Outside Julie's window, a group of people was milling about the baseball diamond. Turtle Ted stood on top of a long bench, with a blow horn in his hand, barking orders, but it wasn't until Gwen took it away from him that they saw two lines of people form up on either side of home plate.

"Trust Gwen Sheridan to sort that one out," Michael said with a little laugh. "Think I'll give it a miss, though. I'm not much good at baseball."

"I'll take you to the library if you like," Julie said. "All my parents have already been here."

"Great. I have no idea where that is."

Julie felt Michael's hand in the small of her back as they left her classroom and went down the hall.

"Did you get Joy to her friend's house?"

"I did. Although, I'm pretty sure they aren't working on a project. You should have seen this boy. He's like an Adonis. Tall and blond, with muscles everywhere."

Julie couldn't help laughing. "Do you think there's something going on?"

"She insists they're just friends."

"But just in case, his parents are home, right?"

Michael gasped. "Should I have checked that?"

"Geez Doc, yes."

He laughed then. "This isn't my first rodeo, you know. I'm picking her up at eight. Are you still okay with taking Faith and Hope home?"

"Of course."

She left him at the entrance to the library. "I'm going to get a hotdog. See you later?"

"I'll catch up with you before I leave to get Joy."

While Michael headed into the library to find Faith, Julie made her way back down the hall and outside to wait in the lineup of people wanting hotdogs. She was at the condiments table a little later when Vince came up behind her.

"Did you see Dr. Adams?" she asked, wrapping a napkin around her hotdog.

"Yes, just now. Nice man." Vince slathered a generous amount of relish on his hotdog. "Darn it!" he said as it spilled over onto the table.

Just as Julie handed him some napkins to clean up the mess, she heard a woman shouting in the distance. Vince's head snapped up at the same time as Julie's.

"Who's that?" he asked, when they saw Michael talking to a woman near the primary entrance to the school. He seemed to be losing the battle to calm her down.

"A patient?" Julie guessed. An angry patient, she thought when the woman threw something at Michael.

"I don't recognize her," Vince said.

"Shouldn't we put a stop to it? It isn't the kind of behaviour we want going on here."

"Maybe they're leaving. They're heading toward the parking lot."

"I don't think so. Neither one of them is getting in a car." Julie put down her hotdog, intending to go to the parking lot, but Vince held her back.

"Look, Julie, it's his problem. Don't make it yours." He moved on to the drinks table, helped himself to a juice box, and headed toward the ball diamond.

Julie would have taken Vince's advice if she hadn't noticed Hope, out of the corner of her eye, who was running toward her father and the open gate to the parking lot. Not wanting to alarm anyone, Julie hurried in their direction. Michael couldn't have seen Hope from where he was standing, nor could he have seen that a car was backing out of a parking space and straight toward Hope.

Julie launched herself into a full run and made it there just in time to scoop Hope up and set her down again, out of harm's way. The car jolted to a stop and a young woman jumped out of it and raced toward them.

"I didn't see her!" the woman cried. "I'm so sorry. Are you alright, sweetheart?"

"I'm fine." Hope said.

"Are you sure?" The woman asked, then turning to Julie, she said, "I didn't see her. She's so little, I just…"

"Honestly, she's fine. Not a scratch," Julie said.

"Well. Alright. If you're sure she's okay." The woman was about to get back in her car when she looked back at Hope. "Little girl. You shouldn't run out like that. Where's your mother? Why isn't she looking after you?"

Hope's eyes filled with tears as she reached up to take hold of Julie's hand. "I don't have a mother to take care of me," she said softly.

"Come on, sweetheart," Julie said. "Let's get an ice cream treat."

"I want to see Daddy," Hope insisted. "Who's that lady?"

Julie urged her back toward the food tables. "He'll come and find you in a few minutes, I'm sure. Look, there's Ali. She's looking for you. Why don't the two of you get an ice cream?"

"Do you want one, Julie?" Hope asked, as they caught up with Ali.

"You go. I'll get one later."

Hope scampered off after one last wary glance in her father's direction. Julie wanted to scream. Michael was so busy arguing with this woman he hadn't even seen what had almost happened. She was about to walk away when the woman raised her hand to strike Michael across the face, but he caught her by the wrist to stop her.

What the…? This was not happening on school grounds, with so many people there.

"Hey!" she called out, working her way between parked cars. "You need to take this somewhere else."

The minute she heard her coming, the woman snatched her hand away and turned to leave. As she did, she looked up at Michael and said, "You have no right to keep my girls from me."

"It's called custody, Grace," he said, just loud enough for Julie to hear.

So, this was the infamous Grace. Not in prison anymore.

"I'll fight you on this," Grace shot back.

"Good luck with that," he snapped.

Grace was only a few steps away, but she spun about on her heel. "Don't you dare..."

"Enough!" Julie insisted, now only a few feet away. "What part of *take this somewhere else* did the two of you not understand? This is not the time or the place. This is a family event in a public place and there are young, impressionable children here. So, either leave and sort this out somewhere else, or drop it until you can."

"She's right," Michael said. "You need to leave, Grace."

Grace's icy stare went from Michael to Julie and back again. "You'll regret what you've done," she hissed, then stomped down the driveway.

Satisfied the immediate concern was over, Julie headed back toward the baseball diamond. Maybe watching the game would help slow her heart rate and calm her nerves. She hadn't even reached the gate when she heard Michael coming up fast behind her.

"Julie wait!"

"Your daughter was almost hit by a car!" Julie said, keeping her voice low.

"What? Which one? Is she alright?" His eyes darted as he spun around, searching the grounds.

It was Julie who spotted Hope with Ali across the field, each with an ice cream cone in their hands.

"It was Hope. She saw the two of you. I thought you said she was in prison?" Julie asked, her eyes travelling down the length of the driveway, to see Grace get into a cherry red Ford Escort and drive away.

"She was. Early parole," he said. "For good behaviour, she told me."

It took everything Julie had inside her not to laugh at the irony of that remark. Good behaviour, be damned. This wasn't good behaviour, not on her part or his.

"Well, whatever is going on between the two of you, you cannot bring it into the school like this."

"I didn't. I don't know why she's here. My lawyer should have let me know she was out."

The crack of a ball being hit, followed by peals of laughter from the baseball diamond, sent Julie's gaze in that direction. Vince was running on his way to first base, but was an easy out when Noah Hewitt, who was playing shortstop, caught his low fly ball.

"I can't talk about this now," she told him. "And except for how this pertains to your daughters at school, it's none of my business. I suggest you have a conversation with Vince Sawyer, our principal. If there are custody issues, it should be noted in their files."

"I'm sorry," he said again. His hand reached out to hers, fingers grazing Julie's. "Honestly, if I'd know…"

"I'm not the one you should be saying sorry to." Julie nodded to Hope, who was climbing onto the bleachers with Ali to sit with Joe and Annie Hewitt. She pulled her hand away from his as hot, angry tears burned her eyes. She turned away, unwilling to let him see the anger that churned inside her. Whatever lies he was caught up in, whatever mess lay in his past, Michael Adams had to make this right for his daughters and she could not get mixed up in any of it.

Chapter 11

In the early hours of Wednesday morning, Julie's phone vibrated with such violent urgency she had to grab it to stop it from falling off the nightstand.

"Michael?" she said, seeing his name on the screen. She pulled herself to a sitting position, but almost gasped out when she saw what time it was. She was late and had no time for more excuses from next door. He'd missed running yesterday, having been out of sorts after Grace's appearance at the school. He'd gathered the girls and taken them with him to pick up Joy, saying she was 'off the hook' for taking care of Faith and Hope any further that night.

"Sorry if I woke you. I just assumed you'd be up," he said.

"I should have been. Gosh, it's after seven. Is anything wrong?" She hurried to get herself out of bed and start the coffee. Her morning run would have to wait until after school today.

"Not wrong, exactly. I've got to go to Toronto today and overnight. I wouldn't ask, but after what happened at the school..."

Does this have something to do with Grace, she wanted to ask but didn't. "Of course I'll stay with them."

"I wasn't sure. I thought you were angry with me."

Angry wasn't the word Julie would have used. Disappointed. Annoyed. Confused.

"I'm assuming at your place would be easier for them," she said, ignoring his comment.

"If you don't mind."

"Not at all. Tell Joy not to get the bus home? I'll pick her up after school and we'll have a girls' night out. Supper and maybe a bit of shopping. Is that okay?"

"It's perfect." He sighed and followed with a long pause. "Look. Julie. I..."

"Hey Doc, I'm sorry to interrupt, but I'm running late, so can we talk later?"

Avoidance and denial. Julie chased them away, the words Sirona would have said that were echoing through her head. She wasn't avoiding him, nor was she denying anything. She was late, and she had to get ready for school.

"Yeah, sure. I'm sorry I'm putting you out."

"It's fine, Michael, honestly."

Julie had just parked in her usual spot in the school parking lot when her phone pinged with a text message from Michael. Two words, 'thank you' with a smiley emoji after it. She stared at it for a long minute before replying with a simple NP (of course, it wasn't a problem). She did not add any emojis, smiley faces or otherwise.

She was halfway to the entrance when it occurred to her Rebecca's car was not in her usual spot, nor was it anywhere else on the lot. Other staff cars were parked, as usual. Vince's prized hunter green '69 mustang was in the first spot, Sarah's VW beetle was next, followed by the space where Rebecca's should be and then Julie's SUV. The Airdries walked most days, so it wasn't unusual not to see his pickup truck in the space closest to the fence.

As Julie suspected, she learned in the office that Rebecca had called in sick, and when she went down the hall to her own room, a supply teacher sat at Rebecca's desk, staring at the lesson plans in front of her. She was a tiny girl, no bigger than some of the grade six girls. She had a perky, ski slope nose and a heart-shaped mouth layered with a thin coat of pink. When she looked up at Julie, she bore the innocence of someone who was barely out of teacher's college and Julie felt both sorry and excited for her at the same time. Someone with fresh ideas and enthusiasm just waiting for the classroom experience to boost her confidence.

"First official class, after student teaching?" Julie asked her, stepping into the room.

"Yes. And I'm a little nervous." She stood and reached out to shake Julie's hand. "Olivia Baxter," she said. "I assume you're Julie Wight. Vince Sawyer told me you'd be across the hall. Any pearls of wisdom you want to impart?"

"You'll be fine. It's a good group. Chelsea McCann is always a willing helper and I'm close by if you need anything."

"Good to know."

Julie left Olivia to review the rest of the lesson plans. She would have an easy day of it, since the grade ones had Phys Ed, with Vince, in the mornings, and on this particular Wednesday it was their turn to go to the public library, next door. Olivia only had to get through a few lessons, and the rest of the day would be a breeze.

At two in the afternoon, Felicity came to Julie's classroom to talk about family and show the students how to create their first family tree. After her talk, she handed out blank sheets of paper on which she asked the class to draw the members of their family. Tomorrow, Felicity would bring blank pedigree charts for the children to fill in the four generations as far as their great grandparents.

Julie and Felicity were milling about the classroom, helping where needed while the children worked on their pictures. When Julie stopped at Hope's desk, she bent down to talk to her.

"Want to tell me who these people are?" Julie asked.

"That's Grandma and Granddad. I coloured their hair grey because they're old. This is Daddy with the stethoscope. Joy with her phone. Faith with a book because she's always reading. And this is me, and Blind Bruce, naturally."

"Who's this over here, by the tree?" Julie asked. Hope had drawn a woman with long brown hair, powder blue eyes, with a halo over her head.

"That's Mummy. She's in heaven watching over us."

"Great job," Julie said.

Hope's solemn expression tugged at Julie's heartstrings, remembering the comments the woman in the car had made to her on Monday night and knowing how close Hope had come to actually meeting her mother.

Before Hope could say anything else, Ali's hand jettisoned out toward Julie.

"Miss Wight, I'm finished mine, too." Ali slid her picture to the edge of her desk. "That's Mummy, Daddy, Noah, Ryder, Grandpa Sam and me."

"Nice! I see two dogs in your picture. I thought you only had one, Max."

"The other one is Duke. He comes to see Max all the time, so he's almost part of our family."

"Duke certainly likes to wander," Felicity agreed, looking over Ali's picture.

Minutes later, the warning bell sounded and Julie announced it was time to get ready for home.

"Put your pictures on my desk, please, and remember your reading books go home with you tonight and your agendas. Please ask for someone to sign them."

It was only a few minutes later when the classroom had emptied, Felicity pulled on her jacket and asked if Julie had plans for the evening.

"I do, actually." Julie gathered her purse from her bottom drawer. "I'm minding Michael's girls overnight. He had to go to Toronto and didn't think he'd make it back until tomorrow."

"So, he asked you?"

"Well, he doesn't have any family here."

"I realize that. I just wondered if the two of you were getting close?"

"Like dating close, you mean?"

"Why not? He's an eligible bachelor and you're a single woman." Felicity grinned as she pulled on a pair of leather gloves and adjusted her fingers into them.

Julie shook her head. She and Felicity were more like sisters than friends, but Michael's marital status wasn't something she was about to discuss with anyone. Besides, she'd told Felicity often enough how she felt about complicated relationships. She shouldn't have to remind her of it again.

"He is my tenant. I like his daughters," Julie said. "That's it. And that's how it should stay."

"You could do worse." Felicity put her hands up when Julie was about to protest. "I won't push. You know best, I'm sure." And then she was gone, and Julie listened to the echoing sound of Felicity's chunky heeled boots all the way down the hall.

If there was anyone she might have discussed Michael with, Felicity would have been the one, but Julie wasn't about to do that.

It wasn't her story to tell, so Michael's secret was safe with her, although she suspected it wouldn't be long before tongues were wagging about what had happened on Monday night.

As Julie tidied her desk and stacked the pictures her students had made into a neat pile on one corner, she had the disturbing feeling she was being watched. Hope had gone to the washroom when the other students were dismissed, and Faith hadn't come from her classroom to meet them yet. Maybe Felicity had forgotten something.

She glanced toward the door and stopped, her hand going to her heart when she saw Rebecca watching her.

"Goodness, you scared me half to death!" Julie cried. "I didn't realize you were back. Did you just take half a day?"

"Just picking up a few things from my desk," Rebecca said.

Her hair was dishevelled, her eyes bloodshot, as if she had a fever or had been crying, and her otherwise pale face bore a red mark on one cheek, as if she'd been slapped.

"If you don't mind me saying so, Becs, you look a little worse for wear."

Rebecca shook her head as if to clear the fog from it. "I should be fine by Monday."

"It's not Covid, is it? Because maybe you shouldn't be here."

"No. Nothing like that. It's a weakness that runs in our family. Not at all contagious." Rebecca jerked her thumb over her shoulder toward her classroom. "I should get the stuff I came for."

"Sure. Feel better soon."

Heading down the hall, Julie wondered what was up with Rebecca. That mark on her cheek was definitely from a slap and she couldn't help wondering if it was another date-gone-wrong, although that didn't account for the feverish look of her eyes.

Faith and Hope were waiting for her just outside her door with eager smiles on the faces.

"All set?" she asked, as Hope fell in beside her.

"Where are we going for supper?" Faith asked.

"I was thinking, Mucho Burrito. Is that okay?"

"Yippee!" Hope cried. "I love burritos."

"You love tacos," Faith corrected.

"And burritos," Hope insisted.

"Whatever." Faith pushed open the door.

"What about Joy? Does she like Mexican food?" Julie asked.

"Sometimes, but she won't complain."

Joy confirmed Faith's statement after they picked her up at school. "It's not my favourite, but I'm okay with it," she said.

When they arrived in town, there was no street parking available, so Julie went to the public lot in the block below Main Street and walking back to the restaurant they window shopped. Julie made a game of it, suggesting the girls point out things they'd add to their wish list if it were closer to Christmas. When they came to Mucho Burrito, Joy opened the door to let her sisters go inside first, but held Julie back.

"Do you see that woman behind us, looking in the window of that shop?"

Julie glanced in the direction Joy pointed out to her. "The short woman with the red jacket?"

"Yes. She's been behind us since the parking lot and just as we were going inside, she stopped to look in that window."

"I'm sure it's just a co-incidence." Julie suggested. "Everyone window shops along this street. There's so much to see."

"Maybe."

Julie put an arm around Joy's shoulders and guided her inside the restaurant. "I think you've been watching too many thrillers. I'm sure she's just here as randomly as we are. Let's eat. I'm starving."

But inside, waiting in line to place their orders, Julie kept an eye on the woman in the red jacket, who was now passing the window of Mucho Burrito. She slowed long enough to read the signs in the window, then her eyes met Julie's. She smiled then, as if they knew each other, though Julie was sure she didn't recognize her.

Strange.

It was stranger still when they'd finished eating and went into a Hallowe'en store, at Hope's insistence, because the woman was there too. Hope scampered off the minute they were in the door, with Joy quickly following along behind. Julie and Faith perused the racks closer to the front of the store and the woman in the red jacket disappeared into the crowd of people waiting to cash out.

Julie stuck close to Faith, who was pulling costumes off the rack and replacing them again. The woman wasn't Grace. Of that she was sure, so whatever threats Grace had made the other night, she wasn't going to carry them out tonight. Still, an uneasy feeling settled over Julie and she sent a text message to Joy asking her not to let Hope out of her sight.

"Do you know what you want to dress up as?" Julie asked Faith, who was considering a Vampire costume.

"Does anyone go trick-or-treating all the way out to our place?" Faith asked.

"Not really. But we'll have a dress-up day at school and the Hewitts always have a party at their lodge. They decorate the place up like a haunted house, have party games and creepy music."

Julie pulled an outfit off the rack. "What about this? I could help you with makeup if you want to be a dead cheerleader."

"Maybe. I was thinking of Katniss Everdeen, but I'm not sure what her costume would look like."

"I've seen those. It's a body suit, black with white sleeves and a grey chevron in the middle. Then you just need a bow and arrow or something to go with it."

"That could work, or that dress she wore in the movie, you know, the one where she spins, and it lights on fire."

"But you can't have a dress that catches fire."

"No, but I could paint the bottom to look like it was on fire."

"That would look really cool." Julie moved on to see if they could find something suitable Faith could paint.

They were about an hour browsing when Julie noticed Hope yawn and realized it must be getting close to bedtime. "It's getting late. Time to go," she said, though Hope protested that she wasn't tired at all.

They left the store in a fit of giggles over the costumes and what they might wear that year, and what they absolutely would not want to wear. Ever.

On the way to Julie's car, she noticed the same woman they'd seen earlier getting into the passenger side of a car two rows over from where she had parked. It looked like a man was behind the wheel, but she couldn't be sure because the overhead lights of the parking lot cast shadows over the windshield, preventing her from getting a good look at the driver.

"There she is again," Joy said, nudging Julie's elbow, when they reached Julie's vehicle. "Now I'm really creeped out."

"I'm sure it's just a coincidence," Julie assured her, but just to be on the safe side, she decided to get some pictures of the car.

"Hey, I've got an idea. Hold up those silly masks we bought, and I'll send a picture to your dad. He can guess which one of you is behind each of them."

Julie lined the girls up along the side of her car, got out her phone and when she took the pictures, she made sure the woman and her car were also in the shot. She took two more photos as the car sped past. One she would send one to Michael and the other would go to Darren Meyers.

Chapter 12

Hope did her best to prolong bedtime by asking for a glass of water, taking an inordinate amount of time to brush her teeth, and because she was *hopelessly* addicted to bedtime stories, two chapters from *Charlotte's Web*. Faith went to bed at the same time, wanting to finish Catching Fire and once they were settled, it left Joy and Julie alone in the kitchen. Julie filled the kettle and asked if Joy wanted a cup of tea, too.

"Sure. Thanks." Joy pulled a package of chocolate chip cookies out of the cupboard and set two mugs out for their tea, while Julie rifled through the selection of teas.

"I should bring you some of my special blend," she said, when they'd made their choices from Michael's collection. "Annie Hewitt used to work at a tea shop, and she still orders her tea from there. Whenever she's getting some, I put in a request of my own. It's an apple blend. Next time you're at my place, you should try it. It's herbal. No caffeine to keep you awake."

"I like herbal teas. Dad says they're good for us, antioxidants and all that, but I just like the taste."

When their drinks were ready, and they were seated, Joy cupped her hands around her mug and stared into it.

"Anything I can help with?" Julie asked, wondering what was on Joy's mind. She dunked a cookie and waited.

"I was just wondering if you knew why Dad went to Toronto?"

"He didn't say."

"I think it has something to do with Mum."

"What makes you say that?"

Joy shrugged and dunked a cookie into her tea, too. "She's not dead, you know. She had a car accident, and she was drinking, but that part about her dying isn't true. My grandmother told me, but I'm not supposed to tell my sisters. I just don't know why Dad didn't tell me himself."

"Have you asked him about it?"

"Tried to, but he just changes the subject."

A hint of sarcasm laced Joy's words. Julie couldn't help but wonder if there was a link between Joy's questions and Grace's appearance at the school a couple of days earlier.

"There must be an explanation, Joy."

"But why can't we see her? I mean, if she's not dead, then what's the big deal?"

"I imagine whatever your father's reasons for that are, he thought it was best given the circumstances."

"What circumstances?"

Prison, for one, Julie thought, but she wasn't about to tell Joy that. She had no idea what crime Grace had committed or how long she'd been in prison, but she guessed it had been a while since Joy seemed to know nothing about any of it.

"Maybe you just need to give him a little time and trust that he's doing what's best for you and your sisters."

"You don't think that woman tonight has anything to do with my mum, do you?"

"Why would she?"

"I dunno. Just a weird feeling. I guess not."

"I'm sure she was just someone who was shopping, just like we were."

"Yeah. Probably. I'm going to bed now," Joy said, getting up to put her cup in the sink. "Thanks Julie, for supper and for the talk."

"Of course. Anytime. Are you okay here for ten minutes while I run next door to get some of my things?"

"Sure. But I'm locking the door while you're gone. That woman is still creeping me out."

"Of course," Julie said, gathering her own keys from her purse. "I'll be right back."

It took Julie only a few minutes to stuff a nightgown, slippers, and the book she'd been reading into a bag, then hurry back to Michael's. She said goodnight to Joy, then went to bed herself. Climbing into Michael's queen size bed, she propped a mountain of pillows behind her head and opened her book to read. But she didn't manage more than a page before her eyelids got heavy and she gave up. It was only nine-thirty, but Julie couldn't keep her eyes open any longer.

The following morning when Julie woke and went to the kitchen, the girls were already there, showered, lunches made, backpacks waiting at the door and bowls of half-eaten cereal in front of them.

"Morning! I was going to make you pancakes, but I see I'm too late for that." Julie picked up a cereal box and scanned the nutritional profile. "These are much better for you that a load of sugary maple syrup, anyway."

Hope put one fist on her hip and shook a finger, lowering her voice so she could do her best impression of her father. "No sugary cereals in this house. Sugar is bad for your teeth and has loads of empty calories."

Julie laughed and gave her a good morning hug. "Well done. Sadly, your father is 100 percent right. Although I wish it weren't true. Apple Jacks is one of my favourite cereals." Julie poured Shreddies into the last bowl on the table someone, probably Joy, had set out.

"I noticed you've already made the lunches?" Julie said.

"Yup. All done," Joy said, getting up to put her bowl in the sink. On the way by, she grabbed Hope's as well.

"Goodness, you're organized, Joy."

She shrugged, rinsed the bowls, then put them in the dishwasher. "I always make our lunches."

"I help too," Faith put in.

"Sometimes," Joy said, tugging Faith's braid. "You could more, though."

"Gladly. You want to make a chore list?" Faith opened a drawer and pulled out a notebook and pen.

"Not now. School silly." Joy snatched them from her hands and put them away. "But it wouldn't kill you to help. You've always got your nose in a book."

"I like reading."

"And I like a tidy house."

"Bet you were up all night talking to Briiiii… an," Faith teased.

"Was not."

"Brian?" Julie asked, looking at Joy. "Is that who you were studying with the other night?" She thought of Michael's description the other night, of the blond adonis who'd answered the door, when he dropped Joy off to study.

"He's a *friend*, and I wasn't talking to him all night. We're working on a project together." She flashed a glare at Faith. "So there!"

As Hope squeezed past her sisters, she sent Julie an eye roll that suggested this went on all the time. Then, grabbing her backpack, she headed toward the door.

"I hear Turtle Ted!" she shouted as the sound of a whining engine echoed across the lake.

There was a whirling of braids, a swish of jackets, the thump of backpacks slung over their shoulders and then the door slammed shut behind them and suddenly, everything went quiet.

"Well, that was fun," Julie mumbled to her spoon.

After tidying the kitchen, she did a quick whip around to make Michael's bed and gather her things. The girls had already made their beds, and the bathroom was tidy and free of damp towels, so she locked the front door, pulled her housecoat tight around herself and followed the path to her place. How did mothers manage to get their kids off to school, then get themselves out the door, every day? She hadn't even made the girls' lunches or their breakfast, let alone go for a run. She'd barely have time to shower and do her hair. Running would have to wait. Again!

Julie arrived at school just in time to see the buses pull into the parking lot and as she crossed the tarmac to go inside, Turtle Ted's bus reloaded with the older children and headed down the drive on their way to Bracebridge.

The playground filled up with the joyful sounds of children at play and she wondered if this was one of the last days she could take her class outside for reading period. Thanksgiving was only two weeks away and Hallowe'en would follow soon enough and then, heaven forbid, it was only a matter of days before the inevitable first snowfall.

Her class was ready to start rehearsals of the Thanksgiving Day play written by Faith, Joanna, and Shelby. Everyone had an equal part to play, which Julie thought was a clever way of writing it. No one was left out. No one would be disappointed not to have the lead role. It was brilliant and apparently, she wasn't the only one who was excited because Joanna and Shelby came running up to her, excited over some costume and prop changes they wanted to make.

"I'm sure we can manage it, but shouldn't you bring Faith in on this, too?" Julie suggested.

"We haven't seen her yet this morning," Joanna said.

"Maybe she didn't come to school today," Shelby offered, sweeping her beautiful blue eyes over the playground toward the parking lot.

"She's here. I saw them get on the bus," Julie said, her gaze following Shelby's.

But she hadn't actually seen the girls get on Ted's bus, had she? She'd only heard Ted pulling around the circle and tooting his horn, and watched the girls race out the door. Something inside Julie jolted and ground to a halt and for a moment, she couldn't breathe. Michael had trusted his daughters to her, they were her responsibility, but she hadn't watched them get on the bus. What if something had happened? What if somewhere between the door of their cottage and the top of the circle, something awful, something unspeakable, something… Grace!

"Miss Wight?" Joanna broke into her thoughts.

"Sorry, I… Why don't we talk about this during morning recess? The three of you can come to my classroom and we'll work through your plans."

Calm down, Julie told herself, doing her best to mask her worry from Joanna and Shelby. If anything was wrong, she would know about it. Someone would have said something before now. Ted would have kept honking, or…

"That's a great idea!" Shelby was saying. "And it will give us time to talk to Faith about it, too. Thanks Miss Wight."

Julie trained her eyes on the groups of children gathered around the playground, the field and the tarmac and finally came to rest on an odd sight. Ali was standing alone below the monkey bars, spotting Ryder.

"She's a bit small to be your spotter, Ryder," Julie suggested, going over to them. "Maybe you should ask Noah, or one of the older boys." Ryder dropped down and went in search of Noah, leaving Ali and Julie alone.

"Why aren't you playing with Hope this morning?" Julie asked.

Ali lowered her head. "Faith said I shouldn't go with them."

"Where did they go?"

Ali pointed toward the fence on the far side of the school grounds. "To talk to that lady. She called Faith over when we got off the bus."

When Julie had glanced across the field earlier, she'd mistaken the small group under the poplar trees for the usual sixth-grade girls who hung out there. This time, her eyes fixed on the same spot, she realized Ali was right. Faith and Hope stood on the school side of the fence. Someone Julie couldn't quite see was on the other side. A few feet away was the same cherry-red hatchback she'd seen Grace get into the other night.

Grace!

That sick feeling in her gut that hadn't quite gone away returned with a vengeance. She started walking as fast as could, not wanting to alert the other children that there was a problem and cause a panic. As she went, she pulled her phone out of her pocket and sent a warning text to Vince's cellphone.

The closer she got, the more she was certain it was the same woman who'd practically accosted Michael on Parents' Night. She was small, barely shoulder height, with the chain-link fence. Her hair, a shade darker than Hope's, was in a ponytail that spilled from under a baseball cap, the brim of it hiding her features. There were holes in the knees of her jeans and she wore a mustard-yellow hoodie with a chocolate-brown puffy vest over top.

Julie picked up her pace, when Grace was distracted from the girls just long enough to see Julie heading her way. Grace saw her coming and bolted for her car. Before Julie got to the fence, the tires of the cherry red Escort were churning up gravel from the shoulder of the road.

"Hey!" Julie shouted after her. But she was too late. She arrived just as Grace turned left and disappeared. Julie waved away the gravel dust and looked at the girls.

"Do you know her?" she asked.

"Come on." Ignoring Julie, Faith took Hope's hand and headed back toward the school.

"Not so fast, you two. Do you know her?" Faith shook her head and dropped her gaze to the ground, so she turned to Hope for answers.

Tears welled in Hope's eyes. "She said she knows our dad. Are we in trouble?"

"She's lying!" Faith shouted.

Her reaction was so unlike the girl Julie was coming to know she couldn't believe what she was hearing; lies, shouting, being sharp with her younger sister. None of this was the quiet, shy bookworm Faith had seemed to be. If this was what seeing their mother did to them, she could understand why Michael had been determined to keep Grace away.

Julie put a reassuring hand on each of their shoulders. "It's alright. You're not in trouble," she sighed. "The school has a policy about visitors. They need to check in at the office."

That's all she would say about it to them, but she would have to file a report at the office and if Vince hadn't already called the police, she'd at least mention it to Darren.

"The bell is about to ring," Julie said. "We should go inside."

The rest of that day, an uneasiness settled over Julie, and she could not get Grace or her visit to the school this morning out of her head. What had she hoped to accomplish by talking to the girls over the fence? If Michael had sole custody, surely, she'd need a court order allowing her visitation rights. Had she told the girls who she was, and asked them not to say anything? It was all one big mystery, and Julie was fed up with it. She was glad Vince had taken charge of the situation and she didn't have to discuss any of it with Michael. The school had a record of the incident, and Darren was aware of the situation.

"That picture you sent me last night," he said, when they were alone in Vince's office later that day. "It was blurry, so I sent it to our tech guys. I'm hoping they can fix it up so we can put it through the facial recognition system."

"It was probably a coincidence," Julie said. "Huntsville is a small town and there were lots of people milling around last night. It spooked Joy and to be honest, I was a little spooked too. And now this."

"Well, we're on it, so…" His phone pinged. "Sorry, gotta take this. I guess we're done here, Julie. I'll keep you posted."

Chapter 13

Friday afternoon, and Julie was looking forward to a quiet, relaxing weekend. Tomorrow she'd go into town, run some errands and maybe call Vivian George and have that conversation over coffee she'd wanted to have the other night. In the evening, she and Sirona would have their usual game of Canasta and on Sunday, she might go for a paddle.

Julie poured a glass of Chardonnay and went to sit on the deck and enjoy the unusually warm temperatures. Twenty-six degrees in late September was rare, and she wasn't about to let anything spoil her evening or the promise of a peaceful weekend. She leaned back and tipped her face skyward and let the late afternoon sun bathe her in warmth.

It was quiet across the lake. Duke had ambled by earlier. He'd come up on her deck and sniffed around a little, and she'd given him a pat and one of the dog treats she kept in a jar on the window ledge. Then, like the happy wanderer he was, he took off. The silence enveloped her, coaxed her into a dreamy state like the kind just before falling asleep. She was sure she could just drift off and would if she could accept that…

Her eyes snapped open at the sound of someone coming up the stairs to her deck.

"Hey!" Michael said, when she almost spilled her wine, trying to sit up straighter to look at him. He stood on the top step, a bottle of wine in each hand. "A thank you gift for watching the girls."

"Jeez, you scared me half to death." She motioned to an empty chair across from her. "You didn't have to give me anything."

"It's just wine and I'll probably drink most of it anyway, if you're still talking to me, that is." He set the bottles down on the table.

"An apology? What for?" she asked.

Michael took the chair next to hers and stretched out his long legs, crossing them at the ankles. "I'm sure you know."

There was a hint of playfulness in his eyes, and it softened the anger she'd been feeling since yesterday. She knew when Michael had arrived home from Toronto because he'd sent her a text and because she'd seen his car at the clinic. And yet, he hadn't acknowledged what had happened at school yesterday, which seemed odd.

"Do you want the wine or something else to drink?" she asked, when it seemed he was settling in for a while. "I have a couple of beers left or there are soft drinks, or I could make coffee, tea…"

"The wine would be great." His hand reached out, grazed her arm, and rested there. "You don't have to fuss, really."

"I'll just get another glass and the corkscrew," she said. "Let's stay out here. It seems a shame to waste this great weather."

"Good idea. I'm keeping an eye out for the girls. They've gone for a paddle."

When she returned with the glass and a small tray of cheese and crackers, she set them down on the table between them.

"Michael…" she said, at the exact moment he said, "You know…"

"You first," he said, opening one of the bottles of wine he'd brought.

"Okay. Probably best to talk about this before the girls get back, anyway."

"Oh dear. Was there a problem while I was away?"

"They were angels. We had a great time. It's about Grace showing up at the school again."

Michael's brow furrowed into a frown. "What do you mean again?"

"Didn't our principal, Vince Sawyer, get in touch with you? or Darren Meyers, the police?"

"No. I haven't heard from anyone." He pulled out his phone to check. "Nothing here," he said. "Unless it went to my spam folder, but I dump those a couple of times a day out of habit."

"Yesterday morning, Grace showed up at the school. She didn't stick around long. As soon as she saw me, she took off. I had to report it. I gave a statement to Darren Meyers. I told him I knew her to be the girls' mother and how I knew that. I had to tell him about Monday night, too."

"It's fine, Julie. Grace is the reason I was in Toronto. I was signing papers to have a restraining order put against her. It's in place now, so she can't come near any of us." His words were reassuring, but a small vein pulsing in his neck suggested he wasn't as calm as he'd have her believe.

"So, it's over. She'll stay away now?"

"If she doesn't, she'll end up back in prison."

Julie nodded. "I'm sorry. If this hadn't happened at school, I wouldn't have gotten involved, but after the incident the other night and now this, I really had no choice."

"You did the right thing, Julie. I'm sorry about all this. I've stuck you in the middle of it, and I didn't mean to."

But he had, she thought, when he asked her to watch his children and when he hadn't insisted Grace leave the school grounds the other day.

"You should have told me the truth from the start," she said. "At least then, I would have been better prepared. I would have kept a closer eye on them, driven them to school myself, yesterday."

He stared at her, angry, pleading his case. "I tried to, but if you recall, you didn't want to know. You shut me down, remember?" His voice softened as he realized he'd been close to shouting. "I'm sorry. That was uncalled for. I know you were trying to help."

"I *am* trying to help, and I know your anger isn't with me."

"You're right. It isn't. I don't know what else I can say. Do you want me to find another place to live?"

"What? No!" she blurted out. "That's not what I want at all. I just…" Her eyes lifted to the shoreline, where the girls were beaching the canoe. In minutes, they'd have their life jackets off and be coming up the steps, and she hadn't even noticed they'd come around the point.

Michael stood up and called down to them. "I'm coming." He turned back to Julie. "I've got to go. They'll be wanting their supper. I…"

Julie put a hand on his arm. "Then why don't you have supper here and maybe we could talk afterwards."

He hesitated for a moment, his eyes questioning hers, until he finally nodded. "Okay then. If you're sure."

"I am. I'll just get things started inside." She gathered their glasses and the cheese and crackers they hadn't touched and started toward the door.

"That was great!" Joy said, coming up the steps. "It's almost warm enough to swim."

Hope was right behind her. "I'm hungry. What's for supper?"

"Spaghetti, if you want some," Julie said.

"Yes, please!" Hope hurried inside after Julie. "Can I help?"

"You sure can."

While Julie heated the sauce and cooked a fresh pot of noodles, Michael and Hope made garlic bread. Joy and Faith set the dining room table so they could spread out a bit more than in her small kitchen. It wasn't long before they all sat down to dinner.

Despite the girls' chatter and Michael's attempts to keep the conversation going, Julie felt the awkwardness that lay between them. Her thoughts trailed back to Michael's offer to find somewhere else to live and she couldn't help thinking that was the last thing she wanted to happen. She cared about the girls and, if she were honest about it, she enjoyed their morning runs, when they had them, and the evenings they spent on the dock. She would miss that and now that there was a restraining order against Grace, surely she'd keep her distance and things would settle down.

"How's your project going, Joy?" Julie asked when there was a lull in the conversation.

"I'm supposed to interview someone who immigrated to Canada. But first I need to find someone."

Julie flashed a smile at Michael, who looked sheepishly down at his lap, but kept his silence. "You could ask your father," Julie said with a nod toward him.

"What?" Joy's fingers played with the rose gold oval earring dangling from her lobe. Julie had noticed them earlier and thought how pretty they were on Joy. "You mean do my project on Dad?" Joy said, making a face. "Eww. No. That would be weird."

"Why? He's an immigrant. Can't you tell from his accent? How old were you when you came?" Julie turned to Michael.

"What accent?" Joy asked, which received an eye roll from her father. "He doesn't have an accent. That's just the way he talks."

"He talks like that because he was born in England," Michael said, speaking about himself in the third person to tease his daughter.

"Oh." Joy's fingers covered her mouth, to hide her embarrassment. "Sorry. I guess I knew that. I did. Honestly. I just forgot. Maybe sometime over the weekend I could interview you?"

Michael smiled. "You could, or you could talk to your grandparents. My father came here for work, so they're the ones with the real story. I just came along for the ride."

"Oh! Of course! I wasn't thinking about them," Joy said. "I mean, it's obvious they came from England. You can tell by their accent." Her eyes widened when she looked at her father and realized the mistake in her thinking. "Sorry, Dad. I goofed up."

"You're alright," Michael said, sending her a playful grin, laced with love and understanding.

When everyone had eaten their fill, Julie began gathering dirty dishes and leftovers. "I have some of Sirona's delicious carrot cake, I think. Who wants more milk, or tea or coffee to drink with their dessert?"

Faith followed when Julie went to the kitchen to start a pot of coffee and get their dessert.

"Did you know Sirona has herbs drying all over her kitchen?" Faith asked. "It smells awesome. She's even got a Chinese medicine wheel on the wall. She explained it to me, but I remember little of what she told me."

"Sirona was a naturopath before she retired. She's all about healing naturally and eastern medicine. I love going over there. It's like having an herbal library right next door."

Faith leaned against the counter while Julie put things away in the fridge. "I love libraries. I used to volunteer at the one in our school in Niagara Falls. I asked about helping in ours, but they don't need anyone. I thought maybe I could work at the public library next door to the school. What do you think?"

"You'd have to get your dad's permission. If he's okay with it, I could go over with you one day next week. You must have met Mrs. Dawson when you went there with your class."

"We did. She's really nice. Okay, I'll ask, Dad." Grinning with anticipation, Faith scooped up a stack of fresh napkins and headed back to the dining room.

When Julie brought in their dessert and the plates, Faith was pleading her case. When he seemed reluctant, she held her ground, insisting that she was almost twelve, and reminding him that she'd done it at their other school.

"Tell you what," Michael said to Faith. "I'll walk over with you and talk to this, Mrs. Dawson. I haven't been to the library yet."

"How am I supposed to look responsible if my dad takes me over there?"

"You'll look like you have the support of people who love you," he insisted.

"Okay," she reluctantly agreed, then shot Julie a pleading *will you talk to him* glance. Michael caught the look and caved.

"Alright. Alright," he said, hands in surrender. "I can see when I'm beat. But I want to know the days and hours you'll work, and who would be responsible for you when you're there."

Faith threw her arms around her father's neck and squealed with delight. "Thanks, Dad," she said, unwrapping herself to give him a peck on the cheek.

"Who wants carrot cake?" Julie asked.

"Can we take it to our place?" Joy asked, sliding her chair back. "We were going to play Monopoly." She shot a glance at her father. "If that's okay."

"And leave us on our own? Goodness, what will we do without you?" he teased. "Go on then. Leave the old folks to our tea and crumpets."

"Crumpets? What are crumpets?" Hope asked.

"Never mind," Michael said. "Go have fun. But remember, I'm the shoe, so don't any of you dare use it."

"Right Dad!" Hope groaned.

Julie sliced three generous portions of carrot cake, put them on a tray with forks, and handed it to Joy.

"Thanks for supper," Joy said as they left through the back door.

Michael followed Julie to the kitchen, opened the dishwasher to start loading glasses into it.

"You don't have to do that," Julie said.

"Yes, I do." He handed Julie a plate. "You rinse. I'll load."

They fell into a rhythm, as if they'd been moving around the kitchen with practiced ease, forever, until everything was tidy and there was nothing left to do but enjoy their dessert and talk.

Michael leaned against the counter, crossed his arms over his chest, and watched her pour two mugs of coffee.

"You made Faith happy about the library," she said, handing him one of them. Then she reached for a small bottle of brandy from the cupboard over the fridge.

"Oh! Good woman!" He took the bottle from her, unscrewed the top and poured a little into his cup, then held it up, offering to do the same to hers.

"Yes, please."

When he capped the bottle and put it on the counter, his hand caught on the countertop, a spot where the trim was coming away. Julie had repaired it once already and thought the Gorilla Glue had done the trick of sticking it down, but when Michael yanked his hand back and blood trickled down the side of it, she winced.

"Oh god. Sorry. I need to fix that again. Here, let me…"

They surveyed his injury together until he grabbed a paper towel to soak up the blood. "It's nothing," he said. "Look, it's already stopping. Just a scrape."

Julie got a pot of Sirona's cure-all salve out of the drawer and opened it. "Here, put some of this on it."

Michael yanked his hand away. "What is that?" He took the little silver pot of salve and sniffed it. "Where did you get this?

There's no label on it. What if I'm allergic to something that's in it?"

"Are you allergic to dandelion and willow bark?"

"What?" he frowned and looked at the tin again.

"It's Sirona's all-natural remedy for burns and minor cuts. I use it all the time."

He sniffed the contents again and put it down, wrinkling his nose. "Polysporin, or iodine. That's what it needs."

Julie took a generous portion of salve from the tin and reached for his hand. "Give it five minutes. You'll see how good it is." She lathered it on his cut, then found a band-aid to put over it. "Better?"

He feigned a child-like pout, then grinned at her. "Thanks Mom," he teased.

"I'd hate to see you when you're sick. But then you know what they say. Doctors make the worst patients."

"And teachers make poor students. But these tinctures of Sirona's and…"

"Stop it, Michael. Really. Give the salve a chance. You'll see I'm right.

He looked down at his hand. "Hey, you know something. The sting is already gone. Maybe there *is* something to this."

"Now he gets it." Julie rolled her eyes. She picked up her brandy-laced coffee and a piece of carrot cake and headed for the door. "Want a jacket? I have a couple that would fit you." She opened a closet by the back door.

"Do you always keep men's jackets around just in case?" he asked, reaching for a brown corduroy coat with a swede collar and cuffs.

"They were Eddy's. About the only thing he left behind that I didn't throw out or donate."

Outside, they settled into comfy chairs and, after a long sip of his coffee, Michael said, "For what it's worth, he's a fool. Has he been gone long?"

"A couple of years. But that's not what we were going to talk about. The girls aren't here and you promised to tell me more about Grace."

"Fair dues," he said, setting his untouched carrot cake on the table between them. "I met her about six months before we were married. It was too fast, I know, but I'd finished school, was in my late twenties. When I was looking to buy a home, I met her at an open house. Grace was a stager working for a realtor and when I saw her, I fell in love with her smile. Then, we got talking, and I asked her out. She seemed so desperate for someone to take care of her and, of course, being in the profession of caring for people it was probably inevitable. I've been through years of counselling to figure that out. I certainly didn't know what I was doing at the time."

"Yeah, I know what that's like," she said. "We learn the hard way, don't we?"

"You can say that again. But we had ten good years. A few ups and downs, as you do. After Joy and Faith came along, it felt like we were a family, and I'd say we were pretty happy. Or I was. But then, just after Hope was born…"

His jaw tightened as he set his gaze on something across the lake.

"After Hope was born?"

He nodded. "That's when things changed. It was the turning point in our marriage, and after that, nothing was the same." He shook his head, as if he still couldn't believe that seven years ago, his life had been so drastically different.

He'd been happy, content in his life. She could see that and was about to say something, but the look on his face said it wasn't the right time. It was as if he'd hit a wall of emotion that had left him speechless.

The moon cast a long beam of white across the surface of the lake and in the distance, an owl hooted, calling to its mate. Except for that, it was so quiet Julie could hear her heart beating in her chest. She waited in case he wanted to say something else, but Michael drank down the last of his coffee and set his empty cup on the table beside his untouched dessert.

Then he fixed his gaze on hers. "Want to play Monopoly?" he asked.

Where did that come from? She wondered. Was that really all he was going to say? Everything changed seven years ago. What about why Grace had been to prison? Had he honestly thought moving three hours away from home was going to stop her from finding her daughters? But then, she hadn't told him everything about Eddy either, had she?

"Monopoly? Sure. I guess."

"Come on," he said, getting out of his chair. "Someone needs to stop Joy from sticking her sisters with all the worthless properties."

At the top of her steps, she reached for the handrail and felt Michael close behind her. She turned to say something to him, to tell him she understood his need to keep some of his past a secret, but in that moment, as their eyes met and she was about to speak, Michael leaned down and kissed her.

She wasn't ready for that, hadn't been expecting it, had remembered his words, adamant and final that he wasn't looking for a relationship, had no time for one and his only thoughts were for his girls. She hadn't wanted this either.

"Sorry," he said, when they parted. "I don't know where that came from." He took her hand in his and gave it a little squeeze. "That's a lie. I do know where that came from, but I can't help thinking it was the wrong thing to do, and I'm sorry."

"It's just…"

"I know. I remember what we both said before. Neither of us wants a relationship right now, but I really do value your friendship, Julie. I wouldn't want to do anything to ruin that, and if I have, then I'm sorry."

It wasn't what she was going to say, but it was close enough. "You haven't ruined anything, Michael. And you can never have too many friends."

Chapter 14

Along with the Humble Pie Bakery, Yummies in A Jar, and a few other shops in town, the library was one of Baysville's most popular attractions for both seasonal cottagers and the locals alike. It was the next building along University Street from the elementary school, with an empty three-acre plot of town-owned land between them.

The building was once the two-storey home of one of the first families to settle in the area in the mid-eighteen hundreds and had been many things after the family no longer owned it. Outside, it still looked much as it had in the early days, although vinyl siding now covered the clapboard, and the windows had been replaced with double panes. The wide verandah still wrapped its way from the side of the house to the front, its railing painted a brilliant white against the pale-yellow vinyl. In good weather roomy padded rocking chairs sat along it with small tables in between, creating an inviting, *welcome to grandma's house* kind of atmosphere.

It was lunch hour on Monday morning, nearly a week since Michael had granted permission for Faith to ask for a position at the library. Julie had called Theresa Dawson to set an appointment and Michael had sent an email to grant his consent, providing she was willing to take Faith on. Faith had been anxiously pacing outside Julie's classroom, unable to eat her lunch. She was so nervous. Julie had given her some busy work, putting up some Hallowe'en decorations to keep her occupied until the appointed time.

At twenty minutes after twelve, Julie reached for her jacket and nodded to Faith, who dropped the tacks she'd been using onto Julie's desk and squeezed her eyes shut.

"Is it time to go?" she asked.

"It is. Are you nervous?"

"A little, but I'm excited too."

The weatherman boasted that this was the warmest autumn on record, and when they went outside, after Faith's short stop in the restroom, the nip in the air suggested Mother Nature had something else in mind. Winter was coming. The scent of crisp leaves filled the air as Julie and Faith made their way out of the school gate and down University Street toward the library.

As they walked side by side, talking about what Baysville had been like when Julie was growing up, she couldn't shake the feeling they were being watched. She thought Michael might be watching from the clinic. After their Monopoly game the other night, he'd walked Julie home and expressed his concern about Faith working at the library.

"It's not the work. I'm sure she'll be fine with that. I worry about her going from the school to the library on her own," he'd said.

"She's nearly twelve years old and a lot of the kids walk home from school every day, much further than the library," Julie had protested. "And if it's Grace you're worried about, you have the restraining order against her. She'd be crazy to show herself here again."

"Crazy just might be the word."

She had stopped in the middle of the path. "Don't you think it's time you told me everything? One friend to another." They'd smiled, and he'd grazed her hand with his, and when she looked in his eyes, she knew he wanted to kiss her again. She'd moved on then, wanting her earlier words about friends to sink in for him.

"It would take more than a two-minute walk between our cottages, Julie. If you really want to know, I'll tell you everything, but for now, I just need to know my girls are safe."

"You don't have to tell me anything you don't want to, Michael, but you can't take this opportunity away from Faith. Not unless you're going to tell her everything, so she understands."

"Could you make sure she gets there?" he had asked. "Walk with her until she's safely inside. She obviously doesn't want me there."

"I'll walk with her myself if that will make you feel better, and if for some unforeseeable reason I can't, then Rebecca or one of the other teachers will."

"Every time she goes to the library?" he'd asked.

"Every time. Until the situation with her mother is resolved."

Now, as Julie glanced around her for the eyes she couldn't see, she realized it wasn't Michael, since his car wasn't even in the clinic's parking lot. But was it someone else, because that's how a lurker would be. Out of sight, hidden behind a pole or a building or a... Julie shook off the feeling, telling herself she was letting all of this get to her. The library's porch steps were lined with oversize potted mums. When they reached the door and Faith pulled it open, Julie followed her inside. No one else followed. No stirred behind them. No shadows shifted in the distance. Surely, she was just imagining things.

Theresa Dawson was nearing retirement age. Once she'd wanted to be a schoolteacher, if there had been money for university when she was young, she'd told Julie. As there hadn't been, she'd gotten a job at the local library and, little by little, put her earnings toward night classes and part-time schooling until she'd earned her degree in Library Science. She had years of experience working at one of the large Toronto libraries, and when they were cottaging here during the summer months, she had volunteered at this library. Eventually, when she and her husband sold their home in Toronto and moved to Baysville permanently, she became the librarian full-time.

The Dawson's owned a cozy bungalow on the water, where Bay Street met Baysville Trail and every morning when her husband went off to work in Bracebridge, Theresa walked up to the library and opened its doors. When she wasn't busy with patrons, she wrote stories, novels, and a bit of poetry, which she secretly told Julie she'd planned to publish, if she could ever find the time. She got down from a counter height stool, when Faith and Julie came into the main room of the library.

"Hello Faith," she said.

"Hello Mrs. Dawson." Faith's approach to the counter was timid, but she stiffened her shoulders and seemed to summon up her courage. "I was wondering if you needed after school help. I have experience working at the library in my other school. You could ask them if you need a reference."

Julie let go of the breath she'd been holding on Faith's behalf and silently applauded her for getting her request out. She had been that same shy, insecure child once, and knew what it felt like to face your fears, especially when it involved approaching adults.

Mrs. Dawson seemed equally proud of Faith's courage. "Well now. I hired a part-time helper just a couple of days ago. But I'm sure there's enough work for both of you."

"You have an employee?" Julie asked, surprised and pleased, since Theresa had told her more than once that the hours were taking their toll and she'd been thinking of retiring.

"Yes," Mrs. Dawson said. "She's new in town, and she thought working here, she'd get to know people and help me at the same time. So, I'll be training you both at the same time. You're in grade six, aren't you, Faith?"

"Yes, Ma'am. I am."

"Well then, you're eleven years old, or nearly twelve, I'd imagine. That's a wonderful age to be." She shuffled some papers on the counter, looking for something. "Somewhere here, I have an email from your father granting his permission for you to volunteer, so everything is in order. Can you start today, after school?"

Faith was nearly bursting. Her face beamed as she looked from Mrs. Dawson to Julie and back again. "Yes! Yes, I can." A look of pure bliss spread across her face. "I'll be here as soon as I'm dismissed. Thank you, Mrs. Dawson. I'll work hard. I promise."

"I'm sure you will, dear." She held up the piece of paper she'd been looking for. "Ah, here it is. Your father has asked that you only work on Mondays, Tuesdays and Wednesdays. He's going to pick you up at five. So, I'll add you to our roster on those days. How would that be?" Theresa Dawson folded her hands on the counter and smiled at Faith.

"That's perfect. Thank you. Thank you so much!" In her excitement, Faith squeezed Julie's hand and Julie squeezed back. She couldn't have been more thrilled for her. She sent Theresa Dawson a grateful glance before she and Faith left the building.

On the way back to the school, Faith's nervousness was gone, and she seemed to Julie to have found her niche. It was more than her love of books that had been sparked. It was her confidence in herself, in her ability to go after what she wanted, and Julie couldn't have been prouder of her.

"Well done," she said as they walked along University Street toward the school.

"I couldn't have done it without you, Julie. I was so nervous."

"You were great, and I know Mrs. Dawson is getting a great worker in you."

"Joy thinks I don't do anything to help around the house, but I do, in my own way. She likes to clean. Hope likes to help Dad in the kitchen, but I'm his thinking daughter." She grinned. "That's what he calls me."

"I can tell that about you," Julie agreed. "You're the strong and silent one."

"Maybe, but I won't let people push me around."

"That's good," Julie said, unsure why Faith was picking that exact moment to emphasize that. "Is there something you want to talk about?"

"Not really. I'm just happy for once. Because being in the middle isn't always fun, but now I get to go home and tell Joy that my love of books has got me something I really want."

"Yes, it has, Faith. You know everyone has some special talent. We don't always know what it is and sometimes we spend most of our lives figuring it out. You're lucky to have found your love of books at such a young age. Maybe one day you'll write your own books."

Faith grinned. "I've already started. I have three journals filled with ideas of stories I want to write."

"That's wonderful. Maybe one day you'll be a famous author."

"Or maybe I'll write for the theatre or screenplays for the movies." A smile crept across Faith's features.

Julie's arm went around Faith's shoulders and she gave her a little squeeze. "You can do anything you want to do, my dear. All you need is the desire and a little faith."

"I'll always have faith, because it's my name. That's why Dad picked it for me."

"It was a good choice," Julie agreed.

They'd reached the entrance to the school's driveway when a car passed by, going too fast for being in a school zone. Julie hurried Faith onto the grounds and watched as the car headed toward the main road. And then she frowned as she recognized the car, or at least she thought she had.

"Everything okay, Julie?" Faith asked when she'd stopped dead in her tracks.

"Look, there's Joanna. She'll want to hear your news," Julie said, but what she was thinking was, what on earth was Eddy doing in Baysville? And was that why she'd had the feeling someone had been watching her?

Chapter 15

Julie woke on Thanksgiving morning, as she often did on special occasions, reminiscing about her mother and the wonderful family traditions she'd given them all before she passed away. When Julie and her sister were growing up, they never sat down for a holiday meal with less than twenty people around the table. Preparations began days before the big event because there was Grandma's silver to polish, shopping for all the ingredients, table decorations to be dragged down from the attic and, of course, the endless dusting and vacuuming.

On the day, while the turkey or ham cooked, her father made the rounds in their eight-seater van collecting the great aunts and great uncles who didn't drive anymore while those who did, arrived in their own cars, bearing bottles of wine, bowls of salad, and sumptuous desserts. Julie's mother set a Hallmark kind of table, with all the trimmings, including the good dishes, the polished sterling silverware and the sparkling crystal glasses.

Julie loved helping her mother, especially when it came to making the stuffing, and because of that, when Michael had invited her to his family Thanksgiving dinner, she offered to make her mother's special recipe. Joy said she would like to help, so now the stuffing recipe, secret ingredients and all, would be passed along to her.

Julie had just made a fresh pot of her apple tea and was pouring a cup when Joy knocked on the back door.

"You want some?" Julie asked, holding up an empty cup.

"I'm okay," Joy said. "I just gulped down a glass of water. I'm trying to lose some weight."

"Tea has no calories, but if you're sure."

Joy was already a little too thin in Julie's mind, but telling her that wouldn't help, so Julie tried something else. She eyed Joy up and down, put a finger to her lips and then she wiggled one in a follow me motion.

"I bought a top the other day that doesn't fit. I was going to take it back, but you might like it. You want to see it?"

"Um. Okay. Sure. But…" Joy followed her upstairs and into Julie's room at the end of the hall.

When Julie opened her closet, Joy gasped. "Oh, I love that organizer."

Julie had ordered it online from a closet company and installed it herself. The system of wire racks and shelving maximized the small space of the closet, leaving her room for all her clothes and a section of shelves down the middle for miscellaneous things. The middle shelf held three photo albums and an old shoe box. When Julie reached in to get the blouse, she accidentally knocked the box on the floor and all the contents spilled out.

"Oh gosh. Look what I did."

Joy bent to pick up the box while Julie scooped up the contents. Amid a pile of old black and white photos, Joy noticed a little pink photo album. As she picked it up to hand it to Julie, a photo slipped out of it.

"Is that an ultrasound photo?" Joy asked, explaining that an adult student in one of her classes was expecting.

"It is," Julie said, her face flushing. She shoved everything else back into the shoe box and reached for the picture Joy was still holding.

"Is it your baby?" Joy asked, then seeing Julie bite her bottom lip, she added. "Sorry. It's none of my business."

"No, it's okay." Julie led Joy to the bed to sit down. "There are only three people who know about her. Me, Felicity and now you."

"I won't tell anyone. I promise," Joy said, eyes wide, obviously respectful of Julie's privacy. "Can I ask what happened?"

"I was only fourteen weeks. There were complications and…" Julie sucked in a breath of air and brushed at the tears that threatened.

"I'm so sorry, Julie. I shouldn't have asked." Joy handed the picture back to her.

"You didn't know."

"Where's her father? Didn't he know?"

"Eddy and I split up a while ago now, but no, he didn't know. He didn't want kids and I... well, that doesn't matter." She sighed. "She would have been seven now. Hope's age."

"Did you have names picked out?"

Julie smiled and nodded. "I did. I made a list and left it out for Eddy to find. It wasn't a very direct way to tell him I was expecting, but I was too nervous. I crossed a different name off the list every so often until it was down to just one. Lily. That's what I called her."

"Lily is a pretty name."

Julie sighed and rubbed her hands on her thighs. "Now, about that top." She went back to the closet, put the box in its place and drew out a hanger. "Here it is. What do you think?"

Joy slid off the bed and took the top off the hanger. "It's nice, actually." The surprise in her voice made Julie smile.

"Why don't you try it on? The bathroom is down the hall."

Joy returned a few moments later, and while Julie lifted Joy's hair out of the collar, she turned her shoulders to look into the full-length mirror.

"What do you think?" Julie asked, though she could tell by the smile on Joy's face she loved it.

"It's pretty, but I don't think I should. I mean, you could get your money back and get something else."

"I could, but..." Julie sat down on the bed. "Consider it an early birthday present."

"My birthday is weeks away."

"Then it's a Thanksgiving Day present. Or a non-occasion present, because it's nice to give something for no reason at all and besides, I'd like you to have it."

"Thanks Julie." Joy gave her a hug, then returned to the bathroom to change into her own top.

On their way back to the kitchen, she said, "You know, I've got a pair of jeans that would look great with this, and my rose gold earrings that would match perfectly."

"You see? It was meant to be yours. Now, let's get that stuffing made before your father wanders over here looking for it. I'm guessing he wants to get the turkey into the oven."

In the kitchen, Joy peeled and cored and chopped up apples while Julie did the onions. Julie steered the conversation to school, how her project was going on immigration, and wondered if she'd talked to Michael about that. Joy had, but she'd also talked about other things.

"I asked him about Mum," she said.

"How did that go?"

"It's a bit weird because Dad talks all the time, about everything, even stuff you don't want to talk about, like sex and pregnancy and birth control." She gave an actual little shudder then and rolled her eyes.

"He's a dad and a doctor, remember? Of course he's going to talk about those things."

"I know. But this stuff with Mum is different. I told him what my grandmother said, and I promised not to tell Faith or Hope. Julie, Mum has been to my school. So, I had to tell him. And I want to know what's going on. I'm nearly sixteen. I'm not a baby."

"When did you see your mother?" Julie asked.

"Last week," Joy said. "Faith told me she was at their school, too. I'm surprised I even remember her." She pushed apple core bits from her cutting board into the compost. "Dad doesn't keep any pictures of her around. I was just a kid when she… went away, but Hope looks like her, so it wasn't hard to tell who she was."

"What did she say, if you don't mind me asking?" Julie scraped onions into the bowl of stuffing bread and reached for the apples Joy had chopped.

"She wanted me to go with her to pick up Faith and Hope, to go to a park or something."

"But you didn't?"

Joy shook her head. "I didn't want to skip school, but I also think she was drunk or high or something. Something about it didn't feel right." She moved on to chop some celery. "Do you think it was Mum Faith saw in the window the night of the sleepover?"

"Oh, I'm not sure about that. The police seem to think it was a squatter staying in a vacant cottage."

"Maybe that squatter was my mother."

The thought had crossed Julie's mind too, more than once since all this had begun.

"Does my Mum have addiction problems?" Joy asked. "Drugs or alcohol or something. Aren't they inherited? Shouldn't Dad tell us stuff like that?"

"I've read that they can be, but your dad is the one to answer those questions."

An annoyance at Michael's vagueness with his daughters was festering in Julie. Joy was right. If their mother had genetically inherited medical issues, the girls had a right to know, especially someone Joy's age.

"I'm just so confused," Joy said, as tears welled in her eyes.

Julie set down her knife and pulled Joy into her embrace. "I wish I could tell you something more."

"I thought maybe he'd told you," she murmured into Julie's shoulder.

"He hasn't." Then she lifted Joy's chin and cupped her face in her hands. "Try to be patient, sweetheart. When he's ready, he will talk about it, okay?"

"Yeah," she nodded and reached for a tissue from the box on the counter. "Thanks Julie. I mean. It's good to get things off my chest, you know?"

"Anytime, sweetheart." Julie needed a tissue of her own. "I think your father is a good man, Joy. I also think that whatever he's not saying, he has his reasons. It's not my place to question what those reasons are. He and I are just friends, neighbours, you know? Sometimes, when someone we love is struggling, like he probably is right now, the rest of us just have to let him sort it out and then, when he's ready, he'll talk about it. Does that make sense?"

"It does." Joy nodded. "It's just that it feels like my whole life has been a big, huge lie and that makes me angry."

"I understand that. But something in my gut tells me this won't be a mystery for much longer."

Chapter 16

The smell of turkey cooking wafted through the open kitchen window as Julie balanced a cheesecake in one hand and Sirona's carrot cake in the other while knocking on Michael's door with her elbow. The cheesecake was from the Humble Pie Butter Tart Factory, where everything was to die for, but cheesecake was their specialty. When Michael first mentioned Thanksgiving dinner, Julie had called right away to order one because they inevitably sold out. The carrot cake was Sirona's contribution to supper. She'd dropped it off with Julie earlier that afternoon, saying she had an errand to run and would be back in time for dinner.

"Happy Thanksgiving!" Michael said, pushing open the screen door to let Julie in. "You didn't have to bring two desserts." He took one, and she followed him to the kitchen.

"As you might have guessed, the carrot cake is from Sirona," Julie said. She felt his eyes lingering admiringly over the new dress she was wearing. It was a shade of soft pink that brought out the blue in her eyes and standing in front of the mirror in the shop's dressing room, the other day, it had made her smile; a sure sign it was the one to pick out of the six she'd been considering.

"You look stunning!" His words came out in a half whisper as he stepped closer and took her shawl out of her hands. "Can I get you a drink? Glass of wine or something stronger?"

"I'm good with wine, thanks."

Michael looked just-showered fresh in Levi 511 jeans and a blue denim button-down shirt. The three-day shadow was a pleasant departure from his normal clean shaven, all business look. It gave him a rugged, outdoorsy appearance, like he belonged out there on Ril Lake with the rest of the all-season cottagers.

When they took their drinks into the living room, he waved Julie to a seat, then busied himself tidying magazines, and books and other papers from the coffee table, until she reached out a hand to stop him. He seemed nervous, as if he was uncomfortable to be alone with her.

"Are you alright?"

"Sure. Why wouldn't I be? Just tidying up, after the girls." He sank into an armchair and rested his glass on his knee, but his eyes drifted to the window and the lake beyond.

She considered Joy had probably cornered him when she got back with the stuffing earlier, and if they had talked, he might still be on edge about it. They sat in an awkward silence until Julie finally broke the ice with something non-committal on neutral ground to get the conversation going.

"I love the openness of this room." She glanced toward the archway that led to the dining room. "It wasn't like this when I was little, but my father opened that wall after he added the Muskoka room. It makes this whole area feel more welcoming."

"Did you tell me this when we first came to look at the place? I don't remember."

"I'm sure you didn't care at the time. Maybe you don't now."

"No," he said. "I do. Tell me."

Julie was aware she'd lost his attention a couple of words into her short, albeit boring, story, but she carried on anyway, describing how her father had redone this cottage with the plan of living there all year round once he and her mother retired. But her mother hadn't lived long enough to see her retirement or to enjoy living out here year round.

Michael seemed lost in thought at first until he said, "You said when you and your sister were kids. You've never mentioned her before."

"You never asked." She took a long sip of her wine.

"No, I guess I didn't."

"She prefers city life, and since her husband is high up in the Marriott Hotel chain, they move somewhere new every couple of years, so she's content. Right now, they're living in Athens."

"Greece, I assume, not New York."

"Yes. She wants me to visit. I like the idea of seeing other countries, but I never want to live anywhere but here."

"I can see why." Michael's eyes drifted to the window and the shadows that were closing in as the sun worked its way toward the horizon.

"Can I help with the table?" Julie asked when it seemed they'd run out of things to say. Or at least he had. Glancing toward the dining room and the bare tabletop, she couldn't help thinking it was the first thing she'd have done that morning—but apparently it wasn't a priority for Michael.

He flashed her a sincere look of relief. "Would you? I've become surprisingly good at the cooking end of things, but table setting is not my forte. It's usually a bit of a free-for-all with just us." He pushed out of his chair and set his half empty glass on the table. "I'll get the girls to help."

With a little dad coaxing, the girls met Julie in the dining room and, while Michael went to *mind the turkey*, as he put it, Julie and his girls set the table.

Her grandmother's dark cherry wood hutch, matching table and twelve cane-backed chairs, had been brought down from the other cottage when her grandma passed away and her parents moved into the bigger place. Her mother would have burned the entire lot of it until her father suggested it was still in good enough shape for renters. So here it stood.

Julie tugged on one end of the table, opening it up for two more leaves, which she knew were in Michael's bedroom closet, the only one deep enough to hold anything other than clothes. Once they were in place, they unfolded Grandma's Irish linen tablecloth and got all the dishes out of the hutch. Joy set out the plates, Faith did the silverware, and Hope folded napkins and put one under each person's fork. Julie set out the glasses, water, wine and juice, for young diners, and then they stood back to survey the results.

"It's missing something," Faith said, arms crossed and tapping her fingers on her elbows.

"Flowers, candles, or a centrepiece," Joy suggested, lips pursed and a frown across her brow.

Hope scrunched up her nose. "But where would the food go?"

Julie had an idea. "Come on, jackets and rubber boots. It rained last night."

In the woods between the cottages, they collected leaves of every autumn colour they could find, bright oranges, golden yellows, and brilliant reds. They added sprigs of fresh pine and cedar to bring in the scent of the outdoors. They cleaned up any traces of dirt, dried the leaves as best they could, then scattered everything over the tablecloth.

When they finished, Hope stood back and sighed a huge, little girl sigh. "It's so pretty," she said, grinning up at Julie.

Michael came in from the kitchen, his hands shoved deep into his jean pockets. He flashed her a grateful smile. "Nice," he said, and his girls beamed back at him with pride.

It was Joy who suggested they should make place cards for their guests, so they went off, leaving Julie and Michael alone. His gaze stayed with her for just a little too long.

"Julie," he began, moving closer. "Thank you for doing this. It's wonderful. You're wonderful. I…" He came closer still and Julie held her breath.

"Michael I…"

"Ali's here!" Hope squealed as she raced through the dining room and headed toward the front door.

He smiled, then grazed her cheek with a kiss, leaving a hint of something warm there. She took a deep breath as he left the room to greet his guests, then followed along behind.

There was a bit of a scramble to gather coats, put the food Annie brought in the fridge, and get drinks for everyone. Hope dragged Ali off to her bedroom, which left Noah and Ryder to stuff their hands in their pockets, wondering what to do with themselves until Joy came to the rescue.

"Hey guys, do you like Monopoly?" Joy asked mischievously, expecting some new fish were about to be snared.

They scampered off while the adults settled into the living room to talk and enjoy the drinks Michael poured them. They had barely sat down when Sirona arrived.

"Yoo Hoo!" she called from the door. Michael went to let her in and while Julie put Sirona's coat in the closet, he offered her something to drink.

"If there's some brandy going, I wouldn't mind that," Sirona said, a little gleam in her eye. "There's a bit of a chill in the air tonight."

Less than an hour later, Michael announced dinner was ready and when they all gathered around the table, he placed an enormous, perfectly roasted turkey in front of them. The girls beamed with pride as they followed him into the dining room with other dishes. The guests looked for their place cards, which had been carefully orchestrated by the girls. Julie was sure it wasn't a coincidence she was sitting next to Michael, but she kept her silence, remembering back to their dinner weeks ago, when Michael had explained their matchmaking attempts. She wondered what they were thinking now, since they'd been spending so much time together. It wouldn't be fair to get their hopes up if they were just going to be friends.

"Well, now, isn't this table lovely?" Sirona said, a little breathlessly as she unfolded her napkin and set it on her lap. "Did you girls do all this?"

"With a lot of help," Hope said, glancing up at Julie.

Seated at the head of his table, Michael wore a look of pride and contentment. He asked Sirona to give the blessing, and she obliged.

"Bless us with good food, the gift of gab and hearty laughter. May the love and joy we share be with us ever after. Amen."

"Amen!"

After that, there was a great rush to carve the turkey and pass the food around the table. When their plates were filled, Joy insisted everyone should take a turn to say what they were thankful for.

"You start, Hope," Joy said, nudging her sister's elbow.

Hope was glad of her new best friend and Ali echoed that, then the two of them giggled and whispered behind their hands, as if to prove that it was true.

Faith was glad of her new position at the library, even if it wasn't a paid job, which she'd really like to have one day, so she could start saving some money.

"What would you buy with your money," Joe asked her. "Do you have something special in mind?"

"I'm saving for university," Faith said. "I want to go to Oxford and that costs a lot of money. Dad says I have a great aunt there and maybe she would let me stay with her while I study."

There was pride in Michael's smile, just then, and something wistful, as if the thought of his daughter leaving home was almost too much for him.

"Don't worry, Michael," Joe said. "It's not for another six years. She might change her mind."

"Faith never changes her mind," Michael said, not taking his eyes off his daughter. "Do you, darling?" Faith shook her head as her cheeks pinked.

Ryder and Noah were thankful the hockey season was about to start and for the new equipment Joe had just bought them, because last year's gear was too small.

Sirona's speech was brief and highlighted her gratitude for nature, her plants, her lovely little cottage, and the company of good friends.

Joe and Annie held hands and told the others they were grateful for each other, for Annie's father Sam who was mending after a stroke last year and for their family being back together again with the addition of Ryder who'd fit in as if he was one of their own.

Joy was glad her immigration project was finished and hoped it got the A+ she thought it deserved.

When it came to Julie, she honestly didn't know what to say. She had many things to be grateful for, but nothing really stood out, other than the obvious, so she did the corny thing.

"I'm thankful for all of you," she said. "And that there's cheesecake for dessert." That got the laugh she hoped for. She turned to Michael. "Your turn."

"Last but not least, am I?" he said. "Well, the list of things to be thankful for is long this year, but, if I have to choose, after my girls, of course…" He tipped his wine glass in their direction. "I'd have to say I'm thankful for Julie." His eyes found hers over his glass. "It wasn't easy to change jobs and homes and be so far away from everything that was familiar to us, but she has made the transition easier and for that, I'll always be grateful. So, let's have a toast." He raised his glass. "To family and friends and all that we are to each other. And may there be many more celebrations like this one."

"Here, here!"

Noah seemed to think things were getting a little too serious, and that it was time for one of his jokes.

"Knock, knock," he called out above the din.

"Who's there?" Everyone chimed.

"Norma Lee."

"Norma Lee who?"

Noah rubbed his belly and, with much feigned effort, grunted, "Norma Lee, I don't eat this much food!"

Everyone burst out laughing and those within reach ruffled Noah's hair.

"Dessert anyone?" Michael called out when the laughter died down.

Chapter 17

When everyone had eaten their fill, they all got up to clear the table and get coffee and the desserts. As they were bringing things into the kitchen, someone knocked at the front door and Joy went to see who it was. A moment later, Darren Meyers stood in the kitchen, hat in hand, a sheepish expression on his face.

"Hey Doc, I'm sorry to interrupt your party, but could we talk outside?"

Michael set the turkey platter he'd been holding next to the roasting pan. "Of course."

"Dad?" Joy looked up at her father, a worried expression on her face, until he rested a hand on her shoulder and kissed her forehead.

"It's alright, darling. Help Julie get coffee on and the desserts, okay?" He threw a concerned glance in Julie's direction, then reached for his jacket and followed Darren outside.

Joy and Julie went to the kitchen window, where they could see Darren and Michael in the driveway. They were talking in such low voices that even when Joy slid the window open a crack, letting in a blast of cool evening air, they couldn't hear what they were saying.

"I'm sure he'll just be a minute," Julie said, reaching to fill the coffeepot. Then she got dessert plates and mugs out of the cupboard while Joy filled a sugar bowl and the cream jug. "It's probably something about the clinic. Maybe someone tried to break in or something."

Julie's attempts to distract Joy weren't working because, just as she picked up a tray to take it to the dining room, they both saw Darren open the back door of his cruiser. He tucked Michael's head down, just like they do on TV, and then he urged him inside. No handcuffs. No arguments but also no explanation. Joy let out a gasp that brought Joe into the kitchen. He stood behind them, watching as

Darren closed the door of the car. Michael glanced up toward the kitchen window and Joy reached out to touch the glass.

"What on earth is going on?" Joe asked.

Julie raced to the door and got there just as a grey sedan pulled up next to Darren. A short, stalky woman got out and leaned into the window of the cruiser. She spoke to Darren for less than a minute, then stepped back from the car.

"What's going on?" Julie pushed open the door and called out. "Where is Darren taking Michael, and who are you?"

The engine of Darren's cruiser turned over, and they were gone, out of the circle and onto Ril Cove Road.

"Miss Wight?" The woman said, coming toward the door, her hands outstretched as if to block Julie from running after them. "Let's go inside, shall we?"

"But what...?"

"Inside. Please."

The others had gathered in the kitchen, just as anxious as Julie to know what was going on. Joe was the first to demand an explanation.

"What's happening? Where has Darren taken Michael?"

The woman slipped out of her shoes, leaving them by the mat with everyone else's, and went into the kitchen.

"My name is Sherry Chaney. Please call me Sherry. I'm a Family Liaison Officer. I work with the police department in cases where families might need support."

Joy gasped out loud while Julie stifled one of her own. "Why would we need support?" Joy asked.

"Where have you taken Michael?" Julie demanded.

Sherry skimmed the crowd that was gathered in the kitchen until her eyes came to rest on Joy's. "Maybe we could talk, in private. Just the family."

"No!" Joe said. "We're not leaving until we have some answers."

Annie flashed him a *stay out of this* look. "Why don't I take the kids home? Unless you'd rather we stay, Julie."

"Maybe Joe could stay," Julie said. "In case one of us has to go to Michael or…"

"Where is Daddy?" Hope asked, huge tears welling in her eyes. "Why is everyone so upset? Who is she?" She pointed to Sherry, who bent down to eye-level with Hope.

"You're the youngest. Hope is it?" Sherry stuck out a hand to shake Hope's.

Hope pulled her hand away, instinctively not wanting to shake hands with this stranger. "I want to know where my daddy is?"

They were all looking at Sherry as she straightened up again. "He's helping the police," she said. "He'll be back before you know it. Maybe we'd all like a cup of tea?"

"I'll do that," Julie said, filling the kettle.

Annie ushered her kids to the closet in search of their coats, and Faith and Hope went to help.

Sirona was quick to offer help. "Joy, maybe you and I could finish clearing the table."

Alone with Sherry, Julie watched the woman as she gazed around the kitchen, reading notes attached to the fridge and eyeing the mail on the counter. Julie gathered it up and shoved it into a drawer, out of sight.

"That's private," she said, giving Sherry a disapproving look.

"What's your role here," Sherry asked.

"I'm a neighbour and friend," Julie said, dropping tea bags into a pot and filling it with boiling water from the kettle.

"So, you and Mr. Adams aren't…?"

"Not that it's any of your business."

"Not the children's guardian, either?"

"No. I own this cottage, and Dr. Adams is my tenant. But we're friends, if that makes a difference." Julie would like to have exerted her rights to kick the woman out, but even more than that, she wanted to know what was going on. She leaned against the counter, waiting for the kettle to boil.

"Why are you being so mysterious? What do we need a Family Liaison something-or-other for?"

"All in good time," Sherry said. "Got any cookies?"

"No, but you may as well have the cheesecake, since none of us are going to want it." Julie cut her a generous slice and slapped it onto a plate. It landed upside down, so that the filling was smushed, but Julie didn't care. She was angry and frustrated. She stuck a fork in it and handed it to Sherry.

"Thanks," Sherry said, licking the filling from her thumb where it had slid to the edge of the plate. "From Humble Pie Bakery?" she asked.

"Of course. You know it?"

"You bet I do."

Perhaps Sherry had a redeeming quality after all.

When the tea was made, the leftovers wrapped and stored in the fridge, Sirona took Hope and Faith to the dining room and got out a deck of cards. "Let's play Old Maid," they heard her say as the rest went to the Muskoka room and closed the door.

A concerned and protective Joe stood sentry in the doorway, arms folded across his chest, as his eyes darted between Joy and Julie, who took the couch. Sherry sat in the chair opposite. When they all had a cup of tea in their hands, wanted or not, Julie looked at Sherry.

"Now, will you please tell us what this is all about?"

One-handed, Sherry pulled a notepad out of her suit jacket pocket. "Can I just get your names, please?" Her gaze met Julie's over her cup.

"Julie Wight."

"And you're the... neighbour," Sherry said, setting down her teacup to write.

"She's our friend, and she takes care of us when Dad's away," Joy interceded.

"Okay. That's great. Thank you. And you're Joy, the eldest daughter, right?" When Joy nodded, Sherry turned to Joe. "And you, sir? How are you connected to this family?"

"A friend of Michael's, we are neighbours. We're all friends here. We were invited to Thanksgiving Dinner. It's why we're here. Whatever you've got to say, say it, please."

"Okay. Thank you. And the woman in the other room, with the girls. Who is she?" Sherry asked.

"That's Sirona," Julie said.

Sherry wrote it down. "And her surname?"

Julie glanced up at Joe, then back again. "I don't think she has one. She's never told me what it was."

"No surname. Like Cher, you mean?" Sherry said, eyeing them suspiciously.

"You'll have to ask her yourself. I don't know it." Julie took a sip of tea, hoping it would steady her nerves. "Look, can't you tell us what's going on? Why has Michael been taken away? Was he arrested?"

"I'll tell you what I can." Sherry set her notepad aside and wrapped her stubby fingers around her teacup. "There's been an incident," she said.

"What kind of incident?" Joy asked.

"The body of a woman was found in a vacant cottage. She'd been staying there for some time, we think. There are food containers, a few groceries, and some clothes."

"Is it the same cottage where my canoe was found? Darren said there were some squatters living there."

"On Muskoka Bob Road?" When Julie nodded, Sherry did too. "The ID we found in the cottage suggests that three people were living there, a Mia Sanders and..."

"My mother?" Joy cried out.

"Yes, dear. Grace Walker," Sherry said.

Joy frowned. "Walker, but that's not our name."

"It's the name she goes by now. Apparently, Walker was her maiden name," Sherry said. "The thing is, one of them was found dead and we need your father to tell us whether or not it's your mother. I'm sorry. I know how that sounds harsh, and that this is difficult for you."

Joy sucked in a gulp of air, her eyes welling with tears as she set her teacup down on the table. "You have no idea how this is for me or for my family."

"It might not be your Mum, Joy," Julie said, squeezing Joy's hand. And then she turned to Sherry. "How, and when did she die?"

"We're still investigating. We don't have a time of death yet, just…"

Something inside Joy seemed to ooze to the surface. She balled the fist of one hand and squeezed Julie's with the other. "You think my father had something to do with it, don't you?" she hissed at Sherry. "Well, he wouldn't. He's not like that. He's…"

Sherry shook her head. "Please Joy. It's best if you remain calm. Look, let's all take a breath here." Joe sat on the arm of the couch and put an arm around Joy's shoulders, while Sherry continued. "Dr. Adams has not been arrested. He's been asked to identify the body. Do you understand what that means, Joy?"

Joy nodded soberly. "But why take him away in the police car like that? Why couldn't he come inside and talk to us? He didn't even get his cellphone, or say goodbye or…"

"Let her explain," Joe mumbled. "I know you're worried, but it will be alright. Remember, your dad has been here with you all day. Even if he could kill someone, which he couldn't, he could never have done this."

"Like I said, it's an ongoing investigation. Dr. Adams will know if it is or isn't your mother, and an autopsy will tell us more. I can't speak for Officer Meyers or what happened outside earlier, but that's about all I can say at this time."

"And you're sure you don't know when the death occurred?" Joe asked.

"It was within the last twenty-four hours. I shouldn't even be telling you that."

As Joy slumped against her, Julie's mind raced over the past twenty-four hours, doing her best to recall where she had been, wondering too, where Michael and the girls had been.

"I hope it's her," Joy announced, finally able to brush away some of her tears. "She deserves to die after what she did."

Julie squeezed her hand and tried to comfort her, but nothing seemed to work. Joy broke free of her grasp, got up, and stormed from the room. Joe was about to follow when Julie grabbed his arm.

"I think she needs some time alone, just for now."

Joe nodded, then looked at Sherry. "Are you sure there isn't anything else you can tell us?"

"Like I said, it's an ongoing investigation and we currently have no more information than this. Dr. Adams is not under arrest. He's assisting the police with their investigation. My office was made aware there might be no one to stay with the girls, which is why I'm here. My role is to help the family through what might be a difficult time. And like it or not, I am obliged to remain since neither of you have legal guardianship over the girls."

Chapter 18

Hours later, after the girls had gone to bed and Joe and Sirona had left, Michael came home. Julie had been at the kitchen window when the police car pulled into the driveway. She held her breath as Michael got out. He'd been in the front passenger seat this time. He said something to Darren, then went inside.

Sherry had left since her part in things was over, and when she stopped at the door, she sent Julie a look of approval and a small nod of respect before she stepped outside. It wasn't until the taillights of her car disappeared down Ril Cove Road that Michael let out a long, low sigh. And then he leaned against the kitchen counter and looked at Julie. His features were shallow and drawn and there was a look about him of a man who'd been through a mental war zone.

"You look like you could use a stiff drink," she said, reaching for the bottle of scotch on the counter.

"Yeah."

His voice was rough and growly, as if a rasping tool had somehow slid down his throat. His brow furrowed, and she felt him watching her as she got two crystal glasses out of the cupboard and set them down. He reached for her hand when she went to pour their drinks.

"Change your mind?" she asked. When she looked up at him, her heart ached for him. He was a troubled man, one whose secrets were not just catching up with him but taking their toll. Would sharing his troubles lessen them? That's something her grandmother used to say, although then Julie's problems were little more than being angry at her mother about something, or her younger sister's nosiness. Adult problems were not so easily solved, even when shared.

Michael shook his head. "No, I want it. But first I need to say thank you. I don't know how I can ever repay you for your kindness, for all you've done for the girls, for staying here when I had to…"

Julie set the bottle down and put her arms around him. A friendly hug. A hug of compassion. A hug that says, I'm here for you. He pulled her closer, rested his chin on the top of her head, and sighed.

"Whatever you need," she said softly. "Do you want to tell me what happened?" she asked, looking up at him. He nodded, then released her so she could fix their drinks.

"But I don't want to keep you. It's been a long day."

"I'll manage." She poured two fingers of Scotch in each of their glasses and followed him to the Muskoka room, where they wrapped in warm blankets against the chill of the night air. Julie waited, her hands wrapped around her tumbler, giving him time to gather his thoughts. Finally, after a few moments, and a long gulp of his drink, Michael seemed ready. His eyes flitted to the window, where nothing but the darkness of the night stared back at him. And then he turned to her.

"The things your mind can conjure up when you're riding in the backseat of a police car," he said. "Like, has there been a case of mistaken identity? Was I caught on a drone shot or on CCTV somewhere and now they're going to throw me in jail?"

"Surely you didn't think that?"

"I didn't know what to think. Darren told me they wanted help to identify a woman's body and that she might be Grace." He lifted his glass and drank the rest of his whisky in one gulp, then ran a finger over his lip to catch a drip. He blinked hard, as if he couldn't quite grasp the memories of what had just happened. "I was so nervous."

"Anyone would be."

"No, you don't get it. Julie." Her body stiffened at the sudden sharpness in his tone. "I'm sorry. I'm not mad at you. I don't think I could ever be angry with you. It's me I'm mad at, because all the way to the morgue, I kept hoping, praying, wishing it would be Grace. I know that sounds cruel, but the difference it would have meant to our lives, to the girls…" He turned to look at her then, his eyes filling with tears. He brushed at them angrily, as if he had no business shedding tears, for himself or for anyone. "But it wasn't

Grace." He paused for a long moment and held her gaze. "It wasn't Grace," he said again.

"That's good then, isn't it?" she asked.

"Yes. It's good that it wasn't Grace. I mean, despite what I was thinking on the way. I always hoped that the girls could have some kind of relationship with her, one day, if things were… god, I don't know what I was thinking." He buried his head in his hands, unable or unwilling to say more.

Julie leaned forward, reached out, and set her hand on his knee. "But surely this dead woman has nothing to do with you. The police will leave you alone now."

He looked at her again, eyes bloodshot and undoubtedly burning. "I'm not so sure. They asked if I knew a Mia Sanders. Apparently, she was one of three squatters at the cottage where they found your canoe. I'm guessing she is the dead woman."

"But what does she have to do with Grace? Did they think Grace was squatting there too?"

"The name means nothing to me, but it's been years since I've seen or talked to Grace. I don't know who she's friends with now, so I suppose she could have been."

"But you don't know anyone by that name?"

He shook his head and did his best to steady his trembling hand as he set his empty glass on the table.

"Whoever she was, she came to a brutal death. You'd have thought after years of carving up cadavers in medical school, I would have been prepared for anything." He shook his head again, as if that would force the sight of the dead woman out of his mind. "She was…" He blew out a lungful of air and raised his hand to one side of his face. "She was all bashed in here. Her cheekbones smashed against her skull, like someone had punched her, hard. Brutally hard. There were a lot of knife wounds in her torso, Darren said. And that fits with Grace's past, so we went over everything that happened seven years ago. That's why I was gone so long."

Julie shook her head, not understanding. "Grace's past? Is this the secret you've been keeping? Do the police think Grace killed this woman? Is she capable of that?"

"Honestly, I don't know what she's capable of now, but back then…" He nodded. "Back then, yes."

"Jeez, Michael. Does that have something to do with why she was in prison?"

He nodded and dropped his head. "But she's done her time now and I might have to consider visitation rights, eventually."

"You don't want to do that?" Julie watched his face for more, but he wasn't forthcoming. "Is that why you moved up here? So she wouldn't find you, because I can't imagine it would be too difficult to find out where a doctor is. Social media. Government listings of doctors and so on."

"Confession time." Michael leaned forward and took her hand in his. "We've only been living in Niagara Falls for the last five years, Julie. We're from Vancouver. And I had our names legally changed. We weren't always Adams, and the girls weren't born Joy, Faith, and Hope. Those are names I chose for them when all this happened."

"When all what happened, Michael?"

"When…"

Confession lingered on his lips and in the way he looked at her, and Julie knew she was about to hear it all. She hadn't wanted to know, before, hadn't wanted to get involved in whatever complications came with this man and his family, but things had changed. She'd become attached to the girls. She worried about them, and though she tried not to, she cared about him, too. This was as far from a simple life as it could be, but something about the man she'd come to know told her that whatever he was about to reveal, none of it was his fault.

The words were on the tip of his tongue when another of Faith's ear-piercing screams sent shockwaves through the cottage that echoed off the lake. They shot out of their chairs, tipping the table between them, their glasses tumbling to the floor. Julie stooped to pick them up and set the table upright.

"I've got to see to her," Michael said. "I'll be back in a few minutes. Please wait."

A second scream sent shivers running up and down Julie's spine. "She needs you, and it won't be a few minutes. I'll just go."

"Are you sure?"

She nodded, then pleaded with him. "Don't let her cry out a third time, Michael. Go to her."

When he left the room, Julie sat down again, willing her heart to cease its incessant ramming against her chest. She was alone in the room and suddenly it felt as if Michael had taken all the air with him. She gasped for breath, hearing his words repeatedly in her mind. Adams wasn't their last name. They weren't from Niagara Falls. Grace had done time for something involving knives and stabbing and now she was here, in Baysville, or somewhere nearby demanding to be with her children.

It was one thing to rent her cottage to help pay her mortgage, and quite another to have allowed this madness into her life. She didn't want to see any harm come to Michael or the girls, but knives, stabbing and murder was beyond complicated.

As she slipped out onto the deck and down the steps, her thoughts shifted to their lease and what it would cost her to break it. It was a selfish thought and as quickly as it came, she pushed it away. Michael would get on with things in his own way and no matter what, for the girls' sake, she would not put them out, but she wanted nothing more to do with the nightmare that seemed to plague them all.

Chapter 19

Except for seeing Hope in class and Faith in the halls at school, Julie saw nothing of the Adams over the next little while. There hadn't even been a wave across the driveway when they got in the car, and Michael had stopped running in the mornings, or perhaps he was just going at a different time. It was as if she didn't exist, as if everything that had happened Thanksgiving night and before it was forgotten. She reminded herself that it was she who'd left without a word to him that night and she who'd kept her distance since then. She who'd been thinking of breaking his lease, just to rid herself of the complications she didn't want in her life.

She couldn't say what she expected Michael to tell her when they'd sat in his Muskoka room that night, but she wasn't prepared for what she'd heard. She'd thought herself a caring sort of person, someone who would stand by her friends through anything, but not this, not murder, not whatever was in Michael and Grace's past that had made him lie to his children and change their names. Surely Joy and Faith, too, were old enough to remember they'd once had other names, even if Hope wasn't. She had questions; so many questions, but she would not ask them. Instead, she ignored the twinges of guilt that pinched at her heart, when she thought of Joy and Faith and Hope and their innocence in all this, and told herself that they weren't her responsibility, except at school.

Without question or comment, Michael had made sure Faith got to the library for her shifts after school. He was also driving the three of them every day, no longer allowing them to take the bus. She didn't question his reasons. Until they knew for sure that Grace was no longer in the area, she would have done the same.

Julie couldn't deny she had a million questions floating through her mind at any given time, or that she'd spent hours scrolling the internet for information or news about Grace Walker. Michael's social media was surprisingly non-existent, even since he'd changed his name from whatever it used to be. Joy had an Instagram profile that was curiously generic, no pictures, and nothing that would suggest who she was now, or had been before. How did people stay off the social media grid, especially a girl of Joy's age, who seemed to always be on her phone?

By the weekend following Thanksgiving, Julie had run the whole gamut of emotions, gone down the guilt trip path and eventually come full circle back to where she'd started. She told herself that the intimacy she'd felt when she was with Michael had been misguided, a longing for what she'd had with Eddy in the early days of their relationship, but not what she needed or wanted anymore.

On Saturday morning Sirona spread her Tarot deck on Julie's kitchen table, to do a reading for Julie; not that Julie believed any of it. Sirona's salves and tinctures were one thing, but telling someone's future with some funny looking few cards was quite another.

"The Ace of Cups," Sirona insisted, bringing Julie's attention back to the cards between them. "It means a new love interest."

"Must be someone I haven't met yet," Julie told her.

"Is it?" Sirona's eyes flitted to the window. Julie knew she was referring to Michael.

"Be serious," Julie snapped. "There's too much going on over there. The last thing I want is the baggage of a crazed ex-wife."

"But if she weren't in the picture…"

"But she is! And whatever has happened, it must be bad, or why would he have changed all their names and moved from Vancouver?"

"You sound angry, Julie."

"Wouldn't you be? Who am I renting that place to? What do we really know about them? They have a one-year lease. That's ten and half more months of this."

"Take a deep breath. I'm sure, when all is revealed, things will look quite different."

"You see that in your cards, do you?" Julie sneered, then instantly regretted it. She didn't believe in the cards, but Sirona did, and it was wrong to insult her. She mumbled an apology.

"It's alright, dear. I can see you're upset." Sirona said, getting up to refill her tea. "Want more?"

"No, thank you. If I drink any more tea, I'll float all the way to China."

Sirona sat down with a half-filled cup. Gathering her cards, she tucked them into the little silk bag she always carried with her.

"I found a listing in an old Vancouver yellow pages directory," Julie said. "For a plumber with the last name, Walker. The number's not in service anymore."

"You called it?"

"You bet I did.

"Ah. Right."

"You don't suppose they're in the witness protection program?"

Sirona frowned and drummed the sides of her cup with her fingertips. "It's not impossible, but I doubt it. Didn't you say Michael changed their names? I think the government would have given them new identities if that were the case. And would they let him practice medicine so publicly?"

"Normally, all you have to do is bring up your local health care system and an entire list of doctors comes up, along with photographs and bios." Julie got her phone from the counter to prove her point. "Except for his. It's odd, don't you think?"

"It isn't odd if he's trying to keep a low profile."

"Whatever. I'm finished worrying about this. And this…" Julie waved her hand toward the silk bag. "This Ace of Cups business is a crock. Remember when Eddy left, and I said I wanted to be alone?"

"Don't be ridiculous. No one your age enjoys being alone." Sirona's gaze flitted to the clock on the wall. "Goodness, look at the time. I've got a million things to do today."

On her way to the door, Sirona patted the pockets of her jacket and called out in surprise.

"I nearly forgot these. I was beach combing earlier." She opened her hands to reveal three little treasures: a button Julie recognized from Hope's bathing suit, a shepherd's hook bookmark that had been sticking out of the book Faith was reading the day they arrived, and a rose gold earring Joy had been wearing just the other day.

"I don't think anyone is over there just now, but the girls will be happy to see those."

As if on cue, Michael's car pulled into the circle and down the lane next door. The engine shut off, followed by the sound of four doors opening and closing again. There was a flurry of footsteps across the porch, the mutterings of soft voices, and finally, the door of the cottage closing behind them.

"They're home now," Sirona said, watching Julie closely.

"Mm hmm."

"It's not what it seems, with him, you know." Sirona's eyes locked with Julies and as she stared into the steely grey, Julie couldn't help wondering what Sirona wasn't saying.

"You know something," Julie said. "You've been keeping something from me. What is it?"

Sirona shook her head. "Nothing at all, but I know people. And if you ask me, Michael Adams or whatever his name used to be, is a good man, and you'd be a fool to let him slip out of your hands."

"I can't, Sirona. You know I can't. Not after Eddy and what we went through. I deserve better."

"But Michael isn't Eddy."

"Of course, he's not Eddy. But he's… it's… well, it's…"

Sirona placed a motherly hand on Julie's cheek. "It's only complicated if you let it be." She nodded toward Michael's cottage. "Everything you've ever wanted in life is on the other side of those trees, and there's nothing complicated about that."

Julie took a long breath and closed her eyes before saying anything more. She didn't want to argue with Sirona. She loved her like a mother, respected her and knew Sirona only wanted what was best for her.

She knew before she opened her eyes again that Sirona had left, by the sudden rush of wintery air. And then she heard the click as the latch of the door caught and the cold air dissipated into the room.

With a heavy sigh, Julie put the dirty cups in the sink and filled them with hot water to soak. It was then she noticed Sirona had left the girls' treasures on the counter. Julie scooped them up and hurried to the door, intending to give them back.

"Sirona!" she shouted when she reached the top step of her deck, but there was nothing more than a set of footprints in the sand, heading toward the little cottage on the point.

"Well, I'm not going over there," Julie muttered to herself, heading back inside. She put the girls' things on the window ledge, then went on with her Saturday chores.

It was hours later, after she'd finished her to do list, eaten supper and done her dishes, that Julie filled the kettle to make tea and thought about the solitude of her back deck. She was reaching for a cup when the light of the moon caught the gold in Joy's earring resting on the window ledge. Her eyes lingered there as she thought of Sirona's meddling and her insistence that Julie was wrong about Michael.

Well, if Sirona wasn't going to give the girls their things, she would. It was just some trinkets that needed to be returned. That's all. She didn't need to talk or settle anything with Michael. She could just go over there, give them these things, and leave. She might only see Joy, or Faith, or maybe Hope would answer the door. Yes. Hope. She wouldn't be in bed yet. It was Saturday night, no school tomorrow and it was just... Julie glanced up at the clock... seven thirty-three. No, Hope would not be in bed.

She scooped up Sirona's finds, her best wool shawl, and summoned her courage. *Get over yourself,* she mumbled, as she wrapped the shawl around her shoulders and slipped out the back door, down the steps and across the woods between her place and his.

Julie had been going back and forth across this path since she was old enough to walk. Then it had been familiar, a part of what was hers, but now it felt strange, as if what was on the other side belonged to someone else. As she emerged from the trees and stepped onto the grass on Michael's side of the woods, it felt as if she was treading on private property.

Smoke curled from the firepit as she drew nearer, where all the Adams were gathered around a roaring fire, roasting marshmallows. A dry twig snapped beneath her feet, giving her away, and they turned to watch her cross the yard.

"I'll get another chair," Joy said, eagerly jumping up.

Hope gave a little wave and flashed one of her usual brilliant smiles. Julie waved back. Shadows flickered across Faith's solemn face and Julie sensed she wasn't in the mood for what was probably supposed to be an evening of family fun. She'd been out of sorts at school this past week, too, and Julie had chalked it up to a disagreement between friends, but maybe she'd been wrong because just then, Michael seemed quiet too. He was concentrating on adding more wood to the fire and stirring up the embers so the pieces would catch. He hadn't even acknowledged her arrival and despite the heat from the fire, the chill from him was enough to freeze the blood in her veins. She desperately wanted to give the girls their things and leave.

"Sirona found some things that belong to you," she told Hope and Faith, opening her hands to reveal their lost items.

"My button!" Hope squealed. "Oh, thank you, thank you."

"You can thank Sirona next time you see her." Julie held the bookmark out to Faith. "This is yours, I think."

"It's all rusty," Faith sniffed.

"You might soak it in some vinegar and then use some steel wool on it. If that doesn't work, I have a few of these in my desk drawer at school. You could come and get one on Monday."

"Whatever. I don't really care." Faith got out of her chair, stomped past the rest of her family and nearly collided with Joy, who was on her way back with the extra chair.

"Faith!" When Michael shouted, Julie flinched and the hair on her arms stood up. She'd never heard Michael raise his voice before, not to anyone, let alone his girls. "Back here, now," he continued, when Faith ignored him.

She stopped, turned and glared at him, but eventually, she did as she was told.

"You owe Julie an apology," he said. "She was being kind and trying to help."

Faith softened, but only slightly and only when she looked at Julie. "Sorry," she said. Then, with a sigh of resignation, she added, "I shouldn't have been rude. I'm not angry with you."

Julie didn't need Faith's heated glance toward her father to know it was Michael the girl was upset with. There was something in her look that sent Julie back to herself at that age and her own difficult pre-teen years when her parents had thought she should act grown up, yet she was still very much, an awkward, shy child.

She reached out to graze Faith's shoulder tenderly. "Apology accepted. Come by on Monday and pick out a new one, okay?"

Faith nodded and then, without a backward look to her father or her sisters, went inside.

When Julie placed Joy's earring in her hand, she smiled fondly at it. "What a shame. I threw the other one out. I thought this was gone for good. But thanks. Maybe one day I'll get a second hole in one ear, and I'll be able to wear it." She tucked it into the pocket of her hoodie.

"Look Joy. My button!" Hope jumped up to show her sister.

"Cool. Come on," Joy said. "I'll help you sew it back on your bathing suit."

Mission over, Julie was ready to go home, but when the girls were out of earshot, Michael patted the empty chair Joy had set down beside him. And then he apologized again for Faith's outburst.

"People have bad days, even kids," Julie said, her eyes flitting between the empty chair and the woods. She didn't want to sit down and chat, didn't want to sip wine, or talk about childhood memories of growing up here, or her family or any of the other things they'd talked about other evenings. She just wanted to go home. But when his eyes flitted to the chair again, and he seemed to really want her there, she resigned herself to keep it a brief visit and settled into the chair.

Michael turned his gaze back to the fire, mesmerized and unable to look at anything else. "It's been a terrible week for her," he said eventually. "She's at that age, you know."

"I wondered if there was a boy at school or something."

Michael dropped the stick he'd been poking the fire with and looked at her. "It isn't a boy or a friend. It's the other thing common among girls her age."

"Oh! That problem. Her first?" Something in Julie's memory clicked. She'd seen Faith argue with Joanna the other day and that, just like tonight, had seemed odd too. "Gosh, I remember my first one. Boy, I was… Well, never mind. You don't want to hear about that."

Michael twisted in his chair to face her. "I'm glad you came over tonight. I got the impression you were angry with me, so I've been keeping my distance, but I hope we can talk about it."

"I'm not angry." Confused, maybe. Unsure of a lot of things, but she wasn't angry. "After everything that's happened, I was trying to give *you* some space."

A slow smile crept over his face, and a little corner of her heart twinged. No matter how she tried, or what she told herself, she could not deny the attraction she was feeling at that moment. But neither could she deny the mystery around Grace and prison and the rest of it, whatever *it* was. The frustration returned, and she remembered why she'd wanted not to come over in the first place.

"I could, if I hadn't lost my phone."

"You still could have come to the door," she insisted. Then she relented, just a little. "How did you lose your phone?"

He shrugged. "I don't know. It was plugged into the charger the other night and now it's gone. I thought Hope or Faith had borrowed it. Faith has been begging for one and Hope sometimes likes to play a game on it, but they don't have it. I've ordered a new one. It just hasn't arrived yet."

"Well, I'm sorry to hear that. Phones are expensive."

"It's fine. It'll show up eventually, under the bed or down the side of the couch or something. I'll give it to Faith if she promises not to be so grumpy."

Julie smiled. "That grumpiness will pass, at least until next month. Would you like me to talk to her, give her a woman's perspective on things?"

"What are you going to tell her I haven't already?"

Her grin spread even wider across her face. "What exactly did you tell her? You didn't say something like she's a woman now, did you?"

He grimaced. "I might have."

"Michael! For goodness's sake." Julie pushed to the edge of her chair. "How can a man ever explain this to a woman? Do you mind if I speak with her?"

"I was hoping you would," he confessed.

As he reached out, his fingers covering hers, a playful smile crept into the corners of his mouth and suddenly, watching his face as shadows from the fire danced across it, Julie realized that this was what he had been hoping for all along.

She wiggled an annoyed a finger at him. "You sneak. You were hoping I'd say that, weren't you? I have a good mind to go home and let you sort this out yourself. For Faith's sake, I won't, but you, Michael Adams, owe me big time."

"A debt I look forward to repaying," he said, leaning forward in his chair to kiss her on the cheek. "Will that cover it?"

His eyes searched hers, his face impossibly close, his breath laced with the sweet scent of marshmallows. He was going to kiss her again, and this time, not on the cheek. For a moment, she held her breath. Seconds ago, she'd been angry with him, frustrated, unsure of everything. What had changed? Nothing, except for that damned charming smile of his. Her mind wandered back to the tarot reading earlier that day and the Ace of Cups staring back at her from the table.

Had Sirona been right? Was this really as complicated as Julie thought it was? Did it need to be or...

Suddenly, the fire hissed and crackled. A hot ember shot out of it and landed on the back of Julie's hand.

"Ow!" She pulled away to shake it off. "Damn! That hurt." She sucked at the flesh the spark had singed.

Michael took her hand in his, caressed it, checked the tiny burn, and kissed it softly. Then his eyes met hers. "Better?" he asked.

She nodded, certain that her hand was fine, but she couldn't say the same for her heart.

Chapter 20

The following morning, Julie did something completely out of character. She slept in. She was normally an early riser. Even without setting an alarm, her body seemed to know when she'd had enough sleep. But that morning it was ten-thirty when she kicked back the covers, went to the bathroom, then made her way to the kitchen to make coffee.

Michael's car was already gone, and she recalled their conversation at the door last night.

"We're going to try the movies again tomorrow. There's a Sunday morning show in Bracebridge." He'd asked her to come with them, but she'd politely declined. She had things to do, namely the garage to sort out, so there would be room for the four boats. Two canoes and two kayaks took up a lot of space, even when they hung from the ceiling or from hooks on the wall.

He'd persisted using Faith's predicament to convince her to join them.

"Faith will be fine, now," Julie had told him. "I reminded her that Joy could help if she needed someone."

He'd hung his head in jest. "Not her dear old dad."

"It's not your fault you were born a man," she'd said, reaching for the door.

He was about to say something else, but she'd stopped him, because whatever it was, they both knew there was too much unspoken between them and it was far too late for long conversations. She had suggested dinner the following day though, then headed for home. He had stood on his porch, watching until she was inside and had shut off her light.

Now, she lifted the overhead door of her garage, popped in her Air Pods and cranked up her playlist. Then she began hauling things out, sorting them according to the order they'd go back inside, and admitting that one or two things needed to go. The lawnmower, for instance. She didn't use it now that there was no grass on the property. Wally could service it for her and then she could sell it, so she put it in the back of her SUV and on her way into town, she'd drop it off at the garage.

The weed-eater belonged on a hook on the wall not too far from the door. She might need that once or twice more before the snow fell. Her cross-county skies, the snow shovels and snowblower would go in last, for easy access in the winter months. Her flowerpots and other gardening supplies, which she hardly ever used, went a little further back on the shelving unit because they needed tidying, and because she wasn't quite ready to part with them yet.

An old dresser stood against the east wall, an item she'd bought at an auction sale more than seven years ago. Her plan was to strip it and paint it white and add pink porcelain handles. But then the miscarriage had happened and, in the months and years that followed, the dresser regressed deeper into the back corner. Julie covered it with a tarp and put three boxes of her grandmother's crockery on top of it. Minutes later, she thought better of that and put the crockery in the back of her car alongside the lawnmower. She'd already kept everything of her grandmother's she'd wanted to. This could go to charity

Now with her music cranked, her broom as her dance partner, as Kylie Minogue belted out *Can't Get You Out of My Head*, Julie pushed her broom across the floor, stopping now and again to sway to the music. It felt remarkably freeing to have the garage in order again, and she was celebrating in her own quirky way. She swept and danced and gathered all the bits and dust to the middle of the floor. When the music paused while the next song came on, Julie bent to pick up a stray nail. As she stood up again, a shadow crossed the threshold of the doorway behind her. She was not alone, and someone was coming up behind her.

Adrenaline soared through her body, and in one swift and clean motion, Julie shifted the broom to her left hand, whirled around, and grabbed her assailant's arm. She swung it upward, hard, and twisted the offender over her leg and onto the floor.

"Michael!" she gasped, seeing who it was. "I'm so sorry. I didn't realize it was you."

He blinked up at her, dazed at first, until he grunted and rolled over onto his stomach, then pushed himself to his knees. Julie reached down to help him up, but he pushed her arm, angrily groaning as he stood up.

"Jesus, Julie. What the fu…" He stopped short of saying what he was about when she gave him her sternest teacher look. "Fudge!"

"I'm sorry," Julie said again, pocketing her Air Pods and shutting off the music. "You should have said something, given me a warning that it was you."

"Who did you think it was, for crying out loud?"

She reached out to dust the dirt from the back of his shirt. "That's the thing. I didn't think. I just reacted. I told you I have a brown belt in karate, and I took kick boxing."

Dusting the dirt from his jeans, one half of Michael's face broke into a grin while the other grimaced with pain. "You weren't kidding when you said you could take care of yourself." He checked all his limbs, walked a few paces around the garage and decided he was fine, except for a bit of discomfort in the arm she'd grabbed. Finally, he conceded he wasn't too badly hurt and there was no great harm done. "It's fine. I'm just a little…" He put a hand on his back, caressing his kidney area. "Stiff, I think." Then he walked around the garage a little more, shaking one leg, then the other, working out the kinks.

"Give it a rest," Julie said, watching a smirk creep over his face. "You're not hurt."

He continued to poke and prod his back, while the smirk grew and she protested even more. "I'm not so sure… Could be internal bleeding or something. In fact, I think I hurt my jawbone."

"What's the matter with Daddy?" Neither of them had heard Hope come into the garage, but she stood in the doorway, a box of popcorn in her hand.

"Just a minor accident," Julie told her. "He'll get over it."

"I can't finish my popcorn," Hope said, holding the box up for his inspection.

"Put it in the kitchen in case you want it later. And can you please tell your sisters where I am? I'm going to give Julie a hand putting the boats away. If I can walk." He sent a teasing grin Julie's way.

"Okay," Hope said, spinning around twice before she hurried away.

"You don't have to help with the boats," Julie said. "I thought I might leave them out just a little longer. This mess needed to be sorted, boats or no boats. I'm afraid I've been putting it off."

"Okay, but I could help with the rest of this."

"Only if you're not in too much pain," she teased.

When they'd put everything back inside, leaving enough room to get the boats in, whenever Julie was ready to do that, Michael stood back and rubbed the back of his neck.

"Are you sure you're okay?" she asked.

"I'm fine. Honestly. Shocked, though. Maybe I should take some lessons, too. So, I can fight back."

"Maybe you should."

"Ha. Not a bad idea. But right now, I think I need a soak in some Epsom Salts."

"Okay, stop. I feel terrible enough already."

"Okay. I'll let it go. Wait here. I'll be right back."

While she closed the garage, Michael went to his car and returned with two bottles of wine for their dinner. "A peace offering," he said.

"Does this mean I'm forgiven?" she asked.

"It's me who needs to ask for forgiveness, Julie."

"Michael, I wasn't the one on the floor of the garage. I hope you'll forgive me for that."

"Oh, I forgave you the minute it happened but reminding you about it will be fun for a long, long time."

Chapter 21

Janie Woods, the kindergarten teacher, floated into the lunchroom and flipped a dry cleaner bag over the back of a chair.

"Your costume for Thursday?" Sarah asked her, peeking into the top of the bag and letting out a low sultry kind of whistle. "Nice!" she teased. "The kids won't believe it."

The rest of the staff were in various states of eating, marking workbooks, or in Julie's case, monitoring some leftover stew at the microwave, when Janie flopped into a chair and crossed her arms over her chest.

"What is it with men?" she asked.

"We're all vampires, don't you know?" Vince pulled a set of plastic fangs from his pocket and stuck them into his mouth, then grabbed Janie by the neck, pretending he was going to drink her blood. She pushed him away and gave him a playful slap.

"Get off me Dracula or I'll have my union rep after you."

"Good. I hope she's as tasty as you are." Smacking his lips, Vince retrieved his lunch from the fridge and sat across the table from Janie. "So, who was it this time?" he probed. "Some poor guy you met on Tinder who didn't know what he was getting into?"

Janie flipped her hair over her shoulder and shook her head. "It wasn't, as a matter of fact. And it wasn't our first date. We were having a great time until…"

"Until… you slept with him." Vince tossed her a look of annoyance, then shook his head. "Why does your generation think it's okay to go to bed when they first meet someone? Julie, help me out here."

"Nope," Julie chirped from her side of the room. "You're on your own, Vince."

Janie stiffened her body and her lip. "It wasn't *that*. *That* was great, but here's the thing. When guys want… *that*… they're all over you, but when it comes to your needs, they have the emotional capacity of a lampshade."

"Nice analogy." Vince said with a sarcastic grin as he un-wrapped his salmon sandwich. Janie was momentarily lost for words while Vince took a huge bite and grinned at her. Sparing during lunch breaks was something Vince and Janie seemed to enjoy, but it put Julie off her food. That, and the smell of Vince's salmon, sent her to the window for a breath of fresh air.

"Thanks for opening that," Rebecca said. "Reminds me of the sandwiches my mum made my sister. G.G. always liked salmon sandwiches too, but to this day I can't stand them." Rebecca's hand went to her throat as if she was about to retch, then she gathered her things and left the room.

"Now look what you've done, Vince," Julie said, returning to the microwave. "So, who is this man you're talking about, Janie?"

"Does it matter? They're all the same," Janie was saying. "But since you asked, it was a guy I met at the pub the other night." She tossed her pop can into the recycling bin on the other side of the room. It landed with a clink against the ones already there, and she grinned and held up two fingers. "Two points! I should coach the basketball team."

"I don't think it's fair to make a blanket statement like that, Janie," Vince said. "You wouldn't like it if I said all blonds are dumb, or women can't manage money, or old people are forgetful. So, by default then, not every man is an emotional klutz."

Janie took up the challenge, which was exactly what Vince wanted.

"So, if your girlfriend…" Janie began.

Vince held up his hand. "I don't have a girlfriend."

Janie cocked her head to one side, blond hair flopping over her shoulder. "Pretend someone is desperate enough to go out with you."

"Okay. I can do that." Mischief played around Vince's mouth as he bit into an apple.

"If she wanted to just cuddle and not have *s. e. x.* …" Janie lowered her voice to be sure a passing student couldn't hear her. "What would you do?"

"Well, it's a moot point."

"Why?"

Vince grinned and examined his apple for a moment. "Because no woman would ever want to *just cuddle* if she was with me." Vince bit deeper into his apple, grinning at Janie.

"What do you think, Julie?" Janie asked, as the bell dinged, signifying the microwave had finished.

"Leave me out of it." Julie stirred her stew. "It's been so long since I've been close to having... *that* ...I wouldn't know."

Julie took her stew and headed for the door while Vince goaded Janie on even more. Just before Julie closed the door behind her, she could not resist the urge to say something to them. "Why don't the two of you just get a room and put the rest of us out of our misery?"

Sarah cheered. "Amen to that." Vince and Janie were speechless.

"My job here is done," Julie said with a grin as she pulled the door closed behind her.

The door to Rebecca's classroom was closed, and the lights were off. Rebecca was nowhere in sight, although the cardigan that usually hung on the back of her chair was gone and Julie wondered if she had gone outside for a bit of fresh air. Who wouldn't want that after Vince's smelly salmon?

Julie put a thick notepad down on her desk as a placemat for her stew and thought about how little she knew about the rest of the staff. She knew Vince, of course, because they'd taught together in Bracebridge. She knew their secretary, Joan Airdrie, and her husband, Miles, who was the janitor. They'd lived in Baysville for as long as Julie could remember. But the other teachers were new to her because they were new to the school.

Janie was fresh out of teacher's college, young enough to be her daughter, which should have meant she was far too young for Vince, but his usual arm candy was someone much younger than him so maybe he and Janie were a good fit after all. Janie's perky personality and her rapport with young children certainly made her the perfect person to teach kindergarten. Rebecca, who was closer in age to Julie, had spent all her life in big cities until last year, when she decided to try small town life. Sarah Gillespie, the grade three/four teacher, had come from a school in Hamilton. Miles and Joan Airdrie made up the support staff.

As if he knew she'd been thinking about him, Miles rolled a bucket of soapy water down the hall toward the boys' washroom. "Plugged toilet again," he mumbled as he passed her open door.

Julie sat down to eat her lunch and mark this morning's math worksheets. From her desk, she had a clear view of the playground all the way to the fence where the grade six girls had resumed their place under the popular trees, just far enough away from anyone who might overhear their gossip.

Her spoon was halfway to her mouth for the third time, when Julie dropped it into her bowl and gave up eating. The smell of Vince's salmon had turned her off her food. She was done. She replaced the lid, intending to return to the staff room, but a glance out the window stopped her in her tracks. Pulling up alongside the fence on University Street was a cherry-red Ford Escort, the same one Grace had been driving on Meet the Teacher Night. As she squinted into the noon hour sun a woman got out of it and approached the fence, there was no doubt in Julie's mind it was Grace. She stood at the fence, hands cupped around her mouth as if she were shouting. Julie's eyes followed Grace's gaze and there, a few yards from the monkey bars, stood Hope, her arms raised to take something from Ryder.

To Julie, what happened next seemed to be in slow motion, as if they were all in a nightmare. While her feet seemed frozen to the ground, she saw Hope's face light up with recognition and her curls bounce around her face, as she turned to look toward the fence. Seconds later, Hope was on the run.

"No," Julie shouted, the container of stew slipping from her hands. It landed on the floor, splattering liquid everywhere. Reaching for her phone, she stepped over the mess and headed down the hall, dialling 911 as she ran. Passing the lunchroom, she shouted, "AMBER", the code word they used for someone on school grounds that shouldn't be. Chairs scraped across the floor, the door flew open, and Vince was racing alongside her.

"Janie, get the bell," he shouted over his shoulder as they reached the front door. To Julie he asked, "What's happening?"

Together, their hands pushed on the bar and the door flew open.

"There," she pointed, just as two sets of three sharp warning bells echoed across the playground.

"Shit!" Vince hissed, mostly under his breath, as Hope reached the fence, arms outstretched toward Grace.

Julie thrust her phone at Vince just as the 911 operator answered. "I'm going after them," she said. Her only thought was to get to Hope before Grace got her over the fence. She was running before she realized her feet had moved, past the basketball nets, off the tarmac and onto the grass. She sprinted across the playground, eyes fixed on Grace, watching as Hope's shoe caught on the fence. Julie's eyes followed the shoe as Grace tugged and yanked at it and finally pulled it off Hope's foot. The shoe fell silently to the ground on the schoolyard side of the fence. Grace's eyes met Julie's across the distance and as her features turned stone cold, Grace lifted Hope the rest of the way over the fence. Hope turned in her mother's arms, reaching for the lost shoe, her backpack slapping against her mother's face as she did.

"Wait!" Julie screamed, still running at full speed. Faster, she thought. Run faster. "Grace!" she screamed. "Don't do this!"

In the distance, the flashing blue and red lights of a police car caught Julie's eye. Darren must have been at the diner for lunch. He tore out of the parking lot and onto University Street, his tires squealing. Julie was only steps away from the fence, now, and suddenly she was slamming into it. She reached for the diamond-shaped spaces, fingers grasping the wire, feet gripping the holes as she climbed. With one hand on the top of the fence, she was about to jump over when she saw Michael rushing down the clinic steps.

"Grace!" he screamed, racing toward the car. He reached out, his hand slipping as he tried desperately to open the driver's side door. When he couldn't, he slapped the window with both hands. "Don't do this, Grace," he shouted.

There was a pause when the world stood still, and Julie held her breath. She scarcely had time to think, but wondered fleetingly if Grace would give up and stop the car. And then just as quickly as it had all begun, Grace's tires were spitting up gravel and there was nothing Michael, or Julie, or anyone else could do.

Julie let go of the fence and landed back on the ground just as the Escort's tires caught the pavement and Michael was thrown away from the car. She squinted through the dust, trying to get the number on the license plate, but she needn't have bothered because Darren was hot on Grace's trail. As he sped past, Julie bent down and picked up Hope's pink Barbie running shoe.

"No. No. No. Oh my god no!"

Chapter 22

Michael appeared at her side, huffing and panting. "Where's Faith?"

Still clutching desperately to Hope's running shoe, Julie looked up at him. "Faith? I only saw Hope. Maybe she's inside."

"Hurry. We have to find her."

They sped across the field to the tarmac and stopped just short of the door to the school, where Vince was waiting to let them inside. Lockdown meant all the doors were closed and only Vince could admit anyone.

"Dr. Adams. I'm so sorry," Vince said, pushing open the door. "The police are sending someone to take statements. You can wait in my office."

Panting, Michael said, "Someone was in the car with Grace, but she threw a blanket or a coat, or something over them, so I didn't see who it was. Could it have been Faith?"

"I've sent someone to get her. Please." Vince waved them into the outer office, then through a door into his.

Vince's office was a relic from the days of long ago and part of the one-room schoolhouse Baysville Elementary used to be. Over the years, it was expanded and renovated several times, but the offices hadn't really changed. He'd refused a shiny new desk when it was offered, in favour of the old style wooden he sat behind every day. Vince pulled his chair around from behind his desk so Julie could sit down and waved Michael toward a brown faux leather couch—a cast off that had seen better days. It was old and clunky and took up all the far wall. Julie dropped into the chair, exhausted and shaken, and put Hope's shoe on the desk. Michael's hands opened and closed fingers clasping and unclasping as he paced the room, three steps one way and three steps back.

"Dad?"

When Faith appeared in the doorway and his arms flew around her. "Thank god!"

Faith took one look at the running shoe, another at Julie, and then she collapsed against her father. "Where's Hope?" she asked. "Julie? Dad? Tell me. Where is she?"

"She's…" Julie couldn't get the words out. How did you tell someone their little sister has been taken. Kidnapped. By their mother?

Faith's head tipped up to her fathers. "Dad? Tell me."

Michael pulled her to the couch and urged her to sit down next to him. "Hope has gone with your mother," he said. "Did she say anything to you when you saw her that day? Did she tell you a day she'd come and get you? Or…"

"No. But…" Faith's bottom lip trembled. She bit down hard to stop it until it bled. "I'm sorry, Dad. I should have told you, but she said not to."

"Tell me what?" Michael asked.

"She said you wouldn't like it. She said it was the only way we could see each other."

"Who, Faith?" he asked, taking her hand in his.

"Mum. She works at the library. I've been seeing her there."

Michael's body stiffened, as his face went from pink to ashen. His temples began pulsing and Julie wondered what he was going to do next. Faith must have sensed it, too. She pulled away from him and buried her face in her hands.

"I'm sorry. I'm sorry. I should have told you."

He pulled her back to him and wrapped her in his arms, whispering soothing words to her, kissing the top of her head.

"No, darling. This isn't your fault. It's not."

"But you're angry."

"Not at you. Never at you. Never." He wiped her tears with his thumbs until Julie handed them a box of tissues from Vince's desk.

"I'll just be a minute," she said, slipping into the outer office and closing the door behind her. She picked up the phone on Alice's desk and dialled Theresa Dawson but before the call was answered, Michael was at her side. Julie put the call on speaker. Theresa picked up on the second ring.

"I spoke with Alice Airdrie already, Julie," she said. "When I heard the bells, I called to see what was going on and ask if I could help. I didn't know. Honestly. The name Grace Walker meant nothing to me when she applied. Her references checked out. She and Faith got on well, but I never dreamed there was anything other than a working relationship between them. I've already called the police and told them everything I know."

"Okay, Theresa. Thanks." Julie disconnected the call and looked up at Michael, who was already at the door to the office. "Where are you going?"

"Stay here and take care of Faith," he said. "I'm going after her."

"Don't," Julie said. "Let the police handle it."

Suddenly Vince was there, blocking the doorway, forcing Michael to take a step back. "She's right. Besides, that officer is due here any minute to take statements."

Michael pushed against Vince, their noses almost touching. "Unless you're coming with me, I suggest you get out of my way," he said.

"Be reasonable," Vince said.

"Listen to him, Michael," Julie insisted, tugging his arm.

Michael's eyes narrowed. "I'm only going to say this once. No one comes between me and my daughters, so get out of my way, sir, or I'll knock you down, if I have to." He turned to Julie then. "Either of you."

It was fear talking. Julie realized that, but it was also the truth. No one would ever mean as much to Michael as his girls. *Blood is thicker than water*, her grandmother used to say, and that is how it was always going to be.

"Go then," she said. "But I really wish you'd let the police handle it. Driving in the state you're in is not a good idea. Especially when you have no idea where you're going or what direction Grace has gone."

"I can't stand here and do nothing." Michael pushed past Vince, hurried into the hall, and pushed open the front door of the school. Julie followed him outside.

"It's cold out here." He glared at her. "Go back inside. I don't need company and I'm not a crazed idiot. I can drive."

"Please Michael. You're in panic mode and you're terrified. I don't blame you. I know you're not a crazed idiot, but this isn't the thing to do."

Michael wasn't buying into her reasoning. He started to run toward the gate. He was headed for his car across the road at the clinic.

Julie's phone pinged then, and she chased him down to read a message from Darren, eyes darting between the screen of her phone and Michael's face.

OPP are in pursuit, north on hwy 11

"Where is that?" he asked

"Miles away now."

Michael slammed his palm against the school wall. "Damnit to hell."

"Breathe," Julie said softly. "Take a deep breath, hold it and let it out slowly."

"I can't do this, Julie. You do these things, meditate, talk to Sirona about all this witchy-woo stuff, but I can't just shut everything out by taking some deep breaths."

"You're no good to Faith or to Hope, if you're a basket-case."

He turned back to her then and gripped her arms. His face softened as he realized he was hurting her. Instantly, he released his grip. "Sorry. It's just…" He shook his head, ran a hand through his hair and looked back at her again.

"It's okay. It will all be okay."

"How can you know that?" he shouted. "My worst nightmare has come true. She's taken my baby." And then Michael buried his face in his hands and wept. Julie put her arms around him, and they stood there, shivering in the cold, the skies that had been sunny, moments ago, now threatened rain. It seemed like ages before Michael finally relaxed and his tears subsided.

She took his face in her hands. "The police will find her, Michael."

He shook his head, eyes roaming to the field and then to the road, as if he might see her somewhere in the distance.

"I did everything my lawyer told me to do, changed our names, moved all the way from Vancouver, and then up here to the middle of nowhere. I took a job I'm overqualified to do, just to keep my girls safe and now…" He threw his hands in the air. "I can't even do that."

He turned away from her, wiping his face with the sleeve of his shirt. Julie steered him back toward the door. "We should go back inside," she said.

"You're right. I have no idea where I was going. I just felt like I had to go after her, you know?"

She nodded. "I would have done the same if Hope was my daughter."

By two-thirty that afternoon, the police had taken statements from everyone they deemed essential and told Michael they would send a car to pick up Joy. When he called to tell her what had happened, Joy went into immediate panic mode, worried that Grace was going to show up at her school too, until he told her a police car would pick her up in a few minutes.

"We'll see you at home. I love you, Joy," he said, just before hanging up.

Michael had been sitting on the arm of Vince's couch, his head bent, his voice soft as he spoke to Joy. When he finished the call, he looked up at Julie and the police officer who'd taken their statements.

"Can we leave?" he asked.

"Yes, Dr. Adams. There's an FLO waiting outside your house."

"A flow?"

"F. L. O. Family Liaison Officer," the officer said.

"Let me guess. Is her name Sherry Chaney?"

Chapter 23

The sun was sinking fast over the tree line when Julie's car followed Michael's into the circle. Joy raced out of the cottage to meet them and for a long while, she and Faith and their father stood together, arms wrapped around each other.

It took all her strength and resolve for Julie not to put her arms around them, too, but she knew she wasn't a part of them. Michael had been clear earlier, and she'd had plenty of time to think about what he'd said. She decided it was better if she went home and left them alone. Sherry, who'd gotten out of her car the moment they'd all driven in, was better qualified to help them get through these next few hours and maybe there were things they should be doing. Her presence might interfere with that. She put her car in reverse, turned back into the circle and parked in front of her own garage. When she got out of the car, Michael was blocking her way.

"You're not coming in?" he asked, eyes searching hers.

"You don't need me over there," she said, looking over his shoulder toward the cottage. "Sherry will want to talk with you and…"

"I can't do this without you," he pleaded. "Please. I need you."

"I'm not…" She was about to say family, but something told her that would hurt him, and when the time was right, they'd talk about all this, but not now. Not while his youngest daughter was missing. She'd been selfish, she realized. She'd been thinking about how all this was for her and that was wrong.

"Okay," she said softly. If he really needed her, she wouldn't step away now.

He took her hand and led her back down the path through the little stretch of woods and went inside. In the kitchen, Sherry had the girls doing busy work, as Julie had heard it called. Making tea nobody would drink was busy work. Getting out cookies no one would eat was busy work. Filling the milk jug and sugar bowl was busy work. It kept the hands occupied, so the mind couldn't wander too much.

Faith hurried to her father when he and Julie hung up their coats. Michael's voice was soothing when he pulled both of his girls into his arms, then reached for Julie, too.

"It'll be alright. You'll see," he soothed. "Everything will be okay."

Faith was the first to extract herself. "What if we never see Hope again?" she moaned.

Michael took her face between his hands and tilted it up to his, drying her tears with his thumbs. "Hope is fine, my darling. You must believe that. She'll be back with us soon. I promise."

Joy pulled her sister toward the living room but glanced back with tear-filled eyes, Julie knew she was doing her best to be brave for her sister but wasn't feeling very brave at all. Julie felt that way, too. She wanted to be strong, for Michael and for the girls, but every part of her was crumbling inside. She could not close her eyes without seeing Hope's arms reaching out for her lost shoe and the look on her face when her mother shoved her into the car and closed the door. And there was Michael, hands pressed against the window, his face angry, fearful, so unlike the kind and loving face she saw now.

With the girls in the other room, Michael leaned against the kitchen counter, his hands bracing the edge for support. His face was ashen, his eyes darting from item to item across the kitchen.

"I think you should sit down," Julie said, urging him into a chair.

"Tea is ready," Sherry said. "I'll pour him a cup."

"Take the tea to the girls. I think he needs something stronger," Julie said, reaching into the cupboard where Michael kept the good stuff.

It didn't take long to brew a pot of coffee, pour two cups, and lace them heavily with brandy. She set one down in front of him, the other she kept for herself, and leaned against the counter to sip it.

When Sherry came back a few moments later and suggested she could make some sandwiches, they rejected her offer.

"I couldn't eat at a time like this," Michael said.

Julie's thoughts echoed his words, but she longed for something to do, otherwise her fears would take over her reason. "Tell us what we can do, Sherry?" Julie asked.

Sherry took her own teacup and sat down at the table. "Is there any detail you might have forgotten to give in your statements? Anything at all."

"Nothing," Michael said, getting up from the table. "The police know everything."

Julie followed Michael to the living room, where he turned on the TV and the first thing to come on was a news flash. Hope's face loomed on the screen, a ticker tape running below it with a hotline number to call if anyone knew the whereabouts of Hope Adams and a woman called Grace Walker.

"I don't want to watch that," Joy snapped.

He found them a movie on Netflix and went back to the kitchen. This time, Julie sat down at the table opposite him and when a knock came to the door, Sherry went to get it. She returned a moment later with Joe Hewitt.

"Hey," Joe said, giving Julie a hug.

"Thanks for coming." Michael stood up to shake Joe's hand, but Joe pulled him into a hug.

When he let go, Joe said, "I just came to see if there's anything I can do."

Sherry went to sit with the girls while Joe pulled out a chair and sat down. "Just tell us what we can do," he said. He kept his eyes on Michael, watching, waiting. "Anything. Name it. I'm at your disposal and so is my entire crew."

Julie's heart swelled as she thought of what a good friend Joe was now and for as long as she'd known him. She reached out to squeeze his hand. "It's good of you to come over."

Michael shrugged. "It means a great deal that you've come, Joe, but right now, I don't know what you can do. None of us know what to do. We're all going crazy here." He shook his head and raked a hand through his hair. "I'm not sure I can just sit here doing nothing much longer."

Joe pulled a flask out of his jacket pocket and uncapped it. "Need something a little stronger than coffee?"

Julie could have said the coffee was already laced, but she didn't. Michael needed someone else to talk to. Another man who just might understand things better than she could. So she got down two crystal tumblers and set them on the table. Joe filled them, then handed one to Michael.

"Outside? On the porch?" Joe said, nodding toward the front door. "Bring a coat. It's cold out there."

Michael didn't need to be asked twice, and Julie knew that the only thing better than talking to a mate right now would be to see Hope's smiling face. His hand grazed her arm as he followed Joe to the door.

"Won't be long," he said, softly.

"Take all the time you need," she said. When they were gone, Julie filled the sink and began washing cups. It was busy work, but it was just what she needed.

Chapter 24

It was after nine when Michael came back inside. He lowered himself onto the couch and instantly his girls were there with him. Faith sat on one side, Joy on the other, all of them motionless until Faith began chewing the side of her thumbs. She insisted, repeatedly, that it was her fault, that if she'd told her father sooner about Grace working at the library, maybe Hope wouldn't be missing. No amount of reasoning could convince her otherwise and, sadly, there was truth in what she said, though no one would ever admit it. It was already a heavy burden for her to carry. She was so overwrought with worry, her thumbs bled from her gnawing on them. Michael fixed her up, put band-aids over them so she couldn't chew them anymore and suggested she lie down.

"There's too much of Hope in our room," Faith said. "Can I lie down on your bed, Daddy?"

"Of course you can."

They made her comfortable under the covers in Michael's bed and he joined her, lying down next to her, to hold her close. Faith reached for Julie's hand, asking her to lie down beside her as well. So, Julie and Michael created a cozy cocoon around her, until her body eased, and Faith relaxed into sleep.

For a moment, Julie thought Michael might have fallen asleep too, but when she glanced over at him, he was staring at the ceiling, the back of one arm resting on his forehead, the other cradling Faith. He caught her gaze, nodded, and they gently slid their arms from around Faith and left her to rest.

Just outside the bedroom door, Michael stopped Julie. "Thank you," he whispered. "I honestly don't know what I would have done without you."

"You don't have to thank me," Julie protested.

"But I do. You've been so patient, and so understanding."

The air between them seemed to close in on her. Julie didn't like false praise, and that's what this felt like to her. She had done nothing any friend or neighbour wouldn't do. She didn't want him making more of her being there than it was. And as far as understanding went, she was far from that.

"To be honest, Michael, I don't understand any of this."

"Any of what?"

"This whole situation with you and Grace and the girls. I understand marriages fall apart, and people fall out of love, but what I don't understand is why you needed to change your names and move clear across the country. How does a man convince his eldest daughter to go along with the name change and two life-altering moves, without an explanation? And what kind of mother kidnaps her own child, unless it's a custody issue, which you have assured me this isn't?" Julie shook her head. "I'm sorry. I don't get it, Michael. And all of this, whatever it is, is way too complicated for me."

A veil of exhaustion clouded his face as he hung his head. "I owe you an explanation. I've been trying for days but…"

"No Michael. You don't owe me anything. I'm an outsider here, remember? I'm just the landlady, the neighbour, the friend. It's your daughters who need the explanation. Especially Joy. She knew her mother wasn't dead before you moved up here and she's terribly confused. You've got to talk to her."

"I know."

"Do you though? Because from where I'm sitting, it looks a lot like avoidance and denial. If you avoid talking about it, deny it exists, the problem will just go away. But obviously it hasn't."

"I get it. I hear what you're saying. It isn't anything I haven't said to myself a hundred times over. I just thought I had more time." He reached for her hand, entwining his fingers in hers. "I know it wasn't fair of me to involve you in this, but like it or not, you're in it now. Your Hope's teacher. My girls love you. And I…"

"Don't." Her hands flew up to stop him from continuing. "Please don't. Go to Joy and tell her everything. She needs to know."

She squeezed by him in the narrow hallway, on her way to the living room, but he caught her arm and pulled her gaze to his.

"You're right," he said. "Everything you just said is right and I will tell Joy everything, but I would like you to hear it, too.

Please. No matter what you think of me afterwards, I need you to know the truth." When she sighed heavily and looked away, he pleaded. "Please, Julie."

"If that's what you want."

She followed him to the living room and selected an arm-chair facing the window. Outside, Sirona's porch light glowed in the distance, the only dot of light against an otherwise black night. An inviting red and black plaid blanket lay over the arm of the chair and, feeling a sudden chill in the air, Julie pulled it around her. She heard Sherry banging around in the kitchen, refilling the kettle, opening and closing cupboards. It was her job to be there for the family, Julie knew that, but she prayed Sherry would not try to force another cup of tea onto them. It might be Grandma's cure-all, but just now, if Julie wanted anything, it might be a good stiff drink.

Joy released the throw pillow she'd been hugging and looked up from her phone when her father sat down beside her. She had been scrolling the internet, searching through social media and anything else she could find that might provide a clue to Hope's where-abouts.

"Is Faith okay?" she asked when Michael reached for her hand.

"She's sleeping and right now, that's the best thing she can do." He put an arm around Joy's shoulders. "Darling, I need to tell you about your Mum and me. I'm sorry I haven't told you sooner. You're growing up, and as much as I wish you'd stay a little girl, there are things you should know. So, it's time for me to tell you everything."

Uncertainty hovered between them as Joy set her phone on the coffee table in front of her. "I've been asking for ages, Dad."

"I know. I know. Just listen. Please."

Joy nodded. "Okay."

"It's a long story, but I'll sum it up as best I can." Michael took a deep breath before continuing. "It would be easy to say that your mother's medical problems are the cause for all of this, but I must accept blame as well. After we had you and Faith, I wanted a third child, a boy, if that was possible. Your mother was reluctant. She thought the two of you were enough, and you were. We loved you both. But I was persistent. I couldn't let go of the idea of having a son, so eventually, she agreed, and we had Hope. After she was born, I was so excited I gave up caring about a son. She was perfect, like the two perfect girls we already had. We were a perfect family."

"Perfect, huh? What changed?" Sarcasm laced Joy's words, as if she wasn't quite ready to forgive him for keeping her in the dark.

"A woman goes through a lot of hormonal changes during pregnancy and afterwards, when her body is getting back to normal. As a doctor I knew that, but as an orthopedic surgeon, my understanding was little more than the average man's."

"I thought you were a GP?" Julie said, more than a little confused. She hadn't planned on saying anything, expecting she would just listen, but this was something new, and like everything else she was learning about Michael, his job was a lie, too.

"I am now," he said, meeting her gaze. "I needed to stay out of the news and the medical journals. In Vancouver, I was involved in a lot of research studies, writing and publishing papers. Doing things that had my name attached to them. When we moved to Niagara Falls, I went back to family practice, to stay out of the limelight, so to speak."

"What about Mum? What happened to her?" Joy pressed.

"Have you ever heard of postpartum depression?" he asked.

Joy nodded. "In health class, we've talked about it. There's a lady in my class who's come back to school as an adult student to get her diploma. She's having a baby, and my teacher wanted us to know about it. I gave you the paper to sign. Don't you remember?" Joy raised a questioning brow at her father.

"I don't recall what I signed. It doesn't matter. I'm glad you're aware, because it might help you understand. You see, your mother had it severely, after Hope was born. She had mood swings during her pregnancy too, which I attributed to her changing hormones. She was happy one minute, completely depressed the next, and there were fits of anger, too. But after Hope was born, everything got worse, and her mood swings were off the charts. I consulted colleagues and eventually suggested she talk to her psychiatrist about it."

"Her psychiatrist! Mum was seeing a shrink?" Joy asked.

Michael nodded. "She was dealing with loss. Her sister died at a very young age and her parents were killed in a car accident. She'd been seeing someone long before we met."

"Wait." Joy held up her hand. "You're just telling me now that Mum had a sister? You always said she didn't have any family, that our grandparents on that side were dead, that she had no siblings."

"All true, because when I met your Mum, she was completely alone in the world."

"What was her name?" Joy asked. "The aunt that I won't ever know."

"She never told me. I'm sorry."

"Well, maybe she will tell us. If she ever brings Hope back."

"Joy, I know you're angry, but please listen to the rest of this. I want you to know that I did everything I could to protect you girls when your mother was sick. That's why you spent a lot of time at Grandma and Grandpa's house. I was sure it was just a matter of getting her on medication to help her cope. But even that didn't seem to work. She was either exhausted and sleeping, or she was violently aggressive. She got abusive, punching and kicking, throwing things. Anything I did started a scene. I hired a woman to help with the housework, but your mother accused her of stealing and let her go. She thought I was putting something in her food that made her sleepy. She accused me of a lot of other things, too.

"But the biggest problem was I couldn't get her psychiatrist to believe she was as bad as I described. When he saw her, she seemed to cope. So, I put nanny cams in all the rooms and started recording everything. On one of her better days, I showed her a recording of a violent attack when she came at me with the poker. And I'm ashamed to say that I told her if she didn't do something about this, she wouldn't see you girls again. But I also told her when she showed some stability, the three of you could come home. She was desperate to have you back, so she agreed to let me show the recordings to her doctor and to do what he recommended.

"When he saw the videos, he agreed she was not the same person in their sessions as she was at home. It took time, lots of tests and appointments, but eventually we got a diagnosis. Her Postpartum depression had progressed rapidly to severely manic Postpartum Psychosis. He prescribed some new meds for her and some tablets to help her sleep at night and, for a time, she seemed to be on the mend. She still had some bad days, but overall, she got out of bed, showered and dressed, and even managed some simple household tasks each day. Thankfully, the next woman I hired to help didn't aggravate her. I brought you girls home, and things seemed to be okay. Not great, but at least manageable with lots of outside help."

"Is that when she had the accident?" Joy said. "Grandma said she'd been drinking."

"She had. Do you remember when Faith had scarlet fever?" He didn't wait for Joy's response. "I took you and Hope to Grandma's so you wouldn't catch it. One night, something woke me up and my first thought was that Faith was worse. But when I checked on her, she was sleeping soundly in her bed. Your mother wasn't.

"She was in the kitchen, with an empty wine bottle on the counter. I asked her about mixing wine with her meds and she said it didn't matter because she hadn't been taking the pills. And that's when she came after me with a knife. She was so... Well, she wasn't in her right mind. We found out later that she'd been hiding her meds in a drawer, so..."

"She had a knife. Dad! What did you do?"

"The only thing I could. I reached up to block her arm. I thought if I could do that, she'd drop it, but she swung it low and swiped it across my leg."

"Your scar!" Joy said. "I always wondered how you got that."

"It was bad," he said. "Between the blood all over the floor, and the screaming pain in my leg, I could barely stand, but I got to the phone to call 911. By that time, she was out the door and getting into the car. I saw her taillights from the kitchen window when she braked at the end of the driveway. The accident was a few minutes later, but I didn't hear about it until I was in the hospital waiting for surgery. A police officer came to tell me she'd been helicoptered to another hospital. She was in critical but stable condition, but the man she'd pinned against the tree had died instantly."

"Oh my god, Dad. Shit. Shit. Why didn't you tell us any of this?"

"She was in a bad way, Joy. A terrible way."

While Joy took a moment to absorb this, Julie did, too. She understood the severity of what had happened, could understand why Michael had wanted to protect his daughters, but what was the point of the secrecy? It was horrible and tragic, but it wasn't the thing a man changes his name and moves across the country for. There was obviously more than Michael was saying.

"So, that's why she went to jail?" Joy asked.

Michael nodded. "The crown had wanted to charge her with murder. I convinced our lawyer to argue diminished capacity. I hoped that because of her illness, he could get her off on a lighter sentence. In the end she agreed to plead guilty to the lessor offence. She got seven years for vehicular manslaughter."

"But there's something I don't understand," Joy said, looking up at her father. "If Mum has been under psychiatric care and she's served her time, why don't you want us to see her?"

"For a few reasons, Joy. Her psychiatrist's reports to my lawyer suggest she doesn't always take her meds, and that means she's not thinking clearly. Your mother hates me, and she wants revenge. She wants to hurt me, and she knows that taking you girls away from me would be the worst kind of hurt she could ever cause."

"So we changed our names and moved thousands of miles from home to get away from her?" Joy asked.

"Not just her. You see, the family of the man your mother killed threatened us, me, actually. They said because I was a doctor, I should have known what was going on and that I was just as responsible for what happened as your mother was."

"So what if they wanted to sue you? Isn't that why you have malpractice insurance?" Joy asked.

"This is a private matter, nothing to do with my medical practice. He wasn't my patient, and neither was she. Besides, they didn't need money. The man's brother was a real estate developer in Vancouver. He wanted revenge. An eye for an eye. The lawyers talked and when mine came back to me, he suggested the name change and the move. He wanted us in the witness protection program, but we hadn't witnessed a crime, so we were of no use to the government. He tried to talk me into moving back to England, but like an idiot, I didn't listen. I didn't want to go that far away from your grandparents. I didn't think the man's family would ever act on their threats. I thought it was just grief talking. So, John suggested the identity change and that I should take a job as far outside the medical field as I could, but I don't know how to be anything other than a doctor."

"You know how to be a good dad," Joy said, wrapping her arms around him and nestling against his shoulder. "You could have told me this before, you know. I would have understood, and I wouldn't have been such a spoiled brat about moving."

He kissed the top of her head and said, "Thank you, darling."

Michael's body slumped against the sofa. Telling the story had exhausted him, or perhaps it was the worry of how Joy would react. When Julie looked at him, the shadows around his eyes were nearly gone, what remained was the man she'd first thought him to be, the loving father, the caring doctor, the generous and kind friend. Was this the man Grace had known when they first met? Or had she been too sick to see this side of him and know he would have taken care of her forever? What Julie was hearing and seeing in him now was a man who would go to hell and back for the people he loved, just like he'd said in Vince's office a few hours ago.

"You haven't told Faith any of this, though, right?" Joy was asking.

Michael shook his head. "But I think she must have heard your mother and I arguing that night, because I realized, far too late, that she'd come downstairs. She was in the kitchen, standing in the middle of all that blood. When she saw me, I was bleeding and nearly unconscious. She started screaming, and she didn't stop until the ambulance arrived and they gave her something to calm her down."

"Do you think it was Mum at the window the night of the sleepover?" Joy asked.

"I'm pretty sure it was."

"But how did she know where to find us?" Joy asked. "Do you think that someone from that man's family is helping Mum?"

"Why would they?" It was Sherry's voice they heard. No one had noticed her standing in the doorway. "Sorry, I didn't mean to interrupt, but I can answer Joy's question about how Grace knew where to find you."

"Please," Michael said. "Tell us anything you can."

"The dead woman, Mia Sanders, was Grace's cellmate. She was released about eight months before Grace. We believe she tracked you to Niagara Falls, although we aren't sure how she knew you'd gone there. We're still investigating that. We think she's been stalking you for the past eight months and we have CCTV footage of her meeting Grace at Pearson Airport and again up here. We cannot find a connection between Mia and the dead man's family, but it hasn't been ruled out. We just don't know everything yet."

"But she's dead now," Joy said. "And you think my mother killed her?"

"I can't discuss that. For now, our focus is on Hope and getting her home safely." Sherry perched on the arm of the sofa. "I know that you've given statements, but can you all dig down deep and think over the details of the past few days? Especially with Grace spending time with Faith at the library. Maybe she or Hope said something you didn't realize was important. Conversations at dinner, in the car, anything that might help us now."

Sherry turned to Julie. "I was wondering about Hope's work at school. Pictures she drew, conversations between her and her friends you might have overheard. Any detail, no matter how small." Her phone pinged then, and instantly their heads snapped to her, hopeful for some tidbit of news.

Sherry looked at the screen. "No," she said, with a little shake of her head. "Sorry. It's my mother. She's not well and I usually call around this time. I'll just take this in the other room."

Michael sank deeper into the sofa, his face going ashen again. "I can't believe that woman has been stalking us. No wonder

Darren kept insisting I should know her. I tried to place her. Was she a clerk in a store, a teller at the bank, the attendant at the movie theatre, or a waitress at The Flying Saucer where the kids loved to eat? Nothing. I just don't remember her at all."

Julie's phone rang then, and she fished it out of her pocket. Her hands were trembling so hard when she saw who was calling, her phone slipped from her grasp and landed screen-side up on the rug. A blond-haired man with piercing green eyes appeared on the screen, while the ringtone, a portion of Gloria Gainer's *I Will Survive,* played on.

"Who is that?" Joy asked. "I know him. I saw him. I didn't think of it before, but he was outside my school the day Mum came to see me."

Julie frowned. "Are you sure?"

"Positive. He winked at me. I thought he was creepy,"

"Who is he, Julie?" Michael asked.

"It's Eddy."

Chapter 25

Julie wasn't aware she'd fallen asleep until she woke stiff-necked and aching from sleeping in a chair. She uncurled herself from the awkward position, vaguely recalling Michael had tried to get her to sleep on Hope's bed. But that had seemed like invading the child's space and, tired as she was, she couldn't do that.

Sherry had camped out on the sofa for the night. A soft snore escaped her lips as Julie passed her on the way to the bathroom. Joy, she assumed, had gone to her own bed. The door was closed and there was nothing but silence from the other side of it. She peeked in to see Faith, still sleeping soundly, then looked into the girls' room, thinking Michael must have gone there to rest. But there was no sign of him anywhere, until she passed the Muskoka room window and saw him, way down at the lake, sitting in a chair on the dock, an empty tumbler resting on the arm of his chair. From her perspective, Julie couldn't tell if he was sleeping or just staring off into the distance. The sun was grasping for purchase in the sky over the tree line, as morning broke over the lake and everything seemed to spring to life.

Coffee, she thought, making her way to the kitchen, remembering she had to report her absence from work today. She fished her phone out of her pocket, recalling the face she'd seen on the screen last night and the conversation she'd had with him.

"Eddy?" she'd said into the phone as she left the living room to speak to him privately. "What do you want?" It had been more than two years since they'd spoken, and just then, she couldn't fathom why he would be calling her.

"I saw the news," he said, breathlessly, as if he'd just gotten off the ice from playing hockey. "Is she alright? They said she was in grade two at your school. I just assumed she's one of yours."

"One of mine?"

"Yeah. You know. One of your kids."

"I'm hanging up now, Eddy. Don't call me again."

"Wait!"

A pause, while she considered blocking his number and wondered why she hadn't done it two years ago.

"I might have seen her."

"Who?"

"The kid and the mother."

"Just a minute. I'm putting you on speaker. There's someone with the police here."

"No. Don't do that. I really don't have time. Just tell them I'm pretty sure I saw her at McDonalds in Parry Sound. I'm there now. A hockey tournament. I just thought you should know."

Eddy had hung up, the disconnection leaving Julie feeling much like she had after her run the day Eddy had left. He was gone. Then and now.

Julie had found Sherry in the kitchen and told her about the call. She didn't want Michael to hear her and get his hopes up in case it turned out to be nothing. Knowing Eddy the way she did, it might be a prank, his bizarre way of trying to worm his way back into her life. Sherry had taken down Eddy's phone number and promised to relay the information up the line to the authorities, assuring Julie that every lead was taken seriously, and someone would check it out. A quick Google check revealed *The Old Boy's Hockey Tournament* was going on in Parry Sound, and hockey had always been Eddy's second love, or perhaps it was even his first.

Now, as the aroma of brewing coffee filled the kitchen, Julie rinsed their cups from last night and loaded them into the dishwasher. She got down clean ones and pulled cereal boxes, bowls, and cutlery out of the cupboards and drawers. The girls should eat something, she thought. She would have made pancakes and bacon if she thought they'd actually get eaten. Somehow, she knew they wouldn't.

The gurgling and rumbling of the coffee pot must have stirred Sherry into wakefulness. When Julie heard a rustling behind her, there was Sherry, leaning on the doorframe, rubbing the sleep from her eyes.

"Morning," she mumbled, shuffling her way into the kitchen.

"Good morning," Julie answered, handing her a cup of coffee.

"Ta," Sherry said, adding two heaping teaspoons of sugar, a dollop of milk and then stirring it all, clanging the spoon against the mug.

"Has he been out there all night?" Julie asked, inclining her head toward the lake.

"Nope. After you fell asleep, he went for a run, and then he chopped some wood. You each have a nice pile for the winter. When he finished that, he paced back and forth between your two cottages until I coaxed him in out of the cold. Then he poured himself a stiff drink and went down there. I think he just collapsed from sheer exhaustion, mental and physical."

"I have no idea what I would do if I were in his shoes. My heart is breaking, and Hope is just my student, my neighbour's daughter."

"Forgive me," Sherry said. "But I thought you and he…"

Wanting to keep her emotions intact, Julie turned away and busied herself checking sell-by dates in the fridge.

"Yeah. Thought there was something," Sherry said. "I think I'll check in with the team up the road," she added. "Mind if I take them a cup? I'll bring the empties back soon."

"Sure," Julie said, filling two more cups of black, steamy coffee. She found an empty jar to fill with milk and fished some restaurant sugar packets out of a dish on the counter. "Here you go," she said, handing it all to Sherry on a tray.

The team up the road were the two officers posted at the corner of South Ril Lake Road, and Ril Cove Road. They'd been there since the incident happened, and would be there for the duration Julie had been told. "Think of them as a security blanket," Sherry had said yesterday when they'd arrived home and saw them there.

In Michael's kitchen, Julie sipped her coffee and did her best to wrap her head around everything Michael had said last night. But every time she closed her eyes, the playground scene played over in her head like a movie reel. She was running toward the fence, toward that cherry-red car, Hope reaching out for her shoe. Hope crying because Grace was rushing her…

Huh! That was new. She hadn't remembered that yesterday. Hope was crying. She grabbed a notebook and pen out of a kitchen drawer, then closed her eyes and forced her thoughts back to yesterday, back to the playground, to the minute details she hadn't remembered before. And then she wrote.

It's sunny, a cloudless day to be exact, but cold for the end of October. Later, the sky will be grey and it will threaten rain, but not yet. In the distance, I hear the whoosh of running water coming from a hose, and there are men's voices to my left. At the firehall, the two trucks are outside, and someone is hosing them down. My heart is pounding, and I hear my breath as I gather a burst of speed, eyes trained on the top of that fence, positive I won't get over it and wondering simultaneously if I have time to get to the main gate instead. I see that I can't, just as I know I can't scale that fence. My chase is fruitless, but I keep going anyway. Maybe I'll cause enough of a stir that the firemen will look our way. I wonder why the warning bells at the school haven't already put them on alert, but I can't think about that now. I focus on Grace.

She is wearing a brown zip-up hoodie. The rim of a black baseball cap shadows her face. I'm too far away to see the logo on it, but I can see the Nike checkmark on the side of her track pants, which are black with a white stripe down the side. Old, like castoffs you can buy at a second hand shop. And there is someone in the passenger seat of the car. A woman? Maybe, but I can't see anything more than long hair falling over her shoulders because of the window tinting. The blood rushing through my body muffles the sounds around me. But I hear shouting and know that behind me Vince is gathering the rest of the children, urging them inside. Across University Street, beyond Grace's car, Michael flies out of the medical clinic and down the stairs. There's a royal blue SUV, the same make and model as mine, parked against the building. I know that car. Whose is it? A patient? My attention shifts back to the fence and Grace, who is struggling to get Hope's shoe unstuck. She tugs. Hope cries out. The shoe drops to the ground. And then, mere seconds before I reach the fence, Grace pushes Hope into the car, and she is… crying. Her arms reach out to me. To me. Not because of her shoe. I see her sweet little mouth form my name. Juuuulllleeeee. But Grace shoves something inside after Hope, then slams the door. That's when I remember something I'd forgotten to tell the police. Hope has her backpack with her. Why? It was noon hour. She had already eaten her lunch and was outside playing. And then I realize. Hope knew this was going to happen. She was prepared to go with her mother because she'd brought her backpack with her to the playground.

Julie reread what she'd written and put a bold question mark beside the royal blue SUV. Maybe this patient was just going in or coming out when all this took place. Maybe she or he saw something. Maybe their view of the car meant they'd seen whoever was in the passenger seat. Because someone certainly was. She knew it and Michael had said so too.

Sherry returned from her jaunt up the road, tray of empty mugs in hand, looking refreshed from her walk in the morning air. Julie handed her what she'd written but gave her no time to read it.

"Michael's patient," she said, breathlessly. "Find out who it was. They might have seen whoever was in the car with Grace."

"Okay. What else did you remember?" Sherry seemed enthused, happy Julie had done what she asked.

"Hope had her backpack with her. She wouldn't normally have had it on the playground at lunchtime. She must have known her mother was coming. She was ready to go with her."

Sherry was already texting someone with this additional news. "This is good, Julie. Really good."

"One last thing. Hope was crying, and she called out to me. So, for some reason, when all this was happening, she decided she didn't want to go with her mother."

"Could it have been losing the shoe that upset her?"

"Maybe." Julie pointed to the paper. "There were firemen outside too, hosing down the trucks. Maybe one of them saw something. I'm sorry it isn't more."

"It's great. Really. This is helpful." Sherry smiled and Julie had the sense she had news of her own. Something good, she hoped.

"You've heard something."

"I should wait until Dr. Adams is up, but under the circumstances."

"Please, if there's an iota of good news, tell me."

"Yeah, alright. It'll be on the morning news, anyway. They found the car Grace was driving," Sherry said. "But only the car, not Grace and not Hope, but it's something. She needed to ditch it, didn't she? Because everyone knew what she was driving. So we know she got as far as Parry Sound."

"So, Eddy was right." Julie's heart skipped a beat. She'd thought it callous of him, that he was being cruel, calling her at such a horrible time. But he'd been genuine in his own strange way, and all she had done was remember the worst in him.

"Looks like it. They've set up roadblocks and they're checking every vehicle in and out of town. Volunteers are being organized for a door-to-door search this morning."

"We should wake Michael. He'll want to know."

"Let the man sleep. Lord knows he needs it. Besides, there's nothing he can do right now. In a couple of hours, there will be something to do."

How do people survive this up and down—good news one minute, bad news the next? How does a family survive the waiting, the unknowing, the worry, the guilt, the constant wracking your brain for the tiniest of forgotten details? And what about Hope? Does she realize the danger she's in, or does she think that her mother has magically shown up like a fairy story and taken her on an adventure? What had Grace told her? Julie had a million questions and not a single answer she could cling to.

She watched Sherry go comfortably to the coffeepot, as if she were in her own home, and pour herself a refill. It was as if Julie was seeing her for the first time, the woman she was apart from the job she was doing. She was a little on the stocky side, which she probably needed to be given the job she did, but what struck Julie most was the kindness that oozed from her, as if she could touch it, feel it, wrap herself up in it.

"I'm sorry," Julie said, when they sat down at the table together. "I never even thanked you for staying with us on

Thanksgiving Day. You were away from your own family, and you were so kind to the girls. Not to mention yesterday and last night."

Sherry smiled. "It's my job."

"It might be, but I suspect there's more to it than that."

"No different from you. You probably became a teacher to make a difference, mold young minds, who will one day shape the future or something like that."

"Something like that," Julie agreed. "I wanted to be just like Miss Mason. She was my Grade One teacher, and I'm sure I was in love with the idea of teaching because I was in love with the idea of her. What about you? Any mentors who inspired you?"

Sherry's thumb circled the rim of her cup, thoughtfully. She didn't seem the type to share things about herself, but for some reason she opened up to Julie.

"I was in the foster care system from the age of eight. Luckily, I stayed with the same family for quite a while. My foster father, Mr. Fitzsimmons, was a youth corrections officer. His wife was a nurse and between the two of them, they made sure I minded my ps and qs. I was better because of it. When we had '*Take Your Kid To Work Day,*' in Grade nine, I went with him and that's when I got an eyeful, let me tell you. He took me to a lockup for juvenile offenders and when I heard some of their stories and saw the anger and bitterness still in their eyes, I knew I didn't want to be like that. So, I buckled down, got decent grades and, with their help, I made something of myself. I will be forever grateful to them for that. So, I guess they were a bit like your Miss Mason."

"We all need someone to look up to, don't we?" Julie said. "Although I suppose anyone can go off the rails under certain circumstances. Like Grace, for instance. It must have been traumatic for her to lose her sister at such a young age. I don't suppose there's anything more about Mia Sander's death?"

"Well..." Sherry drew in a breath. "It's an ongoing investigation and we don't have all the answers yet."

"Is that the polite way of saying, mind your own business?"

She smiled. "It's my way of saying we don't know. Tox screens, all that stuff. It only happens fast on TV. But she won't be helping Grace anymore, that's for sure."

Julie was refilling her coffee when Joy came into the kitchen, followed closely by her sister.

"Morning," they said in unison, then came to give Julie a hug. If they were her own daughters, she couldn't have loved them more, which seemed a little ridiculous since she'd known them for all of two months. But in her heart, it felt perfectly normal.

"Breakfast?"

Joy nodded, but Faith looked up at her. "I just want to shower first, if that's okay."

"Of course it is."

Joy, already fresh from her shower, started the bacon in the oven on a cookie sheet, so it would lay flat and not spatter grease all over the stove, she told them. A trick her father had taught her. Sherry helped chop onions and Julie scrambled some eggs and grated cheese, so together they made a breakfast of cheese and onion omelettes with toast and bacon for everyone.

While they cleared away the dishes, Julie began thinking of the long, arduous day ahead, and the endless hours of waiting with nothing to do. She couldn't bear the thought of sitting idle or of trying to keep herself occupied with meaningless tasks and it made her wonder if she was that edgy, what was Michael going to be like.

"Please give us something to do," she begged Sherry. "We're all going to go crazy, sitting around waiting."

"I don't think that's going to be a problem." Sherry wiggled her finger in a come with me motion and Joy and Julie followed her to the front door. When she opened it, a long line of pickups, cars, and jeeps were pulling into the circle. "I hope you don't mind. I told the Bracebridge office we could use Michael's dining room."

"Of course, but what for?"

"For the headquarters of Operation Find Hope."

Chapter 26

The horizon was a canvas of colour when Faith and Julie went down to the dock with toast and coffee for Michael. Julie put his coffee on one arm of the chair, while Faith placed the toast on the other.

"Morning Dad," Faith said. "Did you sleep out here?"

He shook his head. "Just watching that beautiful sky." He reached out and pulled Faith onto his lap and tucked her head under his chin. "Did you sleep?" He kissed the fingers she'd chewed on so badly the night before.

"Yes." She reached up to rub the whiskers on his chin. "You need to shave, Dad."

"Come here!" Then, he rubbed his face against her cheek, till she giggled and pushed away from him.

"Go and shave!" she insisted, still laughing.

Julie had taken the only other chair on the dock and, watching them together, she felt a softening in her heart. There was sweetness in that tiny moment when the rest of the world was somewhere else and they could just be father and daughter, do their usual things, be their usual selves. The truly sad thing was it couldn't last. There was too much going on, too many worries, fears, regrets.

Faith stayed on her father's knee for a little longer, playing with the strings on his hoodie, not looking into his eyes.

"Joy told me everything this morning," she said, eventually. Huge tears welled in her eyes. "I'm sorry Dad. I should have been watching Hope. I should have known something was going to happen. Mum kept saying one day we'd all go somewhere nice together…"

"No. No, my darling. This isn't your fault. You couldn't possibly have known. None of us knew what was going on in your mum's mind."

"But I did. I knew. She told me. I just didn't think she'd ever do it. I told her I wouldn't go with her unless you came too. So, she said maybe we'd all just go for ice cream or something. You know how much Hope loves ice cream. I shouldn't have kept her secret. I know that now. If I'd told you then, Hope wouldn't be gone."

"Oh. God! No. Faith. Oh, no." He hugged her tighter. "This isn't your fault. If anyone is to blame, it's me. I shouldn't have kept all this from you. Your nightmares. You saw something that night?"

"Blood. That's all I remember. Blood and you were on the floor. And then loud sirens. I think I hid in the closet because after that, it all goes dark."

It was such a raw and intimate moment between father and daughter, Julie had to look away. She was relieved that Faith had finally been able to talk about her nightmares, but worried too, that all her father had done was bury the secret deeper and deeper.

Their foreheads met and Michael said, "We finally cracked your nightmares, haven't we?"

She grinned. "Dr. Bill will be so proud of me."

Michael hadn't mentioned Faith was seeing anyone about her dreams. Julie's gaze flitted from father to daughter. There was so much about them she did not know and never would. She wasn't family, she told herself. These girls were not her daughters, and no matter how much she cared for them, how strong a bond she might someday have, she would never have what he had with them. How could she? She wasn't their mother. She got up and took a step toward the house, but Michael grabbed her wrist.

"Stay. Please," he mouthed as he cradled Faith against him. "It'll all be fine now, Faith. Trust me. If there's one thing I know about your mother, it's that she loves you girls. She won't hurt Hope, and she won't go far. The police are everywhere looking for her."

"I know. They'll find her. I have faith. Isn't that why you chose this name for me?" Faith said.

"It is." He kissed her on the forehead, then, still holding Julie's hand, he urged Faith out of his lap. "I need to talk to Julie for a minute, okay?"

"Sure," she said. "But you should come inside, because there's something you need to see."

He flashed Julie a questioning glance. "What's going on?"

"I think you should let Faith show you," Julie said, as he released her hand and pushed himself out of his chair.

Julie draped the blanket he'd been using over her arm. It was still warm from the heat of his body and carried a trace of his cologne.

Michael hadn't eaten his toast or drunk his coffee, so she brought that along too. Her wrist still tingled from his grip, not because he'd hurt her, but because it seemed as if Michael had read her thoughts. At the very moment she'd felt separate from him and his family, he'd reached for her as if to say, *oh yes you are.* Or was it wishful thinking on her part?

At the bottom step to the deck, Julie glanced over her shoulder and toward the beach where a barefoot Sirona, swinging a pair of shoes at her side, headed their way.

"It's nearly November, you know," Michael called out.

"Your point is…?" She was teasing, but there was concern in her face as she drew nearer. "I'm so sorry, Michael."

Faith was pulling Michael's arm. "You've got to see this, Dad. Come on!"

When they got to the door, Faith reached up to put her hands over her father's eyes and then nudged him forward until he was standing at the doorway to the dining room. "Okay, now you can look!"

Even Julie was surprised because while she'd been down at the dock, more people had arrived until it seemed like the entire village of Baysville and everyone who was still up here in the lake district had congregated in Michael's dining room. The table was against the wall, and over it hung a computer printed banner that read: Operation Find Hope. On the table was Hope's school picture in a black 8 x 10 frame, flanked by boxes of posters, which Joe and Annie Hewitt were handing out to everyone.

Have you seen this child? The headline splayed out over a picture of Hope blown up to fill the poster. In smaller but still very bold type was a hotline phone number to call and a description of what Hope had been wearing: blue jeans and a pink T-shirt with butterflies on it and a powder blue rain jacket with a hood. She carried a pink Barbie backpack with her lunch kit, a sweater, and a library book from the Baysville Library inside.

Julie read the details, as she ran a hand over Hope's features and then she turned to Michael, who looked as if he was trying not to cry and not doing a good job of it. He pulled her to him, threw an arm around her shoulder, and whispered something in her ear.

"Where did they come from?"

"From everywhere, Michael." She knew nearly everyone in the room, had met their gaze over a bakery counter, or laid on their massage table, or played gin rummy with them at the Rec Centre. And there they were. They'd all taken time off work, organized babysitters, closed their businesses, set aside everything else in their lives to come together to help. This was small town community at its finest.

"They've organized search parties," Julie told Michael. "Joe's entire workforce has given up working today. Wally closed the garage. The shops and businesses in town are all closed. Everyone's here to do everything they can. We won't stop until we find her."

Michael swiped fiercely at tears that came unbidden as he navigated the room, shaking hands and thanking people. Felicity and Ben had maps for everyone so they could mark off their search areas. Gwen and Turtle Ted Sheridan were there. His bus was outside and ready to take a load of people north for door-to-door searches. By the time Michael had circled the room, he came to Ali, who was holding Fred, her favourite teddy bear, in one hand and Blind Bruce, who wasn't blind anymore, in the other. She set them on the table, next to the Hope's picture.

"I'm putting Fred here, so he will tell Bruce, and Bruce will tell Hope that we are all looking for her," Ali said. "And when she's home, we won't ever lose Hope again."

We won't ever lose Hope again.

The childlike innocence in her words left Julie speechless. She thought back to that first day of school, of Hope following Ali off the bus and the two of them finding desks side by side. By first recess, they'd told her they were best friends forever, and that had felt just right.

"Thank you, Ali," Michael said. "I'm sure Hope can feel your love wherever she is."

"I just need a quick word," Sherry said gravely, sidling up next to him.

In the kitchen, while Julie heated the plate of food they'd set aside for Michael, he leaned against the counter while Sherry gave them an update.

"A woman working in a corner store in Parry Sound says someone fitting Grace and Hope's descriptions were there yesterday afternoon. They bought food, drinks and two boxes of hair dye."

"Are you saying Grace has dyed their hair?" Panic spread across Michael's face and stiffened his body. "But people will look for a girl with light brown hair. Now it might be auburn or black or who knows what colour."

Sherry was reassuring. "We don't know for sure that Grace has done anything to Hope's hair. She might have bought it for herself. But people usually buy hair dye from a drugstore. The clerk said she hadn't sold it to anyone in years. That's why she paid attention. She kept an eye on them when they left and saw them cross the street to a motel. Before they came out again, the Amber Alert went off on her phone and she knew instantly who she'd just seen. She called the hotline. The receptionist at the hotel told us Grace didn't have enough money for a room and when she suggested a credit or debit card, she didn't have one of those either, so she just left."

"So, they went... where?"

"To the bus station where the guy behind the ticket booth sold them two tickets to Sudbury for today. She'd asked for Sault Ste Marie, but she didn't have enough money. Does she know someone there?"

"Not that I know of. Are you saying she took a bus to Sudbury this morning?"

"No. At least she hasn't boarded one yet. We've staked out the bus depot. There's been no sign of her and there are roadblocks in and out of town. We're also plastering those posters everywhere and the police have organized crews of volunteers to start in the Sault working their way south, while we will work our way north. We've got police and volunteers watching every bus stop between here and there." She finished with a confident, "We'll find her, Dr. Adams."

"What can I do? I can't just sit here," he asked.

"Go out with a crew. Put up posters, knock on doors, ask questions? We're organizing groups of three to six volunteers. I suggest you let someone else drive so you can have your hands free for phone calls, just in case someone needs to reach you." She looked down at the food getting cold on the plate. "There's one more thing."

"Go on," Michael said.

"We found a second location in Baysville, where Grace has been staying. The loft of an empty barn near the school. When she left yesterday, she didn't take all her belongings. She left her medications behind. Her psychiatrist suggests she has about twenty-four to forty-eight hours before, not having those pills will affect her state of mind."

"If she's been taking them at all," Michael said, raking a hand through his hair. "We need to find them now! Why are we all just standing around? There's no time to waste."

"Agreed. But food first," Sherry reminded. "You need to keep your strength up if you're going to be of any use."

Michael took the plate from Julie and shoved food into his mouth. He didn't stop to chew it, but swallowed it down, put his plate in the sink with a clang so loud it stopped conversation in the other room, and then he headed for the door. He did not stop to shower, didn't change his clothes, didn't shave, as Faith had asked him to. Michael wanted to get going.

Cam was waiting by the front door, one hand on the knob, the other talking to someone on his cellphone.

"Cam is Darren's father," Julie told Michael when they reached the front door.

The two men shook hands. "My vehicle is right outside, but so is the press," Cam said, still blocking the door. "The cops are trying to hold them back and there's yellow crime scene tape strung up, but they're going to hound you the minute I open this door. So just tell me when."

Michael nodded. "I'm surprised they weren't here sooner."

"There are uniformed officers at the corner, but this bunch came through on foot. I'm sorry Doc."

Sherry came up behind them. "I'll come with you, Dr. Adams. Just tell them no comment or say nothing at all. It's up to you."

Michael nodded. "What if I want to make a statement, a plea for Hope's return?"

Sherry smiled. "If you'd like."

He reached for Julie's hand. "Together," he said.

Sherry had another idea. "I think, if you want to reduce speculation, you might want to do this alone."

"But I…" Michael started. Then his jaw tightened. "Oh. I see." He looked at Julie, then at Sherry. "Very well. I wouldn't want to give them any ammunition to get this wrong. Cam. Open the door and let's get this over with."

Cam nodded and opened the door. Outside on Michael's front porch, Sherry stood on one side of him, Cam on the other. Michael held up his hand to the shouting press and a moment later, there was silence.

"Thank you all for coming," Michael began, though Julie would have told them to take a hike. "As you know, my youngest daughter is missing." His bottom lip began to tremble, and he stopped, looked out over the sea of cameras, and held it together. "We just want her back home, safe and sound. Grace, if you're hearing this, please, don't make this any harder than it is."

Sherry stepped forward when the questions began to hurl from the crowd. She held up her hands for silence.

"As you already know, Hope was taken from the school yard yesterday over the lunch hour, and at last sighting was known to be in Parry Sound. We ask that you respect the family's privacy during this difficult time and let the police do what they have to do to bring Hope home." Sherry held up her hand when someone from the press shouted a question. "Please. We're asking anyone with information to call the hotline, no matter how trivial you think it might be. That's all at this time."

There followed the sound of a thousand shutters clicking and questions hurled in Michael's direction as he and Cam made their way to the car. Julie watched from the kitchen window as Cam opened the door and Michael got in, his face pale, his jaw clenched, his eyes staring straight ahead. When Cam started the engine and he hit the gas, churning up the gravel in the driveway, she whispered, "Please let her be safe."

Chapter 27

Julie headed north, with Joy riding shotgun manning Julie's phone. Her SUV was packed to the rafters with coolers filled with food and drinks for the door-to-door search teams. Humble Pie Bakery had been busy since dawn, putting together lunch packages for all the volunteers. The corner market donated bottled water and cans of pop and Joe brought boxes of high-viz vests for all the searchers to wear. Julie and Joy's job, like Felicity's and Gwen's, who were heading out too, was to make sure the door-to-door crews had food and enough water to get them through the day.

In Port Carling they stopped to fill up with gas and just as Julie was getting back in the car, Joy let out a shriek.

"Is that them?" She threw open her door, screaming her sister's name. "Hope!"

Across the street, a young girl, about Hope's age, with an identical backpack twisted around to face them. Her hair colour was the same, and she was wearing a blue raincoat like Hope's. But the moment the little girl turned, it was obvious she wasn't her. Too late to stop her though, Joy was already bolting across the street and before she got there, the mother yanked her child out of reach.

Julie was only steps behind. "Sorry," she said to the mother as she pulled a poster out of her pocket. "We're searching for this little girl. She has a similar backpack to your daughter's. This was an innocent mistake."

The mother's face darkened with recognition of Hope's face on the poster. "That's the little girl from the news," she said. "You're the teacher. We saw the news." She shook her head. "No. We haven't seen her. I'm so sorry." She looked at Joy then. "My heart goes out to you and I pray you find her." She pulled her daughter a little closer. "Come on Kelly. You'll be late for school."

As they returned to Julie's car, Joy was mumbling, half under her breath. "That was dumb of me. She wouldn't be here anyway, would she? We haven't even got to Parry Sound yet."

"She could be anywhere," Julie reminded her. "And it wasn't dumb. You're on the lookout. Your nerves are shattered, and your emotions are all over the place. It's understandable. Besides, they might have come back this way. You never know, so you were right to keep your eyes open. Remember what Sherry said this morning? Just because Grace bought a bus ticket, doesn't mean she's going to get on that bus. She could have bought those tickets to throw the police off her trail."

By the time they checked in with the crew chief at their first designated stop and left enough lunches and water for his crew, Joy seemed more settled. She was even more relaxed after talking to her dad on Julie's phone. Julie marvelled at how he could keep his calm when talking with Faith and Joy, knowing his heart was breaking and he must be sick with worry for Hope.

"That's the problem with cottage country," the crew chief said. "There are hundreds of places to hide. Cabins, cottages, fishing shacks." Julie saw Joy wince at his words and asked her to get another case of water from the car. The man was right, and most of these places were tucked away in the woods, remote and off the beaten path, but it was the last thing Joy needed to hear.

"She's the little girl's sister," Julie told him. "Hearing that there is no news is enough for her. She doesn't need to know how challenging the search is."

"Yeah, sorry. I didn't know."

"I know you didn't. I'll talk to her."

They drove from checkpoint to checkpoint, continuing past lunchtime and well into the afternoon. It was nearly four, with the sun hanging low in a purple sky, when they got the first bit of news in a text from Sherry. Joy read it out loud, twice.

Confirmed sighting in Port Severn. Return to base.

"Port Severn is south of us!" Julie gasped. "We're going the wrong way."

Joy had hardly put down the phone when it rang. "Dad! You're on speaker."

Static crackled on the line as Michael talked. "She sold the bus tickets and hitched a ride with a guy in a campervan. The police are questioning him now. He said…" He took a deep breath, and

Julie heard the relief in his voice. "The driver said the little girl was excited because her mum had bought her new shoes."

"Michael, she is taking care of her," Julie said in a comforting tone. "She's bought food and found shelter last night. That's a good thing."

"Yeah. I just… Look, we've got to move. She's two hours south of where we thought she was."

"So, we go home and regroup?" Julie asked.

There were muffled voices on Michael's end. Julie located a parking lot where she could turn around.

Michael came back to them. "Cam will take me to Port Severn, but we have two others who need to get home. Can we meet you? They could go back with you."

Joy recalled a place they'd just passed. "Key Marine?"

Julie nodded. "We went by it about ten minutes ago. There's a good place to get off the road there. I'll head back."

"Good." More rustling and then Michael said, "See in you in fifteen minutes."

When Cam's Jeep pulled up next to them and Julie saw Michael's face, she had to force herself not to cry. She had to look away from the mixture of agony, fear and sleeplessness that had aged him ten years. *He must be running on sheer adrenaline*, she thought. She glued her eyes to the horizon over his shoulder to keep her own fears hidden when she handed her keys to Will Jefferies.

"Take Joy home with you, Will," she told him. "I'm going on with Michael and Cam."

"Sure, Julie." Will shook Michael's hand. "Good luck," he said, clapping Michael's shoulder. Then, with a nod to Cam, Will climbed into Julie's SUV and they left.

They wasted no time getting into Cam's vehicle and back on the road. Cam hit the gas and laid a long track of rubber down the highway as they sped toward Port Severn. Julie googled the distance. Two hours and eleven minutes, but at the speed Cam was driving, they'd be there a lot sooner. She reached forward to the front seat and squeezed Michael's shoulder.

"We'll find her," she told him.

He nodded, and put a hand over hers, but didn't look back. Julie knew without seeing his face, there were tears in his eyes.

Chapter 28

The tires of the Jeep beneath them thrummed in a steady rhythm as they sped down the highway. Cam's engine whined as he shifted into overdrive and put his foot to the floor. There was little traffic, but when there was, he maneuvered them expertly around it, eyes focused on the road, none of them saying what they were thinking. They didn't dare.

Julie scrolled through social media platforms on her phone. There were hundreds of posts about Hope and every one of them, with a hundred or more comments below. Most people were praying for Hope's safe return. Others were shaming the teachers at the school for the lack of security. How could such a thing happen, some people said? How indeed? Julie thought as they raced down the highway. Who would have dreamed something like this could happen in Baysville, of all places, and why hadn't she, of all people, been more cautious knowing Grace had been at the school already? She was as much to blame as anyone for what was going on.

On Facebook, she discovered a link from a post to a Go-FundMe on Hope's behalf. She passed the phone to Michael. "Do you know these people? Frank and Avril Adams, claiming to be relatives?"

Michael shook his head as he read the blurb posted on the GoFundMe site. "Who does shit like that?" he asked, handing the phone back to her.

"I'll send the link to Darren." Julie did, and then called him. "You need to shut that down," she told him. "Hope doesn't have any relatives named Adams. It's a cash grab. Those people should be charged."

"I'll take care of it," Darren said, then disconnected the call.

Julie went on scrolling. Instagram. TikTok. X. Anywhere there were posts about the missing girl from Baysville or anything else remotely related. She circled back to the GoFundMe page. It was gone. Good work Darren.

After what seemed like ages, they arrived at the roadblock just outside Port Severn. The line up of cars was over two kilometres long with irritated and unaware drivers honking and shaking fists out their windows at the police.

"Can't you go around this, Cam?" Michael asked. "They'll let us through when they know who we are."

"Yeah, let's try it. Get your ID ready. They're going to ask to see it." Cam pulled out and sped to the front, much to the frustration of everyone else who was waiting. When they reached the roadblock the police officer held up his hands up to stop them. Cam shut off the car, collected all their identification, and went to speak to him. In less than a minute, he was back, and the barricade was being moved away. Julie could just imagine the angry fists waving from the people in the cars they passed as they went through. *If they only knew,* she thought.

It was moments later when they pulled into the Municipal Administration Office on Lone Pine Road, in Port Severn. Police had set up a second Operation Find Hope Centre inside the building, but outside it was a hive of activity. Uniformed police officers and volunteers in hi-viz vests took their orders from a woman who stood on the top step of the building. She wore a navy-blue raincoat over a dove grey suit and barked orders from a blow horn she held in her hand.

As Cam, Julie and Michael passed by, she gave them the briefest of nods, as if she'd been expecting them, but needed to focus on what she was doing. Of course, Julie thought. The officers at the roadblock would have messaged ahead to let them know the father of the missing girl was on his way.

Inside the building, urns of coffee were set on tables, along the far wall of the gymnasium size room. Boxes of donuts, muffins, and scones all bearing the familiar Tim Hortons wrappings were scattered at one end of the table, some empty, some full and some halfway in between. Cam grabbed a chocolate glazed donut and went to get coffee for the three of them. Minutes after he returned, three steaming cups in his hands, they were met by a plainclothes detective who said his name was Gary. He directed Cam to the leader of one of the search parties. He asked Michael and Julie to follow him.

"Word is coming in from all over the area," he said, leading them down a carpeted corridor. "We're dealing with them as quickly as we can. Some are mistakes, some are crackpots, but somewhere in the middle of all that there will be one that's not someone looking for their fifteen minutes of fame. So, we check every single one. And that takes time."

He opened a door near the end of the hall and waved them inside a meeting room with a grouping of swivel style chairs on wheels around a wide oval table. The walls were a muted grey, the carpet industrial style in a shade that matched the walls. A picture of King Charles replaced a larger one of his mother that had once been in the same spot, given the faded paint behind it. Beneath a bank of windows that faced the parking lot were three desks, each of them with computers, but none of them turned on.

"Make yourselves comfortable," Gary said. "It's quiet here, away from all the phone chatter and commotion. You should rest if you can."

"I'm not sure we're going to rest much," Julie said. "Do these computers work?" Two computers sat on desks just inside the door.

"Yeah. Sure." Gary pushed a button on the monitor of one of them and fired up the hard drive.

"I've been scrolling the internet, sifting through the junk," Julie explained. "I can't believe what I've been finding." She told him about the GoFundMe account. "People were trying to make money off someone else's grief."

Gary took her phone then and put a number into her contacts. "Send any suspicious links to that number. We'll deal with it right away."

Then he turned to Michael, who was fidgeting, restless, and wanting to do something to help.

"I should be out there searching," Michael said. "Doing something. Not sitting here *resting*." The word came out laced with frustration and sarcasm.

Gary was quick to placate. "Look, Dr. Adams, let's be honest. It's getting late. It's dark and the searchers will be coming in soon. In the meantime, I need someone here to help verify information. Things like descriptions and…"

"Look," Michael protested loudly, stepping a little closer to Gary. "Julie can help you with descriptions. You don't need me."

Gary took a step back, regaining his stance. "In my experience and trust me, I've done more of these than I care to think about, it's best if we have a parent close by. Now, the driver of the camper-van told us your daughter was fine. A little tired, maybe, but otherwise fine. Please. Let us do our jobs, Dr. Adams. Stay put." He reached out to Michael then, gripped his shoulder and sent him a reassuring look. Michael nodded that he understood and Gary released his grip. "Good man." And then he was gone.

Julie sat down at the computer Gary had started for her and went back to her task of scrolling social media posts. Michael paced the room, and in a loud whisper began reciting things that could only have come from his medical training.

"The systems of the body are nervous, respiratory, endocrine…"

Once, when they'd talked about university life, Michael had told her his secret for keeping calm before an exam. He used to pace his dorm room, reciting the systems of the body, the bones, and the muscles. She wondered if it was working now.

"…Carpals—Scaphoid, Lunate…"

Eventually, he stopped in the middle of the room and looked at her. "I just realized two things."

"Go on."

"The people in Vancouver can't be helping Grace. If they were, she would have money to go wherever she wanted and pay for that hotel last night. She's broke, or close to it."

"That makes sense. What's the other thing?"

He sighed heavily. "We know that Grace doesn't have her meds, but what if she hasn't been taking them at all?"

"They'll find her, Michael. We're so close now."

But were they? Julie closed her eyes and in the darkness behind them saw that little pink light-up Barbie shoe drop to the ground and the sole flash with little bursts of light. She exhaled a long, slow breath and opened her eyes. Outside it was dark, and the blackness of the night seemed to close in on them. How much longer would they search tonight?

Like Michael's pacing, the social media posts were all Julie had, so she turned back to them, sure there would be something there, some clue, some tidbit everyone else had overlooked. If she had to confess it, she would have said her energy peeked with an adrenaline rush every time she read an incorrect or off-colour comment. With a clenched jaw, she read them, angry that people who knew nothing about Michael, his children or Grace had a right to judge and post the garbage they did. To hell with free speech, this was bordering on slanderous. She began skimming the posts, letting the anonymous judgement feed her anger, all the time hoping something someone posted might be a lead.

She found it on an Instagram post from someone with the profile *@4vrjs.*

Bang bang on the door, love shack baby, love shack.

The post was followed by a tiny running shoe emoji. Julie's mind raced through the lyrics of the old song she and Eddy used to sing sometimes. Love Shack, by the B-52s, was one of Eddy's favourites, but who knew that? Was someone leaving them a clue? Had @4vrjs seen Grace and Hope in a shack? It wasn't much, but something in the way it was written, and the little running shoe emoji, caught hold and wouldn't let Julie go. It sent a tremble running up and down her spine.

Goosebumps prickled her arm when she called Michael over to see the post. He peered over her shoulder and watched as Julie scrolled through photos on @rvrjs's account, most of which were generic pictures of lakes, mountains, and scenery that could be anywhere. Pictures with people had blurred faces or showed their backs looking out at the scenery beyond them.

"I don't understand. What's so special about this person?" he said.

"I don't know. It's just a feeling I have. The little shoe emoji, as if they're trying to tell us something through the lyrics of the song."

"I think you're reading too much into it, Julie, wanting to see things that aren't there."

"Maybe."

She sent the link to the number Gary had put in her phone and kept scrolling on through the rows and rows of pictures on @4vrjs's account until she came to some that stood out.

"Here," she cried out. "That's the Hallowe'en store in Huntsville. We saw that display when I took the girls there."

Michael looked over her shoulder at the screen as disappointment shadowed his features. "It could be any Hallowe'en store anywhere. It's a coincidence."

"Is it...?"

He scrubbed at the back of his neck. "Are we grasping at straws? Getting our hopes up over nothing?"

He was exhausted, worried, and eager to be doing something instead of pacing an empty room. Julie knew that. She also knew that he might be right. She might be going down a completely useless track, but she couldn't stop any more than he could stop pacing the room. She hit follow on @4vrjs's account. Maybe it was a coincidence. Maybe not. Either way, what could it hurt?

What was left of her coffee had gone cold. "I'm going for more coffee," she said. "Do you want a refresher?"

"Alright. Sure."

At the door, Michael paused, hand on the knob for a moment, and his face went ash white.

"Michael? Are you alright?"

"No. I'm not. I feel as if a bomb has just gone off. I can't hear anything properly, like everything is muted. And you're..." He put a hand on her shoulder. "You're a little fuzzy." He leaned in closer, his body going limp in her arms, nearly buckling her under his weight.

"Sit here." She urged him toward the chairs, one hand around his back, the other gripping his arm. When he sat, she gently nudged his head forward. "You know the drill, Doc. Head between your knees. I'll go get someone to help. I'm sure you're dehydrated, and when was the last time you ate?"

"I'm alright. I'm just..." He looked up, eyes struggling to focus, his face still worryingly pale.

"Head down, Doc!"

He did as he was told, with a small wave of his hand, but by the time Julie got to the door, he'd slumped over, slid off the chair and was flat out on the floor.

She threw open the door and shouted down the hall. "Help!"

Gary appeared immediately at the other end of the hall. "What is it?"

"He needs medical attention. Get someone. Please!"

A cellphone appeared out of Gary's pocket and while he spoke into it, he hurried down the hall toward her. "An ambulance is coming."

When Julie returned to Michael, he was lying on his back, eyes open, staring at the ceiling. "Someone's coming," she told him. "You'll be okay."

He blinked as if trying to clear his vision, then he frowned and clutched at his chest. But it wasn't Julie he was speaking to when he said, "Jesus, Grace. What have you done?"

Moments later, a pair of medics rushed into the room, toting a gurney and a box of gadgets. They went immediately to Michael and began probing, asking questions, checking his heart, his pulse, his blood pressure. Julie couldn't watch. She understood his grief, his fear and the panic he felt, because she felt all of it too. She lowered herself into a chair as thoughts came unbidden to her mind. Could he have prevented this if he'd just told his daughters the truth from the beginning? Is this what living with lies does to a person? What is the cost of keeping secrets and telling lies? Was Michael realizing the expense?

Restless, she went to the bank of windows overlooking the parking lot where a long row of police cars was parked in the streetlamp's glow. At the end of it was a black sedan, or maybe it was a grey. It was hard to tell because of the rain.

Rain!

It registered like a thwack to the side of her head, as rivulets of water ran down the glass. Rain meant the search was over. Rain meant everyone had gone home. Rain meant footprints and other evidence would disappear. No one would search in the rain.

Somewhere in the distance, a thunderstorm rumbled in the night. Instinctively, Julie counted the seconds between it and the first flash of lightning.

One, one thousand.

Two, one thousand.

Three, one thousand… Three miles away. As if the rain on its own wasn't bad enough, now a storm was on its way.

Chapter 29

When the medics finished assessing Michael, they advised him to eat something, to drink more water and to do his best to stay calm, which, under the circumstances, they acknowledged wasn't a simple thing to do. There was nothing wrong with him that sleep, and nourishment wouldn't fix—physically speaking. They were moved to a different room, one with a sofa and comfy armchairs, and a large screen TV on the wall. It was set to a news channel which showed Hope's picture and the hotline number below it every three minutes. Even though the volume was low, it was a distraction neither of them needed. Eventually, Julie found the remote and switched it off.

Outside, the rain pelted against the building and a gust of wind rattled the window. Julie knew by the look on Michael's face they were thinking the same thing. Had Grace found shelter out of this horrible storm? Were they safe? She had to believe they were, and that there was nothing more anyone could do tonight.

Someone had brought food for them. A plate of sandwiches, another of cheese and crackers, and a bowl of fruit sat on the low table in front of the sofa. Michael picked at a sandwich, eating less than half of it before putting the rest onto a napkin.

"Tell me about Eddy," he said. When Julie reached for a cracker. His hand reached out to cover hers on the arm of her chair. "Please?"

"I already told you about him." She couldn't imagine this was what he wanted to talk about now.

"I need to focus on something else."

She relented and put down the cracker. "Well, you know that I wanted a family. At first, Eddy said he did too, but he kept putting it off. He used to say we'd have them when his promotion came through, or we could afford a *real* house, not a cottage on the lake."

"Ouch, that must have hurt."

A wary smile curved her lips. "You have no idea. I pushed a little harder, and finally the truth came out. In Eddy's eyes, kids cramped your lifestyle, and he was happy the way things were. Possibly worst of all, he thought my students should be enough for me."

"Oh, dear."

"Yeah. He had no idea. But I did something really stupid. I went off the pill. I thought if I got pregnant, he'd get used to the idea of being a father and everything would be okay, but…" For a moment, Julie watched rain streaming down the windows, then she turned back to him, tears welling in her eyes. "It was wrong of me to go behind his back like that. I made a huge mistake, and I paid for it." She heaved a great sigh. "Michael, I lost the baby."

"I'm so sorry, Julie."

"I was only fourteen weeks pregnant when I lost her."

"A girl…"

"Yes, and…After I lost her, everything fell apart. I realized that Eddy and I had no future. We had nothing in common and I'd been wasting my life being with him. I stopped going to his games and to the pub afterwards with his friends, and it wasn't long before he started seeing other women. Eventually, I wised up and kicked him out." Julie sighed. "He moved away, and until that phone call the other night, I hadn't heard from him."

"I'm sorry," he said softly, reaching for her hand. "You could have had a family with someone else."

Julie shook her head and fished a tissue out of her pocket. "Come on, Doc. Surely you can guess that ship sailed years ago."

He squeezed her hand. "I'm sorry," he whispered. "I hope Eddy realizes what he let slip out of his hands." His hand grazed her cheek, his eyes searching hers. "I'm sorry I didn't tell you about Grace in the beginning. I should have."

"We all have secrets, Michael." Everyone did, though it was dangerous to keep them sometimes.

Michael turned away, avoiding her gaze. "There's something I didn't tell you, or Joy. I didn't know this when I met Grace, but it became obvious after a while. She's bi-polar. That was why she had mood swings. I had this ridiculous need to be the hero in her life. My shrink says it's why I became a doctor. To be everyone's bloody hero. That night, when everything fell apart, when I finally realized I couldn't do anything for her, I felt so terribly hopeless. I kept asking myself why I'd missed all the signs. Why I'd pushed her to have another baby."

"You can't honestly think that you're to blame for this," Julie said.

"If we hadn't had Hope, Grace might have been just fine."

"She would never be fine, Michael. You of all people know that bi-polar disorder is not something you grow out of. She might have coped if she'd stayed on the meds, but it was never going away."

He sank deeper into the sofa. "I know that now, but back then, I honestly believed I could help her."

She shifted to look at him more closely, and he reached for her hand, his fingers intertwining with hers. In that moment, Julie felt a shift. Something was changing. Something in his face was different because sharing had closed a gap between them and neither of them were hiding behind their pasts anymore.

"You're a doctor, Michael, but you're not a god. There are some things even you cannot fix."

"I know that, in my head, but it's damned hard, Julie, to admit you can't fix everything for the people you love."

"You were never going to fix Grace because you can't fix someone else. They have to do it for themselves." Sirona had spoken those same words to Julie once and, just now, they had an even stronger meaning.

"Jeez, when did you get so preachy?" he said, a smile creeping into the corner of his mouth.

"Sorry, I don't mean to be, but after Eddy, it was a long road of self-discovery, and it was Sirona who helped me."

"That doesn't surprise me. I'm still not convinced all her tinctures and salves are helpful, but she seems to have a wisdom the rest of us don't."

"She came into my life at a time when I needed someone the most. She was such a comfort and now, it feels as if my life is on track, for the first time in a long while."

"I wish I could say the same. It feels as if mine is spinning right out of control."

"You should try to rest," she said, when there seemed to be nothing more to say. "Why don't you lean back and close your eyes for a while?"

Chapter 30

"Dr. Adams?"

Julie hadn't even heard the door open, hadn't realized someone else was in the room until she heard the woman speak. Julie couldn't recall falling asleep, but she must have. At the sound of a woman's voice, she opened her eyes, stretched and focused on the figure standing just inside the door—a woman of average height, hair pulled into a tight bun and wearing a conventional grey business suit.

"Dr. Adams?" the woman repeated, with a little lift of her pointy chin. "I'm Detective Inspector Nicole Allen. Would you come with me, please?"

"You've found her!" Michael was off the couch and halfway to the door when she put her hand up.

"No. Sir. Not yet." She looked at Julie when she stood up, ready to follow. "You can wait here, Miss Wight. We just have a few questions for Dr. Adams."

"No," he said, reaching for Julie's hand. "Whatever you want to tell me, do it right here, right now. Julie stays."

DI Allen's body shifted. Icy blue eyes assessed them, and after a long moment of studying, she agreed. "Let's all sit down then, shall we?"

When they were settled again, she said, "Mia Sanders…"

"The woman who was stalking us?" Michael said.

DI Allen nodded. "Given the suspicious nature of the woman's death, we have been following several lines of inquiry."

"You suspected me," he said.

"When we thought she was your wife…"

"The first thought is the spouse. I get it." Michael fidgeted in his seat. "And now?"

"We're still investigating several things," DI Allen said, her gaze flitting to Julie and back. Her eyes lingered on Julie for a moment, but she said nothing before turning back to Michael. Her efficient tone was grating, peeling back Michael's soul one layer at a time, as if he were an onion being prepared for the frying pan.

"You told us you didn't know Mia Sanders," she said, setting a folder down on the table between them.

"That's right."

From the folder, she pulled a photo and turned it to face Michael. It was grainy as if it had been taken with a cellphone, then blown up. Julie could almost hear Michael's thoughts scuttling back to when it must have been taken.

"There was a car accident on my way to work. I stopped to see if anyone needed medical help before the EMTs arrived. As it happened, they did. A man pleaded with me to pull his wife out of the wreckage. He was so distraught I thought he was going to have a heart attack right there in front of me."

"When was this?" DI Allen asked.

"Early January, this year. It was snowing like crazy. The traffic was moving at a snail's pace because of the slippery conditions. This black SUV came out of a side street and couldn't make the stop at the corner. It rammed the side of the Honda Civic. They were an elderly couple on their way to a hospital appointment a few blocks away. The sound of metal crunching was so loud it brought people out of their houses."

"And this woman? Where did she come from?" DI Allen tapped the photo, indicating the same unknown woman.

"I don't have the faintest idea." Michael pointed to another woman, just visible in the background, middle-aged, round face and glasses. "But this is Mrs. Barnes. She lives in the bungalow right where this happened. She was a patient of mine. I know her, but I don't know the rest of these people."

"Would it surprise you if I said the woman standing next to you is Mia Sanders, and that a witness saw her get out of your car?"

"Can't be. The only time I ever saw Mia Sanders was when she was dead, on a gurney. Even then, I didn't look that closely. It wasn't Grace, and that was enough for me." He gave the photo an indignant push across the table. "This woman did not get out of my car."

"We have a witness who says otherwise."

"Who?"

"I'm sure you know I can't tell you that, Dr. Adams, but we don't think it's someone who had a reason to lie."

Michael pounded his fist on the table. "I'm telling you. I don't know this woman. You're trying to link me to her death, but you're wrong. I don't know her."

Suddenly, something clicked in Michael's thoughts. "Which side of the car did she get out of?"

"Pardon me?" DI Allen sat up straighter.

"The witness who saw her get out of my car must have seen if she was in the back, the front, the passenger side, behind me."

DI Allen checked her file. "It doesn't say."

"Because I put this to you, DI Allen. If this woman was stalking us, she could easily have slipped into the back of my car without me knowing. It was a Friday, garbage day. I started the car, and while it warmed up, I went to the garage to get the bins. The engine was running. The doors weren't locked. She could have gotten into the backseat, hunkered down and I wouldn't have known."

"Can I see that picture?" Julie asked. "It's blurry, but this might be the woman who was following the girls and me in Huntsville."

DI Allen returned the picture to her file folder, tightened her lips, and cast a painfully long and deliberate look at the two of them. "We'll check this out," she said. Just before making her way to the door, she pulled a phone out of her pocket and set it on the table. "Do you recognize this phone, Dr. Adams?"

"Yes. It's the one I lost. The screen is scratched. Here. See?" He showed her a long line across the face of the phone.

"It was found with your wife's other belongings in the loft of a barn in Baysville. We'll return it to you once we've finished going through all the calls and messages."

"Ex-wife. We were divorced six years ago," he hissed.

DI Allen headed for the door. It closed with a perfunctory click.

"Jesus!" Michael said, half to himself. "Could this nightmare get any worse?"

Julie's phone had been vibrating in her pocket, on and off, but she hadn't wanted to interrupt DI Allen to take a call. She read her messages and fired a quick response as Michael flopped back against the sofa.

"I've had a text from Cam," she told him. "He has a cabin for us where we can shower and sleep."

"What about Faith and Joy? I can't leave here, but I can't go home either."

"Felicity and Sirona are with them until… until we know. Michael. Trust that Grace is looking after Hope, that she won't hurt her. She loves her."

He nodded and let his head drop. "In my head, I know you're right, but in my heart…"

Chapter 31

Later, when they'd been cleared to leave the Municipal Office Building, Cam drove them all to the cabin that had been arranged for them. He deposited Julie and Michael, then went to find something other than sandwiches to fill the void, not that any of them had much of an appetite.

"It might take me some time. There's nothing but Timmys in this town," Cam said, before heading out the door.

The storm was subsiding, though a light mist still lingered. Julie pulled back the curtain over the kitchen window and looked across the bay to Yellowhead Island. It was a mass of land, with a smattering of cottages hidden among the trees. It was remote, accessed only by boat, and because it would be an ideal place for someone to hide out, it had already been thoroughly searched. Cam told them he'd been one of the crew and while they were at the Municipal building waiting for news, he'd gone across the narrow strait by boat with tracking dogs. They'd found nothing, not the slightest hint of Hope or Grace. Looking at it now, Julie couldn't help thinking that Yellowhead Island was a reminder of just how isolated parts of the Muskoka Region were.

The cabin looked as tired and worn as Julie felt, but someone had gone over it with a scrub brush. The scent of pine cleaner lingered in the air when they went inside. All Julie wanted was to be away from the constant drone of mumbling voices, the shuffling of paper, and the judgmental stares that came from people who found both her and Michael wanting. What parent loses track of their child? What school can't keep track of its students and what teacher would ever have let a child out of her sight, knowing her mother could be lurking nearby? If it wasn't what they were thinking, it was what flowed through Julie's mind.

Cam suggested he and Michael would share the room with the twin beds. "Unless you two are…"

Michael intervened. "Julie should take the double. It's got a separate bathroom."

It did, such as it was, with avocado green 1950s fixtures, and limescale-coated showerhead. The metal-framed bed groaned when she sat on the edge of it and ran her hand over the faded yellow quilt. On the wall above the headboard was a poorly painted landscape of Honey Harbour.

She plugged her phone into the charger she'd brought with her and returned to the kitchen, where Michael sat at the table mulling things over in his mind.

"I lied to her, didn't I?" His face paled. "Shit. She already thinks I'm guilty of something."

"What makes you say that?"

"I think I know that woman. The more I looked at the picture, the more I thought she looked familiar. I think she worked in the hospital. Not a nurse, though, maybe an orderly or a cleaner. I didn't mean to lie."

"You made a mistake. There's a difference. And under the circumstances, anyone would. You must be going crazy trying to remember details, worrying about Hope. It's too much."

"She won't see it that way." The look of horror on Michael's face was gut wrenching. He scrubbed at the growth on his chin.

Julie took his hands in hers. "Don't be so hard on yourself. People who are innocent don't remember details because they never expect to have to account for them."

"Yeah, right along with liars have every detail down pat. And you can't deny, I've been keeping a lot of secrets, and DI Allen knows it."

He looked at her then, with such angst she wished there was something she could say to ease his pain. Something to take the weight off his shoulders. Something to bring an iota of levity into the room. But nothing short of seeing Hope walk through the door could do that.

"I just want my daughter back." His head slumped into his hands.

"We'll find her, Michael. We're close. I feel it in my gut. Sirona always says, trust your gut and you'll never go wrong." *Please let this be one of those times Sirona was right.*

"How on earth did Grace get my phone? You don't think Faith gave it to her."

"No, I doubt it. I mean, she wouldn't, would she?"

His eyes widened. "She must have been in our house. It's the only way she could have gotten it."

"Oh Jeez. Michael. That was weeks ago." Julie couldn't help wondering about the trinkets Sirona had found, Joy's earring, Faith's bookmark and the button from Hope's bathing suit. Had Grace taken those things too? She was about to ask Michael if anything else was missing when his phone pinged.

"The police," he said, a smile spreading across his features. "They're sending a picture. They've got something!"

Chapter 32

A rush of adrenaline surged through Julie's body when a pink Barbie backpack with a matching water bottle tucked into the side pocket stared up from the screen. Hope's backpack. There was no mistaking the little charm on the end of the zipper, the one Hope had chosen from the treasure box on the first day of school. She told Julie she'd always wanted a horseshoe because it was a symbol of luck.

Michael dialled the number that had sent the picture, then put the call on speaker.

"This is DI Allen."

"That's hers!" They both shouted at the same time.

"Where did you find it?" Michael said. "Can I...?"

"Fingerprints. Dr. Adams. DNA. You understand? It's evidence."

"Right. Sorry. Where was it found? Is anyone searching the area? Can I help?"

There was a long silence from her end of the phone, followed by a heavy sigh. "The area has been thoroughly searched, Dr. Adams. And given the late hour, midnight, and the storm that has just subsided, it's our belief that Grace has found shelter for the night."

Shelter. Julie thought of the Instagram post by @4vrjs post. "In a shack," she said. "Because that's what the person on social media posted."

"I'm sorry?" DI Allen said.

"I sent your detective Gary, a link. Someone posted one line of the lyrics to Love Shack with a running shoe emoji after it."

"I'll look into that."

"What's the plan for morning?" Michael asked, obviously bolstered by this bit of news. "Can we help the search? What time will you start? Where can we meet?"

"Six o'clock," DI Allen replied. "Same building you were at today. Look, the roadblocks are still in place, we'll have duty officers patrolling the streets all night long, and the AMBER ALERT is going out tonight and again first thing tomorrow. Try not to worry."

At the same moment the call was disconnected, Cam came through the door with pizza and a box of chicken wings. "Found a place open in Waubaushene. Dig in." He set the food on the table and pulled a thick wad of white napkins out of his pocket.

Michael showed him the picture of Hope's backpack DI Allen had sent, and Cam swiped a tear from his eye. "Tomorrow's the day. I can feel it in my bones." He put a slice of pizza on a napkin and handed it to Michael. "Get that in you. You need to keep up your strength for your little girl."

Chapter 33

Julie woke to the sounds of thunder and flashes of distant lightning, sending shockwaves of purple and white through the night sky. She got up and pulled back the curtain of her bedroom window. Everything outside was soaked. Splatters of rainwater covered the windows of Cam's Jeep while puddles pooled in the ruts of the mud-packed driveway.

It was three in the morning, according to her phone, but she knew she wouldn't sleep any longer. She showered, turned her underwear inside out, and dressed in the same clothes she'd been wearing the day before. Towel drying her hair, she went to the kitchen, hoping there was coffee in a cupboard, even instant would do if there was nothing else. But the stench of stale pizza and leftover wings had her nearly retching, though she couldn't say why. She loved both, normally, but last night she'd had no appetite and now the food was upsetting her stomach. She gathered the leftovers, took them to the dumpster at the far end of the parking lot, and tossed it all in. She was about to head out toward the park across from their cabin when she heard a stirring behind her and spun around, arms raised in defense mode.

Michael was several paces back. He raised his hands in surrender. "Don't throw me on the ground again, okay? It's just me."

"Hi you," she said, when he got closer.

"Want company?"

"You can't sleep either?"

He shook his head. Julie didn't say *we should search those cabins*. Michael didn't say, *what do you think about staring over there*. They just looked at each other and went.

Their cabin stood in a cluster of similar ones, a dozen of them, nestled at the end of Minten Road. They were all in darkness, as you'd expect at that hour, and because most were empty, except for the other searchers who'd stayed over. It was off season, nearly November, and very few people came north after Labour Day weekend, unless it was for Christmas, or for winter ice-fishing. So, it was dark, deserted and mostly just a mass of ramshackle buildings, begging for a lick of paint and pots of flowers to give them life.

They crossed over into Port Severn Park, where they came upon a group of homeless people camped around the picnic tables in the pavilion. They stirred at the disturbance of people walking by, and one tall and rather ominous looking man told them to get lost until Julie explained who they were and that they were looking for Hope.

"Ah. Then I'm sorry," he said. He offered them a chunk of bread, undoubtedly stale, but most likely his last morsel of food. Julie thought it was the kindest, most generous offer she'd ever encountered, and it tugged at her heart, knowing that in the depths of his own despair, this man would share what little he had left in the world.

"Thank you," she said, realizing she should have put the pizza and wings to better use. "But we're okay."

"I hope you find her," was the last thing the man said as he went back to his sleeping bag under the picnic table.

They walked two kilometres or more down one side of Lone Pine Road, a long and lonely stretch unlit by streetlights, or even a dull or hazy moon. At least the rain had stopped, though the ground on the shoulders of the road were squishy with damp earth and loose gravel. There was little to see, even with the flashlight on their phones. Eventually, they turned around and went back, passing the cabins, a small group of houses and a few shops closed up for the night, until they reached the town's only Tim Hortons.

"I wonder what time they open," Michael said.

"At five, according to their website." Julie had looked them up on Google. "Only ten minutes to wait."

"This is crazy." Michael slumped against a streetlamp that flooded light over the parking lot. He was near to collapse, his face grey, his eyes distant and cloudy. "What are we thinking? Grace and Hope won't be out here in the open or lying in a ditch at the side of the road. They'll be in a barn or an abandoned house or…"

"Or a church," they both said at once, a tiny speck of hope in their voices.

"We passed one near Port Severn Road when we got here yesterday."

Just as they were about to leave, someone opened the door and called out to them. He wore a Tim Hortons uniform, and a bright Tim Hortons smile. The nametag over his left breast pocket told them his name was Steve, and he was the owner.

"You're the man on the TV," Steve said. "That doctor whose daughter has gone missing. Come in and get a cup of coffee."

"You get the coffee, Julie. I'm going to start walking." Michael gave a little wave of thanks to the man standing in the doorway. Julie could see he was itching to get moving.

"It'll only be a minute," Steve said. "Where are you headed?"

"St. John's Church," Julie told him

"You think she's there?" He fished a set of keys out of his pocket. "Here Take my car. You can bring it back later or I'll walk down. But get some coffee first. Come inside and warm up."

He pulled the door open wider and waved them inside. Behind the counter, he filled two cups with steaming, freshly brewed coffee.

"Sugar?" Then he shook his head. "'Course not, you're a doctor. You wouldn't put that crap in your coffee." He secured lids onto the cups, put two muffins and some cookies into a bag, then nodded toward the rear of the building.

"My car's out back. Good luck."

"Thank you," Michael said, gathering the cups while Julie took the bag of food.

"Honestly. We can't thank you enough," she called over her shoulder, hurrying to keep up with Michael.

They could have run the short distance down the road to the church, if they'd known how close by it was, but if Hope was there and she was tired and hungry and cold, having Steve's vehicle with a good strong heater wasn't a bad thing. They pulled onto the shoulder of the road in front of the church. The parking lot was deserted, which was to be expected given the hour. Julie got out, stepped over a shallow rain-filled ditch, then onto the front lawn of the church-yard. Michael was close behind.

"Do you see that?" Julie pointed to a broken basement window as they got closer to the building. She ran to it and was just bending over for a closer look when a police car pulled up and an officer jumped out.

"Stop! Police!" He raced across the parking lot, his hand already on his comms, mumbling something into it.

"It's okay," Michael said, hands in the air. "I'm the father of the missing girl and this is my friend Julie Wight. We saw the broken window and…"

The cop's eyes flitted between them and the window, apparently assessing the situation, until he decided they might be lying, but they weren't dangerous. "I'll check it out, but I want you two out of the way."

"But…"

"Look!" the cop said as he widened his stance. "You have two choices here. You can get into the back of my cruiser and wait, or I can cuff you both to the railing on the church steps. Which is it going to be?"

They chose to wait in the cruiser, and he agreed to let them have their coffee. Julie didn't need the caffeine now because of the adrenaline rushing through her body. She itched to climb through that window herself, and knowing she couldn't, was agonizing. Their sightlines, though, showed every possible exit Grace could take, and that was at least something.

It was nearly twenty minutes later when a grey sedan pulled up. DI Allen got out of it and tugged her blue raincoat tighter around her, though it couldn't hide the dishevelled hair or the rumpled look of her clothes. She'd been working all night, Julie realized, as the woman made a beeline toward the officer standing guard. It wasn't long before a pickup truck arrived, and a stocky farmer-type of man in green coveralls got out of it and went to the far side of the building. He came back in less than a minute, with DI Allen and the younger officer in tow, as he fumbled with a set of keys on his way to the church door.

"Come on! Come on!" Michael's words echoed inside the cruiser. Julie reached for his hands to steady them, but she was just as anxious as he was. Their eyes were fixed on the door, waiting, watching, praying.

Michael's face was turned to the window, but Julie could see the worry tracing lines across his forehead, his lips moving in silent prayer. She leaned into him, resting her chin on his shoulder while they stared out the window and waited.

Julie's phone pinged in her pocket, and she let go of Michael's hands to see who it was. She had a new follower on Instagram. @4vrjs had followed her back and there was a message.

I'm sorry

I'm sorry. What did that mean? Sorry for doing something, sorry because they didn't recognize her. Was it a question? @vrjs's way of asking who she was. Or was this person sorry because they had a part in Hope's disappearance? She said nothing to Michael but pocketed her phone without responding. It was probably some crackpot anyway, and the last thing she wanted to do was upset him further.

Just when she thought they were both going to burst, DI Allen appeared at the church door, followed by the officer and then the man with the keys. Just the three of them. No one else. DI Allen spoke into her phone while the officer came across the parking lot and opened the door to let them out.

"The window was smashed a couple of weeks ago. Kids playing road hockey," he said. "The church has been waiting for a glazier to replace the glass."

"So, no sign that anyone was in there? Somewhere else, maybe. Sleeping on a pew or…" Michael would have felt better checking it for himself and Julie wanted to as well, but the officer shook his head.

"There are no signs of that at all. I'm sorry. No one has been in through that window."

DI Allen came their way, her eyes filled with reproach. "I thought I told you both to get some rest."

"Would you?" Julie asked, feeling bolder than she had yesterday. "If it was your daughter, would you be able to sleep, or eat dinner, or sit on your hands, unable to do anything?"

The inspector lowered her gaze and shook her head; the first sign of remorse or understanding. "No, I don't expect I would. I'm sorry. I can understand why you wanted to check the church out. But we went through it already. One of the first places we looked." She lifted her face to the night air and sighed. "Storm's over," she said. "Won't be long before we can start searching again. Please, get something to eat, more coffee and then come to the muster point inside. We'll update everyone and we'll regroup into new search teams. You can both help if you want to."

She took two steps toward her car before coming back. "Look, if it's any consolation, I have children of my own, one about Hope's age. I understand how worried you are. I don't know what I'd do if this was my child, but I promise you this. We will find Hope. I won't rest until we do."

Chapter 34

A caravan comprising one pickup truck, a single cruiser, and DI Allen's unmarked grey sedan pulled out of the church lot and turned left.

"Breakfast sandwiches? More coffee?" Julie said when they climbed into Steve's vehicle. "We have to return the guy's car, anyway."

Michael's face was taut, deeper lines than before furrowed his brow, and the circles beneath his eyes were the colour of deadly nightshade. He made a U-turn and followed the other vehicles back toward the town centre.

"Today's the day. That's what Cam said," she reminded him, as the others veered right toward the Municipal building, and they continued toward Tim Horton's.

Michael didn't respond. She knew his eyes were scanning the road ahead, alert to anything that might be a clue. A plastic grocery bag, fluttering in the breeze, caught his attention, and he pulled over to look at it.

"Who has plastic grocery bags anymore," he said, holding it up to show her it was empty, except for the rainwater that had pooled in it. He shook the water off and shoved it in his pocket.

At the Tim Hortons, Michael waited outside while Julie went in to return the keys. She asked for Steve at the counter.

"He's doing a delivery," a woman named Ester told her. Ester's nametag boldly displayed, *assistant manager,* beneath her name. Except for staff, the place was empty, until a car pulled into the drive-through window and another woman appeared out of the back to take the order.

Julie passed her the keys to Steve's car. "Will you please thank him for us? His car is out back, in the same place it was before. It was kind of him to lend it to us."

Ester pocketed the keys with a matronly smile. "A kinder man never walked this earth."

"Everyone here has been kind," Julie said.

"Well, why wouldn't we be?" Ester tutted. "Especially considering what you're going through. Good luck to you, my dear."

Julie smiled. She hadn't realized Ester knew who she was, but then who else would be there at five-thirty on a Wednesday morning when a little girl had gone missing? She found Michael outside staring into the depths of a garbage can, as if he were looking down a wishing well.

"All set?" Julie asked.

Apparently, he wasn't, because he took the plastic bag from his pocket and put it over his hand. Using it like a glove, he reached into the garbage can and withdrew a small pink T-shirt with butterflies on it.

Their eyes met, and they both froze.

"Is it hers?" Julie asked, coming closer.

He blinked hard, forcing back the tears and held it out to her. "I can't look. Can you?"

Protecting any evidence that might be on the shirt, Julie kept her fingers inside the bag as she looked at the tag. She shook her head. "It isn't hers," she said with a sigh. The name Emily was scrawled across it and the shirt was only a size five. Too small, by at least two sizes to be Hope's.

They dropped the shirt back into the bin. Michael stared after it. "For a minute I…"

"I know. Come on. It's nearly six. They'll be starting to search again."

The rim of orange was just visible on the horizon when Julie and Michael arrived on foot at the Municipal building. Inside, a crowd was milling about, gathering Hi-Viz vests, whistles and other things, while waiting for their instructions. DI Allen stood at one end of the hall, a megaphone in one hand, her cellphone in the other, poised at her ear. The look on her face suggested there was more good news.

"We have a good lead," she said when Julie and Michael stopped beside her. "A woman and a little girl have crossed through someone's property. The girl was wearing a light blue raincoat, and the woman was in a brown hoodie." She handed the megaphone to the officer standing next to her, then wagged a finger in Michael and Julie's direction. "You can ride with me unless you want to wait here."

Chapter 35

In all the years Julie had been teaching, there was nothing more endearing to her than a child's face when they met their parents. All the things Michael had named his children for, Joy, Faith and Hope, were reflected in their faces, and their reward was the approving look that said, *well done, I'm so proud of you.*

She had seen those looks between Michael and his girls, and something more than that. Maybe he loved a little more, tried a little harder, because he was filling the role of two parents, or maybe they craved his love and understanding more than most, for the same reason. Whatever the source of the bond between them, it was both palpable and enviable. Julie felt it oozing from Michael, then, as they headed down the road, in the back of DI Allen's car. The same officer they'd met at the church earlier occupied the front passenger seat. Julie thought it odd that they didn't even know his name, but she wasn't about to ask. Anticipation was high. Nerves were on edge. Tension hung over them like a shroud.

Michael reached for her hand and their eyes met. This is it, she thought. This is when father and daughter will be reunited and end this agonizing journey. Hope would not be one of the taken children who never made it home again. Her father and sisters would not have to live the rest of their lives wondering if she was still out there somewhere. Most of all, this would end well. She squeezed Michael's hand. It'll be alright. We'll find her. Today is the day. But there was doubt in Michael's face she couldn't erase. There was only one person who could.

John Gilmore lived on the edge of Port Severn's town limits, along the road toward Honey Harbour, in a house that probably should have been condemned years ago. He was close to ninety, in a wheelchair and, according to the officer next to DI Allen, got Meals on Wheels, even *way out here in the sticks.* As they pulled up alongside his home and got out of the car, the front door opened, and John rolled out onto his rickety front porch.

"They must have spent the night in my shack," he said, jerking a crooked thumb toward the backyard.

The word shack made Julie's stomach curl. *Love shack, a little old place where we can get together…*

DI Allen didn't have to tell the officer to look. He was already on his way when she climbed the steps and spoke to John.

"Tell us what you saw, please, sir."

"Just what I told the person on the phone. I get myself into my chair every morning and sit at the window until the nurse comes. So, I was watching, you see. I thought it was two girls at first until I saw the face. It was a woman, older, thirties or even forties. But that little one, the wee lass, she looked back at me and waved. Until the woman tugged on her arm and pulled her off down the road."

"And you're certain it was Hope?" DI Allen pulled a photograph out of her pocket. "This girl."

"Yep. That's her. The face of an angel," he said. He cast a look over her shoulder to where Julie and Michael were waiting. "Is she yours?" he called out.

"My daughter. Yes," Michael said, taking a step closer.

"Well, you shudda kept a better eye on her." He shook a crocked arthritic finger at them and Julie squeezed Michael's hand.

"He doesn't know," she reminded him, half under her breath.

John Gilmore did an about turn in his wheelchair and went back inside, slamming the door behind him. DI Allen followed him, opening the door again. "Mr. Gilmore?" They heard her say.

"He's right," Michael said. "I shouldn't have let her out of my sight."

"If anyone is to blame, it's us, the school system. We let her down. You…" Julie hiccupped as the words caught in her throat and tears welled in her eyes. "I should have been…"

"Don't," he said, taking her other hand too. "Don't you dare fall apart on me now. I can't do this on my own. There's only one person to blame here, and that's Grace and no one else. She knew what she was doing. She's responsible. She…" He pulled her into his arms. "Don't Julie. We have to keep it together. We're close now. So very close."

She nodded into his shoulder, knowing he was right. The backpack. John Gilmore. The shack someone had tried to warn them about. Hope was here. It was just a matter of time.

"Let's find out what's next," Julie suggested, wiping tears away.

A van had pulled up, and an officer got out of it. He slid open a side door and five people spilled out and stood in John Gilmore's driveway.

The driver held up a small box and pulled a whistle out of it. "Take one of these each and stay on the road, so we don't mix up your footprints with theirs. If you spot a place where you think they might have gone off the road, let us know. If you find anything, even if you think it's not related, shout out FIND. Or blow those whistles. Got it? Any questions?"

Julie had a million and she expect Michael did too, but nothing this man could answer. They collected whistles and followed the others, spreading wide across the road to cover the shoulders on both sides. It seemed frustratingly slow work, given the pace they walked. Grace and Hope already had a half hour head start, at least, and they would be running while the group inched its way down a long, paved road.

They hadn't gone more than a hundred feet when someone up ahead shouted "FIND!" and everyone hurried to catch up with him.

"There," a small thin man with a sharp jaw said, pointing to a place in a hedge with broken branches. The ground around it was slightly trampled. "Might have gone through there."

The grass was wet and the ground soggy after last night's storm, but the officer led Michael, Julie, and the man who'd spotted the opening through it while the others carried on down the road.

"Look for anything. Torn fabric, hair caught on a branch, anything to verify this was the direction they came."

They focused on the ground, examined the hedge three feet on either side of the trampled opening, and eventually, when they found nothing more, they moved forward, away from the hedge along a strip of weedy grass, until Michael found something. They'd come to a low garden fence, the kind meant to keep the rabbits from eating all the vegetables and just on the other side of it, he stopped.

"Here!" he shouted. "FIND! I mean FIND."

Instantly, the officer in charge hurried over and, extracting a pair of gloves from his pocket, he stooped to pick up a hair clip, a bobby pin type with a purple butterfly on the end. Julie recognized it from brushing Hope's hair at bedtime, the night Michael had gone to Toronto. She'd put them on Hope's dresser right next to the little white jewellery box with the ballerina that twirled and played Greensleeves.

The officer pulled a clear plastic bag out of his pocket and dropped the pin into it.

"We need to get dogs in here," Michael cried anxiously. "Why aren't we using tracking dogs?"

"We were, but after the storm..." The officer's eyes fixed on Michael's for less than a minute and then with a small nod, he spoke into his comms on his shoulder, while signalling for them to back out of the way and make room for the dogs.

In less than five minutes, a van arrived carrying two tracking German Shepherds. They were beautiful dogs, with thick fur, brilliant blue eyes, and their black noses twitching the minute they got out of the van. They sat obediently while their handlers put their leads on them and waved Hope's cardigan. It must have come from her backpack, Julie realized. Once the dogs got the scent, there was no holding them back. Noses to the ground, they sniffed and sniffed and then took off over the rabbit fence, across the backyard, behind a small bungalow and down a long driveway.

The rest of the group caught up to them, crossed over a road, and followed them into a field. On the other side of it, they came to another road where the handlers stopped while the dogs sniffed and turned and sniffed some more. One of them picked up a scent, and they were gone down a shallow embankment and on through a field of corn stubble.

At the far side of that field they came to a main road, one with yellow lines on the shoulders and the dotted line down the middle. The dogs stopped and began circling an area near a hydro pole. Everyone else stopped too, breathless now. Julie couldn't help thinking this was nothing compared to her daily 9K runs, so why was she out of breath?

The sun was barely up, casting an orange glow over the road and the empty field on the other side plowed up, ready for fall planting. It offered nowhere for a woman and her child to hide and apparently no footprints and no scents, either.

"Why are we stopping?" Michael asked one of the handlers. "Have they found something?"

The handler held a library book between his gloved fingers. It was a thin chapter book which Julie recognized right away as one of the Dragon Master series. When he opened to reveal the Baysville Public Library stamp inside it, Michael let out a groan of despair.

"We'll keep searching this area," the handler shouted.

Julie started to move too, but Michael held her back and nodded upwards at the pole. She followed his gaze and as his arms went around her and his body slumped against hers, he said, "It's a friggin' bus stop, Julie. They got on a god dammed bus!"

Chapter 36

It only took a minute to call up the local bus schedule on her phone. There was only one bus out of Port Severn, and it left from the Esso Station at 10:40 every morning. When Julie showed it to the handler, he explained that where they stood was one stop before the town centre.

"But it's only just past nine so they couldn't have gotten on a bus," she said.

The dogs were sniffing the area around the bus stop sign, circling, noses to the ground, then looking up the road toward town. There wasn't a single car on the road, not even a delivery truck coming through. She had to remind herself that they were miles from the nearest major city. Beautiful country for camping, cottage life, or going on a retreat, but it wasn't exactly a booming metropolis.

"This is where the trail ends," the other handler said.

"They must have gotten a ride here," someone suggested.

"So, they were hitching or…" someone else said.

Angry tears filled Julie's eyes as she felt Michael's arms around her, pulling her into his exhausted, sleep deprived body. They stood for a moment, as his breath went from ragged and gasping to a slow, steady rhythm.

"She's always just one step ahead of us," he said.

His words were barely out when Julie's phone pinged. Together they looked down at the screen, surprised to see it was an Instagram message from @4vrjs.

Esso station park bench

"This is the same person who send the Love Shack lyric post," Julie said. "It's the third message they've sent. What if Grace had an accomplice, and that person is trying to help us?"

She showed the handler the message, and he got onto his phone right away. It was seconds later when he came back and asked, "Do either of you know a Rebecca Vickers?"

Michael's eyebrows shot up. "She's a patient of mine."

"And a teacher at our school. Why do you ask?"

"A few moments ago, a car registered to her went through the drive through at Tim Hortons. The woman at the window said she was sure someone was in the backseat, under a sleeping bag, and when the driver seemed nervous, she tried to stall her, but the woman took off. She didn't even wait to get her food."

Julie racked her brain, summoning details of what she knew about Rebecca. She was just a teacher. A flirt, yes, who'd been attracted to Michael enough to worm her way up to Julie's for pizza and drinks and to sign on as a patient. But how did she connect to Grace? Or had someone else stolen Rebecca's car and picked Grace up? Julie had no answers except that someone was obviously trying to help.

"Whoever, @4vrjs is, they're trying to help," she said. "Is anyone checking out their message?"

"We've sent someone to the Esso station," the officer said.

"So, why are we standing here?" Julie asked just as a police van pulled up beside them and the driver hopped out.

"DI Allen has requested the two of you go back to the Municipal Office," he said, opening the sliding door for them.

Julie climbed into the van and Michael got in beside her. "We're close, Michael. So close. They'll get her."

Inside Operation Find Hope, there was an air of excitement hovering. People seemed more casual, and their stares when Julie and Michael entered the large hall were less accusatory and much more sympathetic. Like yesterday, there were donuts and breakfast wraps, muffins and bagels, all courtesy, from Steve at Tim Hortons.

Cam handed Julie and Michael cups of coffee, while Julie blinked hard to fight off a flood of tears as a rush of cars pulled into the graveled parking lot. Michael leaned close, and they both held their breath while outside the building, car doors slammed, footsteps crunched across the gravel, up the steps to the front door of the building and then…

Julie fixed her eyes on the door, as the same man who'd found the trampled bit of hedge called out. "They're back!" Then he turned to Michael and smiled.

Chapter 37

Six officers flanked DI Allen and four more followed behind. They came across the room and stopped just a few feet away from Michael. And then, like Moses parting the waters of the Red Sea, they all stepped aside. And there she was.

Hope.

Her face beamed when she saw her father, her arms instantly reaching out to him. "Daddy!" she shrieked as he lifted her up and her arms went around his neck. "I missed you."

Everything after that was a blur. Tears streamed down Julie's face as Hope reached out and pulled her into their hug. She felt Michael's arm around her waist, tight as if he was holding on for dear life. His body shook with sobs. His head bent; face buried in Hope's hair. They stood for a long time, or maybe it was only minutes, before DI Allen ushered them into the room down the hall, where they'd been just yesterday, away from the celebrating crowd.

"We've been keeping the press outside the town limits, but we're going to let them in now," she told them. "We'll give them a statement and in a while you can speak to them." She kept her voice low, not wanting Hope to hear what she had to say next. "There's a specialist on her way to talk to Hope. She'll know how to ask all the right questions, while nor alarming Hope."

On the surface, she seemed to be the same little girl, but who knew what her mother had told her or what she had been through? Physically, there were no marks, or cuts or bruises, but a woman capable of the things Michael had described, who was off her meds, could hurt anyone, even her own child.

Julie wasn't part of the group who heard Hope's version of the events. She wasn't family, and she wasn't a doctor. Though Michael protested and asked if she could be present, they shook their heads and showed her the door.

"I'll go to the cabin and get our things," she told him and went to find Cam. Like just about everyone else, he was in the main room, eating a donut and slurping back a large double, double. He poured her a cup of coffee.

"You look like shit," he said, a knowing grin spreading across his face as he handed it to her.

"Likewise," she said, taking a sip.

"I'm glad this ended well," he said. "I can't imagine what the doc has been going through. I must have been…"

"Hell," she finished. "It's been pure and utter hell and I wouldn't wish this on my worst enemy." She set her cup on the table, unfinished. "I told Michael we'd get our things from the cabin. Can we stop at a store first?" she asked. "Somewhere I can get some clothes?"

"Not much chance of that around here," Cam said. "What do you need? I've got a couple of bags of things in the back of my Jeep. I was going to take them to a second hand shop. It's my ex's stuff. It was cluttering up a closet."

"That'll do," Julie said, trying to remember what size Cam's ex might have been. It didn't really matter. She'd make something work.

At the cabin, Julie showered, gave up on the idea of turning her underwear outside in and tossed it into the garbage. Cam's bag of leftovers from his ex-wife held a sweatshirt that was roomy, but manageable, and a pair of yoga pants with a string in the waist she could tighten.

"You know, if you want to get rid of this stuff, there's a group of homeless people living in the park across from here. I'm sure some of the women wouldn't mind having these."

"Fine by me," Cam said.

They drove to the other side of the park and found the same old man who'd offered them bread earlier that morning. When Julie told him Hope had been found, he smiled.

"Ah. That's good then. And your friend. Is he alright?"

"He is now," she told him. "This is another friend of mine. Cam has some clothes he'd like to offer to your group. They were his wife's, but she doesn't need them anymore."

"Zat so?" The man eyed Cam up and down. "Well, I'm sure the girls would take kindly to going through them. Thank you. We'll pass along what we can't use."

And there it was, the unbelievable, undisputable, generosity of people who had nothing to give, who were willing to be generous, anyway. Julie's heart thumped in her chest as she held out her arms to him.

"I'd really like to give you a hug, if that's okay."

He grinned, a half-hearted effort with one side of his mouth twisting up into a smile, and then he wrapped his long arms around her.

"Tell you what," he said, before he let go again. "The girls use the public washroom over at Willow Lanes Trailer Park. It's on the other side of the highway. They just came back and said there was a woman there. A small woman, sitting on the floor who didn't look too good, like she was on something, maybe."

"Grace?" Julie flashed a look at Cam.

"I know where that is," he said. "I was there with a crew yesterday. Come on."

"Thank you," she told the old man. "Thank you for everything."

"Aren't you going to call the cops?" Cam said as they sped toward the trailer park.

"Let's see if it's her first. It could be anyone. It doesn't really make sense though, for her to leave Hope on a bench, and then stick around. She'd have gone with Rebecca, wouldn't she, or whoever it was that was driving the car?"

"If the woman is off her head, maybe her friend ditched her."

"And then took Hope to the park bench at the Esso station? But why? Why not just take her to the police?"

"She's an accomplice, Julie. She'd be in huge trouble."

"She still is, if they catch her."

The park was closed for the season, but it wasn't difficult for Cam to maneuver the Jeep around the barricade and drive in through the front gates. It was almost as if the owners had left the place available so the local homeless people could use the facilities.

They found the washroom and showers in a low building near the main entrance. While Cam waited at the door, Julie went inside. It had all the embodiment of a typical campground rest room with a cement floor, painted cinderblock walls, shadeless hanging bulbs, some of them working, most not. It also had the stench of old urine, recent bowel movements and something else that might have been air freshener or ancient and stale perfume.

Six cracked and battered sinks lined one wall, taps dripping at varying degrees of flow, one of them overflowing onto the floor, leaving a stream of water curling toward the central drain. A toilet flushed at the opposite end of the room, where there were two rows of cubicles, one on the left, the other on the right. The flush came from the left.

Later, when this was all over, Julie would take time to think about what she had done, to consider the consequences and the reason she had acted so hastily. It didn't occur to her then, that there was a deep need burrowing inside her to right the wrongs that she felt responsible for, the negligence John Gilmore had spoken of, the not taking care of the children in her charge. But she would do this later.

"Hello? Is someone here?" she called out, inching her way down the length of the cubicles, swinging doors as she went. The clanging of metal against metal announced her as the doors crashed into the walls behind. The sounds echoed through the cavernous building, and out the slots in the roof, meant to dispel the stench. They weren't working, but that was the least of Julie's worries, because from the last cubicle she heard a faint cough, and then the click of metal sliding, the unlocking of the last door of the last cubicle. As it opened, almost in slow motion, she saw a foot first, a dark blue generically branded running shoe, then a hand pushed the door open further, and a body emerged.

It was Grace.

In her hand, poised high in the air to strike, was a knife. A big, huge, butcher knife. The blade caught a glimmer of light from a swinging bulb overhead. It looked sharp. Sharp enough to do some serious damage. Julie clenched her fists and relaxed her jaw.

"Get back," Grace ordered. "Get back or I'll cut you."

Heart thumping. Blood rushing. Head throbbing. Fear-laced adrenaline kicked in as Julie focused on the knife. She hadn't expected Grace to be carrying a weapon, nor had she expected her to be as strong as she looked, or as wild. Grace's eyes darted toward the door, then landed squarely on Julie's chest. Given the chance, she would aim for the heart. Julie was sure of that.

"I'm sure you don't want to do that," Julie said, taking a step back and raising her hands in surrender. "I'm not here to harm you." Her eyes flashed to the bank of cubicles, where a door was still swinging after she'd smacked it open.

Grace's eyes were big as saucers, pupils dilated so that her irises were barely visible. Her matted hair was dull, in desperate need of washing, and her clothes were tattered and soiled. She was a mess, both inside and out.

Julie took a single step forward, noting the tiny tremble in the hand that held the knife. Grace winced, clenched her jaw, and attempted to steady her hand as Julie took one more step forward.

"Hello Grace."

Another step.

They were fewer than six steps apart, two more, and Julie would be close enough to knock the knife out of Grace's hand. Or could she? She'd only practiced those moves in kickboxing class, with a friend holding a sponge brick. But this wasn't class, and that knife definitely was not made of sponge. Julie steeled herself and fixed her gaze on Grace's eyes. Hope's eyes. Faith's eyes. But not Joy's. Joy had Michael's eyes.

Grace's upper lip curled. "I know who you are. She told me all about you. Julie Wight."

The name slid out of her mouth like a skate blade sliding over fresh ice. A smooth, even stroke, a tone so sharp beneath her words, it cut right into Julie's soul. Game on, Grace, she thought. Make your move.

Julie took another step.

Concentrate. Mask the fear roiling in your belly.

Her stomach churned and gurgled as Grace sniffed, turning her nose up like a wild animal, catching a fresh scent in the air. She lifted a hand to her throat as if the smell had disgusted her. Something in that gesture made Julie stop and take a breath. It was familiar, something she'd seen before from someone else. In the staffroom, she realized. It was that day Vince had eaten the stinky salmon sandwiches and Rebecca had said…

Julie gasped out loud. Rebecca had a sister. She had called her G.G.

It came like a slap in the face as she realized it was Rebecca she'd seen in Grace's car and Rebecca, who must have been helping her gain access to the girls all along. She'd probably told Grace where to find them. Of course, she'd been helping Grace. But why had she dumped her here? Was she planning to come back and pick her up?

And who was @4vrjs?

Julie's eyes drank in every detail of Grace's face, every tiny freckle, which, on Hope, looked cute and girlish, but on Grace seemed angry and mean. There was something of Rebecca there, too. The cut of her jaw, the high cheekbones.

Grace matched Julie's squint, and then she nodded. "Worked it out now, haven't ya?" she said. "I knew you were clever. Much smarter than that idiot husband of mine."

She was wavering, ever so slightly, as if the knife were becoming too heavy. Another burden. Too much to bear. Yet her face showed no sign of hesitation. She would use the knife if she felt threatened. So Julie tried a different tactic.

"You can put that down. I'm not here to hurt you. I just…"

And then an odd thing happened. A single tear welled in Grace's eye and slid down her right cheek. It was the first sign she might be crumbling.

Another step.

"You can't have my girls!" Grace screamed suddenly, her words bouncing off the cinderblock. "Rachel and Maddie and Zoe are mine!"

Then, in a rush, Grace stepped forward, thrusting the knife like a madwoman, stabbing the empty air.

With no time to think, Julie simply reacted. She raised her left arm to block, catching Grace's forearm, while her right hand, palm open, slapped flat and hard into her chest. The forward motion sent Grace slamming into the wall behind her as the knife clattered to the floor. Julie kicked it out of harm's way and stood over her.

"I'm not trying to take your girls."

"Huh!" Grace grunted, looking up at her. She raised herself to her knees and flopped back against the wall and sat down on the floor. Slowly, she worked the thoughts of her head and put them into words. Grace looked up at Julie and sneered.

"You think I don't know about you and him? I've seen the two of you. Running every day. He likes that, doesn't he? Someone to run with him, listen to all his whining about how the health system has gone to hell. I've watched the two of you all the nights on the dock, drinking wine, laughing." Grace's face twisted upward, and she raised a finger. "You've got a great laugh, Julie Wight. The kind he likes. Sultry and patronizing, lapping up every word he says."

Julie found it hard to argue with Grace. She was right. That's exactly how it would have looked to anyone on the outside if they'd been spying on her and Michael.

"Look," Grace said, after a while, her tone negotiating. "I honestly don't give a fig what he does. But those girls are mine and you're not getting them."

Julie kept her eyes trained on Grace's. "Maybe if you got your life together, you could see your girls more often. If that's what you really want."

Sirens, shrill and growing louder, filled the air and Grace shook her head. "I should have known you'd called the cops."

"I didn't. But I'm not sorry they're here. You need help Grace. Maybe if you…"

Grace's head jerked at the sound of voices outside.

Pounding on the door. "Police! Hands in the air." The door flew open, and Julie stepped away from Grace, hands in surrender, high above her head.

It didn't take a genius to figure out which of them was the one they needed to arrest. Two female officers cuffed Grace, recited her rights and marched her toward the door. On her way past Julie, Grace fixed her with an icy stare and then worked up a mouthful of stale spit. She let it fly, landing it on Julie's cheek. Julie didn't blink as the spit slid down her face and landed on Cam's ex-wife's sweatshirt.

"You haven't seen the last of me," Grace hissed as she was pulled toward the door.

When the door closed behind them, all the adrenaline rushed out of Julie's body, along with her resolve, and her breakfast. She ran for a cubicle, hurled into the toilet and came out swiping her mouth on her sleeve. This sweatshirt was going in the garbage when she got home.

"Not a smart move," DI Allen said, fishing a pair of blue disposable gloves out of her pocket. "You could have been killed or seriously injured." She stooped to pick up the knife with a two fingered grip.

"There's something I need to tell you," Julie said.

Her brows raised in question. "Go on."

"Grace's accomplice, Rebecca, the one who was driving the car, is her sister."

"We know. But no more heroics, Miss Wight. We'll take it from here."

Cam was waiting outside, hands shoved deep in his pockets, a sheepish expression on his face. "Sorry. I thought the police should know."

"You were right to call. I was a fool. I don't know what I was thinking."

He held the door open for her, but before Julie got in he pulled her into his arms. "You did a very brave thing in there," he said.

"How do you know what I did?"

His head tilted to one side. "You didn't think I was going to let you go it alone, did you? I just kept out of sight. But I was there, in case you needed me." He pulled her away to look at her. "Are you sure you're okay?"

"I will be. But that was either pretty brave or pretty stupid."

He put both hands on her shoulders and looked her straight in the eye, with a concerned stare in his violet eyes. Eyes she was attracted to once. Eyes that smiled even when he wasn't. Eyes that said there was more to Cam than most people realized.

"Brave," he said, his finger lifting her chin. "Soldier-level brave and I'm proud of you."

"If you say so," she said with a half grin. "Now, if you're finished lying to me, can we go?"

He handed her up into the passenger seat, then climbed in behind the wheel and, just as he started the engine, he gave a funny little smirk. "I have a confession to make. You know I had a huge crush on you back in the day?" She grinned. "Well, now I've got an even bigger one."

Chapter 38

Back at the Municipal Office Building, Julie learned that Hope had been asking for her and that she was finally allowed into the room where Hope and Michael were. They were seated at the table. Hope was colouring; a box of markers, pencil crayons and reams of blank paper lay in front of her.

Julie's first instinct was to go to her, to hug her and hold her tight, tell her she would always be there for her, but it would be too much. For herself and for Hope. Julie had to take a step back from their connection and remember the psychologist's words before she let her go into the room.

"Hope," she'd said. "Had no idea of the danger she'd been in. Her mother had made it a game, an adventure and had promised she would see her Daddy and her sisters again soon. To show Hope, our fears just might trigger something deep inside and set off a PTSD reaction in her."

Julie understood completely and had thanked her for helping Hope.

Coming into the room now, Hope looked up from the picture she was colouring. "Hi Julie. Want to see what I made?"

"Of course I do." Julie pulled out a chair next to Hope and sat down.

"I missed two days of school, so I wanted to catch up on my family tree. See, I've drawn all of us. Daddy, Joy, Faith and me."

"Lovely," Julie said. "And who's this, beside your Dad? Is that Mum?"

Hope looked up at her, a matter-of-fact look on her face. "No silly, that's you."

"Me?"

"Of course. Because you're part of our family now."

"Oh, no. I'm just your teacher. A friend, sure, but…"

"Uh, uh," Hope insisted, putting her arms around Julie's neck and holding on tight. "You're supposed to be my Mum."

Chapter 39

On the drive home, Hope curled up in Julie's arms, in the back seat of Cam's car, and was asleep in minutes. Michael rode shotgun. Though he looked about ready to collapse from exhaustion, he'd been texting Joy to let her know they were on their way and to warn her about what the psychologist had said. Hope believed she'd been on an adventure. She'd gone to Boston Pizza where she was allowed to choose any toppings she wanted. She'd had ice cream for dessert, and she had a new pair of running shoes. For now, it was vital to keep fear and talk of kidnapping, or a crime out of the picture, and everyone had to be on board with that.

When they arrived at Michael's cottage, and unfolded themselves from Cam's jeep, Joy and Faith ran to hug their sister.

"It's so good to be home," Hope said, taking each of her sister's hands.

"We've got something to show you," Faith said as they all went inside.

"Tada!" Joy pulled down a white sheet that had been hiding a row of four outfits on hangers hanging from the doorframe between the living room and dining room.

"Hallowe'en costumes!" Hope cried.

Joy lifted them down one by one. "Hope you'll be Wednesday. Dad will be Gomez. Of course. Faith wants to be Grandmama and I'm going to be Lurch."

"We just need Morticia," Faith said, pushing a long black wig into Julie's hands. "Everyone has a black dress, right?"

"The Addams Family. It's prefect." Hope was dancing around the room, holding her Wednesday costume next to her body. "Yes. Yes. Be Morticia, Julie. Please say yes, Julie. Please be Morticia."

With all four of them looking at her, prodding, and insisting, it was impossible for Julie to say no. "I think I can come up with something Morticia-like from my closet."

So, after Hope was tucked into bed and everyone had breathed a huge sigh of relief, Julie went home for a shower and food and a good stiff shot of whisky to calm her nerves.

It was much later that night, the sky purple after a breathtaking sunset, a waxing moon high over the lake, when she looked out and saw Michael sitting on the dock. He was alone, in a Muskoka chair, with his back to her and she thought at first he was sleeping, until he reached down and filled his wineglass from a bottle beside his chair. He turned back as if he sensed her looking his way and tipped the bottle up in a *join me for a drink* gesture. She grabbed a warm shawl and went to join him.

By the time she'd made her way down her steps, he'd already pulled another chair alongside his.

"Beautiful night for the end of October," she said, settling in next to him.

"The best." He handed her a glass and poured wine into it.

"Do you always bring two glasses out when you come to drink on the dock?" she asked.

"I had a hunch you might drop by."

"Did you?"

"Kind of."

"And if I hadn't?"

"I'd have taken the glass inside and put it back in the cupboard, but…"

"But?"

"But I would have been very disappointed and very lonely."

He reached for her hand, caressing the back of it with his thumb, then he drew it up to his lips and kissed it. "I'm so sorry," he said. "I should have told you everything much sooner. I should have been open and honest and…"

"No. You shouldn't have. You should never have to tell anyone anything unless you want to. Okay, the cops sometimes need to know things, but not me or anyone else." She took a breath. "I should have trusted you. I should have trusted and respected your right to say or not say anything."

"I thought I was protecting the girls, but in the end, it did more harm than good. So many things might have been different if I'd been honest from the beginning, with the girls and with you. And I'm afraid I've created a Grand Canyon size rift between us. I want to make it up to you. If you'll let me."

"What's done is done," she said, avoiding the subject he'd opened. "The police have Rebecca and Grace in custody. You had no idea she had a living sister?"

"There was never anyone else around. What an idiot I've been."

"No, you haven't. You've been duped, like millions of others in the past. I don't think you stood a chance. Rebecca set you up. She was on the selection committee for the new doctor. She bragged about how it would help her get to know people in the community, give her a purpose and all that. I just thought she was looking for men to date. But think about it, if she had an influence on that committee, she probably pushed for you to get the job."

"And Mia Sanders?" He asked. "I wonder what her story was?"

"I suppose if they were cellmates, Grace might have had something on her. Maybe she bribed Mia into helping her."

"Did you really knock that knife out of Grace's hand?" he asked in admiration. "Cam told me," he added.

"Cam should have kept his mouth shut about that. It was stupid. I should never have gone in there."

"But he was there, just in case."

"Yes, but I didn't know it at the time." Julie blinked hard, remembering the look on Grace's face, the knife held high in the air, ready to strike. "Was she really like that at home?"

"Not always. There were good times, too. Before."

His voice drifted and, in his silence, Julie saw a reckoning come over his face. When he turned to her, she felt the heat of his gaze penetrating, digging deep into her soul as he cocked his head to one.

"Julie, is there anything going on between you and Cam, because if there is, I…"

"Me and Cam? Gosh no. He's a little too professor-like for me."

"That's rich, coming from a teacher."

"He's, you know, old and stuffy, and he wears cardigans with patches on the elbows." She shook her head. "Not my type at all." Although he had been once. She held back a grin. "But Cam will always be a good friend."

He said nothing for a moment, but stared at her until she couldn't bear the intensity of his gaze. What wasn't he saying? What lay hidden beneath that oh so alluring smile?

"What is it?" she asked. "I get the sense you want to say something, but…"

"Alright. As long as I'm turning over a new leaf in the honesty department, I need to tell you what went through my mind when Cam told me what you'd done."

"Go on," she urged, when it seemed he might reconsider.

"I don't know. It's stupid really," he said.

"Try me."

"Well, my mind went through a huge gamut of things like, if you could do that, were you capable of other things? More intense, more physical and if you were, had you been the one who'd…" He laughed. "It's absurd. So ridiculous, I can't even say it."

"Say it. Was I the one who…?"

"No. I can't. I was exhausted. Overwhelmed. Not thinking clearly."

"Michael. Tell me."

He squirmed in his chair, then turned to face her. "Fine. Just for a fleeting moment, I thought you might be responsible for Mia Sanders' death."

Julie burst out laughing. "That is not at all what I thought you were going to say. Of course, I'm not. I couldn't kill anyone, any more than you could. Honestly, until now I'd only done that move in a class with a friend and a lot of giggling and a ton of missed steps."

"Well, whatever you did and however you did it, thank you." His words were throaty and scratchy from exhaustion, and as the trees whispered overhead, and a shiver of the coming cold of November raced up Julie's spine, she decided it was time to call it a night.

"It's getting late," she said, watching Michael's face in the dim light shining down from the porch. "And I still have to sort out a costume for tomorrow night." He nodded and let go of her hand. "You should get some sleep, too. It's over now. Everyone is fine, home in their beds. Safe and sound."

Michael nodded again but kept his gaze out over the water. "I just want to sit here a while longer."

"Okay. Night then."

She felt his eyes follow her across the hundred or so, yards between their cottages. She valued the tranquillity of this place, the serenity of living alone, of her only neighbour being Sirona, a couple of hundred yards away, who kept mostly to herself. She'd been living like this since Eddy left and until that exact moment, Julie had liked it. Now, this walk, alone, to her empty and cold cottage seemed the loneliest walk of her life. Michael came with a lot of complications she didn't need or want and yet, she was having a hard time thinking of what life would be like ten months from now when his lease was up.

At the bottom step of the deck, she turned and found he was still watching her. She smiled, sure he couldn't see it from that far away. But he gave a little wave of his hand and though she couldn't see his face, Julie knew he was smiling too.

The heat of the shower cascading down her body felt wonderful. Julie lingered there a long time, enjoying the warmth, wrapping herself in the delicious pleasure, relishing the feeling of clean skin, clean hair, clean body. But when she closed her eyes, to let the water run over her face, she was there again, in that dingy, smelly, campground washroom, facing Grace, seeing the knife coming at her, in slow motion this time, like in the movies. She wanted to scream, to let out all the anger, the frustration, the fear, but sounds carried. A snapping twig could echo like cannon fire across the lake on any given day, and Julie didn't want to alarm anyone. So, she sank to the floor of the shower and let the hot water do its work while she sobbed away the tension. When the water ran cold, Julie had nothing left. No strength, no emotion, no thoughts. She reached up and shut off the taps.

She pulled on a pair of pjs, wrapped a towel around her head, and went to the kitchen to make a cup of tea. There was a book on her night table which might make her drowsy enough to fall asleep and keep her from reliving those moments. If it didn't, she had Sirona's *sleepy time* tincture she'd used when Eddy left her. It had worked then, no reason it wouldn't work now.

She switched out all the lights and double checked that the doors were locked. She was halfway up the stairs when she realized she didn't want to be alone. She wasn't afraid, wasn't worried that anyone was still lurking around the property. She just didn't want to be alone.

"Michael?" She said when he opened the inside door.

He looked at her from the other side of the screen. "What's wrong?"

"God, this is going to sound really childish, but…"

"What is it?" He opened the door wider and pulled her inside.

"I just… I just don't want to be alone tonight," she finally blurted out.

"Is that all? You had me so worried. I thought… Well, never mind what I thought. Sure, come in."

As she stepped inside the door and their eyes met, Julie's pulse quickened. "I'm sorry, Michael, shouldn't have come. This was…"

He reached for her hand. "Please," he whispered. "Just lay down with me. Clothes on. No funny stuff."

She grinned. "Sorry, I can't help it. Funny stuff? Are we twelve?"

He grinned too. "Okay, but you know what I mean. I just…"

She stepped closer and circled his neck with her arms, then took a long breath. "I kind of like the funny stuff."

A wide grin spread across his face, and he leaned in to kiss her—a long, slow, deep, inviting promise of a kiss.

When they lay together in Michael's bed, Julie took a slow deep breath filled with the scent of him, as he took her in his arms. His kisses filled her with desire and she yearned for his hands to caress her skin, his breath to warm her neck and his body to mold with hers. And when the funny stuff was over and they lay together, panting and smiling and staring up at the ceiling, Julie felt something she'd never felt before. She felt content.

Chapter 40

Except for perhaps Christmas, there was nothing more fun than Hallowe'en in Julie's book. You could even take the scary parts out of it and just get dressed up, collect sweets and have a party and it would still be as much fun.

They walked together to Annie's Lodge, with Lurch and Grandmama leading the way. Wednesday held Gomez's hand, and he held Morticia's as they made their way through the woods, around Felicity and Ben's place and on to Annie's lodge.

Annie and Joe had outdone themselves turning the lodge into a haunted house with pumpkins lining both sides of the porch steps, fake spiderwebs everywhere, ghosts and ghouls hanging from the ceiling, recorded noises and music oozing from speakers both inside and out, creaking doors, and evil, cackling laughter. They played all the music favourites like Monster Mash, Witchy Woman and everyone all danced to Michael Jackson's Thriller.

The Hewitt family was dressed as gangsters. Annie and Joe were Bonnie and Clyde and Ali, Noah and Ryder, were like mini versions of the same. Felicity and Ben were Fred and Wilma Flintstone and Gwen and Turtle Ted came as Teenage Mutant Ninja Turtles. What else would they be?

There was apple-bobbing, a life-size Snakes and Ladders game, a blindfolded 'tunnel of death', with things you stuck your hands into, or sniffed or swished in a cup, all of which were just creepy enough to be scary and just funny enough to make everyone laugh. It was the most fun Julie had had in ages, probably because for the first time in weeks, she felt she could relax.

For Julie, being there with Michael and the girls, among their friends, felt both odd and comfortable at the same time. Now that the truth was out, it seemed as if Michael was the man he would have been, if he'd never had to lie or keep secrets.

It would have been easy to slip into a comfortable routine of work, home and something close to dating, but something lingered in the back of Julie's mind that said maybe this was all too good to be true. It wasn't complicated now that the truth was known, and Grace was out of the picture, but what about a year from now, when the lease was up and Michael moved on? This place would be hers forever, but what would he do?

One evening in the first week of November, when the first snow was threating in the skies over Ril Lake, Julie was taking advantage of some free time to catch up on some emails. Michael had taken the girls into Huntsville for dinner and to shop for Joy's birthday. The quiet had returned and for the first time in weeks, Julie let herself relax. And then there was a knock at the front door.

Julie lifted the curtain and looked out.

"Eddy?"

He looked the same, as if he hadn't aged a day since they first met at university. His hair was so blond it was almost white, his eyes as lovely as ever as he stared back at her. He might be handsome, but Julie wasn't about to forget the arguments, or the other women in his life.

"Hi Jewls," he said, with his usual cocky grin.

"What do you want?" It wasn't quite a sneer, but Julie saw no reason to be overly generous either.

"Can I come in? It's freezing out here."

"I'll come out. Let me grab a coat."

They sat in deck chairs on her front porch, huddled against the wintery chill. There was something different about Eddy. His features had softened, his eyes were kinder than she remembered and there was a gentleness about him she hadn't seen since they'd first met, a long, long time ago.

"Okay. You have my attention."

"I'm going away," he said, pensively. "For a long time."

"Another volunteer stint in Africa?"

He shook his head. "No. Not like that. I did something really stupid, Julie. I met someone not long after you and I split. I thought she was wonderful. But…" He grinned in that way people do when they realize they've really messed up. "She wasn't who I thought she was. I got caught up in something bad. I thought…" He reached for her hand. "When I realized the kind of person she was, I thought of you and what I'd lost and how stupid I'd been. I wanted you back, but I knew I'd have to do something drastic to show you I'd changed. So, I… Wait. I'll show you." Eddy pulled out his phone and tapped on the screen.

Julie's phone pinged in her pocket.

"Have a look," he said.

She did and found a message from @4vrjs

it's me Jewls

She frowned and looked up at him. "You're @4vrjs?"

Eddy nodded. "Forever Julie's. Because you'll always be in my heart."

"Eddy, that's… I don't even know what to say to that."

He shrugged. "I know you don't feel the same way. I made mistakes. A lot of them, but this was my way of trying to make it up to you. You see, I was dating Rebecca Vickers, and she got me messed up in this scheme to help her sister. I went along because like an idiot I thought, if I was the one who rescued Hope and brought her back…"

"I'd see you as the hero and take you back?" Julie finished.

"Something like that." Eddy lowered his head. "It was only supposed to be for a couple of hours, but then things got out of hand with Grace. That woman is psycho. Right off her head. So, that's why I was sending you messages. I hoped you'd figure it out."

"Why not just call the hotline?"

"I couldn't risk Rebecca or Grace hearing that conversation. I was never alone. There's more. I was the patient in the doctor's office that day. I was supposed to distract the doctor so he wouldn't know what was going on outside."

"But I recognized that car. A royal blue SUV like mine."

"It's Wally's. He was fixing mine." Eddy fidgeted with the zipper on his coat, a habit she recognized which meant there was more to say and he was nervous about telling her.

"Look, Jewls, I came to apologize and to explain, but there's something else."

"Go on."

Eddy flipped through the photos on his phone until he came to the one he was looking for and turned it to Julie. On the screen was the angelic face of a little girl, staring back at her with a wide smile, dazzling blue eyes, and a tuft of blond hair sticking out of a bow on the top of her head. There was no mistaking the child was Eddy's. She even had his birthmark under her right ear.

"What's her name?" she asked, as Eddy scrolled to the next photo and the next and the next.

"Lily."

A stiffness crept up Julie's spine. "You called her the name I planned for *our* daughter?"

"I know. But hear me out, please. Her mother was a one-night stand, someone I picked up in a bar, right after you and I split up. I didn't know anything about her until the day she was born. The mother died in childbirth, but she'd already done the DNA test and knew she was mine. I have the paperwork to prove paternity."

"No one could look at the two of you and not know that."

"So will you?"

Their eyes met as Julie sensed what he was asking. Fear and longing filled her simultaneously, and she thought she might burst into tears because it seemed like the only response she could manage.

"Will I raise her? Is that what you're asking?"

"Please say yes, Julie. Because I'm going away, remember? I've confessed to everything, and I'll do time now. You're the only one I trust. You should have been a mum. You know that. I know that. And I was a jerk not to see it a long time ago. I couldn't give you what you wanted then, but maybe now I can."

While Julie stared down at the photos of Lily on Eddy's phone, he produced a document from inside his coat pocket.

"You don't have to decide today, but here's the paperwork. I've signed everything and there is money for her in a bank account which my lawyer will transfer to you. You just have to sign it and she's yours. Forever."

"Just till you've served your time, surely."

Eddy grimaced. "Do I look like the kind of man who could raise a child? I'm no good for her."

"But you're getting your life together."

"Maybe when I get out, I could visit from time to time. She could call me Uncle Eddy or something." He took Julie's hands in his, eyes pleading with hers. "Please, Julie."

"Let me ask you something."

"Anything. Anything at all."

"Lily is a year old, a little more? Who's been taking care of her until now?"

Eddy's eyes fell. "My sister but…"

Julie stood up and pulled her coat tighter against the cold. "I can't do this, Eddy. I'm sure she's a lovely little girl, but this is not something I can do."

Eddy stood up, too. "I had to try. I see now it was a mistake. Look Jewls, I screwed up royally and now I'm going to jail." His eyes drifted to a police car just pulling into their circle. Eddy lifted his pant leg and showed her the anklet he wore. "Not like I was going to run." Then he squeezed her hand. "I still love you, know you. I guess I always will. But I'll never be good enough for you."

She was still standing in the driveway, watching the police car fade into the distance, when Michael pulled into the circle, then down his driveway. When he and the girls got out of the car, he waved in her direction.

"Everything okay?" he called out.

"It is now," she called back. "Glass of wine on the dock?"

"See you in ten."

Living a life without complications was impossible and if she'd learned one thing that autumn after Michael Adams and his daughters moved in next door, it was that sometimes complications were worth it.

The End…

A word about Postpartum Depression and
Postpartum Psychosis.
I am not an expert, nor do I pretend to be. I was fortunate to
have had relatively easy pregnancies and nothing more than a very
mild day or two of feeling a little low about their arrivals. Others
are not so blessed, and my heart goes out to these women and any-
one suffering from mental illness.
My hope in creating the character of Grace is to cause interest
in others so that we explore these very real issues that
women are suffering from, and that we gain knowledge and aware-
ness.

*In **To Kill A Mockingbird**, Atticus says to Scout.*
"You never really understand a person until you consider things
from his point of view, until you climb into his skin and walk around
in it."
Without knowledge, we cannot understand.
Without understanding, we cannot truly show compassion.
So, knowledge is the key to understanding and understanding is the
key to love.
I gathered information for Grace's character from a variety of web-
sites, but the most useful, to me, was from the Cleveland Clinic.

https://my.clevelandclinic.org/health/diseases/24152-postpartum-psychosis

If you or someone you love is suffering from this or any
mental illness, please urge them to seek help from reliable sources.

About the author

Margery Reynolds is the pen name of Dale Margery Rutherford, the daughter of an Ontario peach farmer. She is the mother of three, grandmother of two, and now lives in Edmonton, Alberta. Her personal reading choices lean toward historical fiction, but she also enjoys light romance, cozy mysteries, and the occasional suspense.

Her years of cottage rentals in the Muskoka Region of Ontario are what inspired the Ril Lake stories. She has also published short stories and is working on a historical fiction trilogy based on a group of Abolitionists in upstate New York and their journeys from the south to the Niagara River to bring runaway slaves to freedom.

Margery is also keenly interested in tea as a natural remedy for many of life's ailments. Having previously owned a bookstore and tea shop in Niagara Falls, Ontario, she has developed many blends, including her Ril Lake blends, which embody the characters in her stories.

Find Margery on
Substack: https://margeryreynolds.substack.com

Facebook: https://www.facebook.com/authouroffiction

Instagram: @writeonreynolds

Website: http://www.margeryreynolds.ca

Goodreads: https://www.goodreads.com/author/show/23190743.Margery_Reynolds

To all my readers...Thank you!

What's the point in telling stories if no one wants to hear them?
I hope you enjoyed One Autumn and if you did,
please leave a review for me wherever you purchased the book.

Author's Notes & Acknowledgements

As always, there is an endless list of people to thank for this novel. The inspiration for the story was flushed out with the help of several people. Beta readers had eyes on it. Editors had eyes on it, and this is the final version, is at last the story. In no particular order, my thanks go to; Kathy, Mark and Joanne who all read various drafts of this manuscript. To Lynn who not only read it but worked with my editor and I on the final round of revisions digging out the flaws and getting it primed. And most especially to Judy, my editor, my sister and my best friend, who tirelessly reads every word I write, and corrects my mistakes over and over and over again. She flushes out sticky plot points, digs into the very soul of my characters, when I don't have them just right and keeps me on the straight and narrow when I rushed and forget to mind the little details. Her red pen is ruthless, but oh, so very crucial and oh so very precious to me.

Next on the writing agenda for me are two more books in this series. One Spring at Ril Lake, followed by Christmas at Ril Lake, then watch for the cozy mystery series on the horizon–The Golden Thread Mysteries—A Dotty Hamilton story. I cannot tell you when they will release, but as always, if you watch my social media sites or my website or follow me on Substack, you will be one of the first to know.

If you're looking for something else from me, check out The Reynolds Journal Collection, which you can find on Amazon, by searching my name–Margery Reynolds. The collection includes some lined journals with lovely covers, which you can use for journalling, two planners, a food journal, to help us on our path to healthy eating, and my favourite "Don't Forget" the perfect gift for a Baby Boomer. It's a place to store passwords, medical information, financial details, funeral arrangements. In short, it's a handy book where you can store all kinds of things you want your loved ones to know when you reach a point in your life where you can't take care of them anymore.

Teaser

Interested in getting a glimpse of the next book in the Muskoka Cottage Novel Series? Read on……….

One Spring at Ril Lake

Chapter One

Michelle

July 31ˢᵗ, 2025

I'd known since I was very little that something was missing from my life. I was an only child, born to devoted parents who did not indulge me but taught me to be independent, to be respectable, and to understand that actions have consequences; all good values to instill in a child. Growing up, I had friends, sometimes more than I wanted, but I begged my parents for a sister, even a brother would do, but all I got was my father's response, *when you're older you can have the family you want, for now, you'll have to make do with us*. Not exactly what I wanted to hear, but what choice did I have?

Our family farm was just on the outskirts of Binbrook, a small town above the Niagara Escarpment a few miles outside Hamilton's southern border. My family has farmed there for four generations, beginning with my great-great-grandfather, who immigrated to Canada in the late 1800s. Traditionally, the eldest son inherited the farm, while any other children married and moved away, some further than others.

My mother lived on this farm until she married, and then my parents took up residence in a two-bedroom bungalow, with a matchbox sized backyard, on the fringes of the town of Stoney Creek. (North of Binbrook and the family farm). They married later in life than most of their friends because Mum had wanted to focus on her teaching career. After I was born, she became a stay-at-home mum who cooked, cleaned and kept a tidy house. I asked her once why she didn't go back to teaching after I'd started school. Her answer was simple. "I was happy to be at home." Apparently, she was because she never complained.

Dad worked at Dofasco, one of the two steel plants in Hamilton. He made good money, took care of all our financial needs and eventually retired with a healthy pension and a Rolex, which he wore proudly wherever he went. I grew up happy and wanted for little, though we were not what anyone would call rich. Comfortable, was the term my mother always used, and that's what we were. Both my parents died the year I turned fifty. What I have left of them is a box of photographs, a few trinkets I keep on the mantel and a lifetime of wonderful memories.

I loved my parents, loved Gramps and Grammy, and all my crazy relatives, yet something was missing, and I could not shake the feeling I wasn't entirely whole. Even marriage and children didn't fill that gap, nor did following in my mother's footsteps in a teaching career. It was that missing piece of me, and of course the letter, that led me down this path and I will always wonder if I did the right thing or should have left well enough alone.

The Muskoka Cottage Novel Series

By

Margery Reynolds